Guilt is having a crabby day ... saying no ... not living up to other people's expectations {or even to} our own ... there is Bad Daddy guilt . . . Bad Mommy guilt ... Being Selfish guilt ... Bad Person guilt ... I can't stand two-year-olds—including my own—guilt ... why does she want another orgasm guilt ... I forgot to call my mother guilt ... envy, jealousy or resentment guilt ... Now don't these guilts sound more like you?

Guilt is an emotion, not a thought process. Normal Craziness can't be dealt with or overcome by logic and reason. Sometimes it can only be conquered by laughter and sharing. *And that's what this book is all about.*

—Paula & Dick McDonald

GUILT-FREE

Paula and Dick McDonald

BALLANTINE BOOKS • NEW YORK

Dedication

This book is lovingly dedicated to those fine friends who willingly gave so much and who kept us honest when it became so tempting to pull the punches—

to Margie and Burt Meldman, who waded with us through the best and the worst of the past two years and kept our spirits from sagging; and with special thanks to Margie for the concepts of small bites and baby steps;

to T. L. Nolan, who was straight and open, always;

to Judy Kloman, who grew before our very eyes;

and to Lynn Sherman—bless her!—who never doubted once.

Thank you all.

Acknowledgments

A list of all those who contributed to this book would be a book in itself. Our special gratitude for their efforts to:

Bob Albrightson, Isabele Appell, Jerry Appell, Father John Banahan, Jay Barrett, Don Bauman, Jim Behling, Yetta Bernhard, Kit Besag, Frank Besag, Ron Busch, Phyllis Chicorel, Ralph Chicorel, Jan Collins, Charlie Davis, Father Tom Fait, Tom Gard, Ellen Gardiner, Curt Gorrell, Pat Grinager, Virginia Halaska, George Halaska, Noel Handel, Terry Heaton, Father Harold Ide, John Kalbrener, Reverend Dave Koch, Ruth Koch, Jerry Kringle, Bob Markel, Peter Matson, Nancy McDowell, Cris Mike, Pat Morken, Darrell Morken, Karen Nelson, Ann Pereles, Diana Price, Harold Roth, Florence Schmitt, Monsignor William Schuit, Father Dick Sklba, Barbara Strain, Norb Studelska, Ben Wattenberg, Cody Wilson.

Special thanks to Eric, Kelly, Randy and Mike McDonald who were perceptive enough to raid the refrigerator instead of our energy during the past year. And special thanks also to their many friends who had the wisdom to do the same, but who also opened their hearts while munching.

To those countless others across America who also contributed so much to this book, but who remain nameless, we are forever grateful.

Contents

Preface

WHO IN THE WORLD are we, your next-door neighbors, to write a book about guilt? For decades, GUILT has been the exclusive province of Freudian psychoanalysts and a few tortured novelists like Conrad who have probed the dark depths of the human mind. How is it that we, two laymen—neither analysts nor novelists —dare invade their territory? How dare we meddle with driving compulsions and unfathomable anguish? We wouldn't dare—and we didn't.

Guilt-Free is instead a book about feeling guilty when feeling guilty isn't necessary—about those tiny pains, awkward moments, little spots rubbed raw; about the common guilts we each experience daily that hang us up, wear us down, and waste our energy; the guilt feelings we don't rush to tell to a psychiatrist, but don't talk to our best friends about either. These common, uncomfortable feelings flicker through our minds so frequently that we rarely even recognize them as guilt. Still, they inhibit and hurt. They stop us from doing all that we could do with our lives, from being all that we could be. Rather than the overwhelming guilts whispered on the psychoanalyst's couch, these are instead the multitude of quiet pangs and hindrances most of us know so well: "I'd like to, but I can't . . . I wish I could, but my mother would feel hurt . . . I want to, but my church taught . . . I want to, *but I'd feel guilty!*"

Invariably, these guilt feelings are based not upon morality or ethics or dastardly deeds done, but upon what others think or once thought years ago, when we, as children, were taught the rules of niceness, rightness, and goodness; when the seeds of our lives today were first planted. "A nice little girl would . . . A good man can be counted on to . . . The right way, of course is . . ." Those innocent words once filled us with impossible expectations and have now returned to haunt us as adults and to stifle us with everyday guilts.

Everybody feels guilty! If there is one absolute in American life, it is that. Most of us walk around much of the time feeling guilty about something: guilty of not living up to our own or to other people's standards; guilty because we don't measure up—at least not consistently—to society's image of the "good mother," the "good father," the "good citizen," the "good provider"; guilty because our hands or hair or teeth will never look like those of the models on television commercials, because our floors will never shine as brightly, and because we can't seem to solve major (or even minor) family problems in an hour like Marcus Welby does; guilty because what we once learned as right and nice and good no longer seems to apply; guilty because unalterable truths have, in fact, altered; guilty because we now inhabit a world of conflicting expectations and can't seem to please everybody. We are living through an intensely painful period of rapid change. Alvin Toffler predicted and described it in *Future Shock*. But how do we handle it now that it's here? We feel guilty about our inability to cope perfectly with that changing world around us. But we rarely reveal those feelings.

If guilt feelings are still virgin territory, the hushed whispers of the world, how then do two people have the audacity to speak for so many others? This book was inspired by the thoughts and feelings of thousands of Americans. The two of us had the unique privilege of sharing those thoughts and feelings with them, almost accidentally. From that experience, a new insight into modern, middle-class American life evolved for us—a unique view of your lives and ours. But, a bit of history is in order.

In 1974, *Loving Free,* our first book, became a best seller, startling everyone—particularly us. The book attempted to share the story of a then thirteen-year-old marriage fraught with all the perils and pitfalls of most marriages today: money, kids, sex, conformity, family traditions, the job, and of course, communication. *Loving Free* talked openly about many subjects that other books on marriage preferred to avoid. Rather than following the format of a how-to manual, we tried to write the how-it-was chronicle of a real marriage: ups, downs, fall on your face today, struggle back to your feet tomorrow, but always keep trying to make it better. Since *Loving Free* was such a highly personal account of only one marriage, its success astonished us. Marriage counselors and psychologists across America began to praise and recommend the book because of its honesty. Virginia M. Satir, PhD., renowned author and trainer in family therapy commented: "I would like to see this book in the hands of all therapists, family life educators, family members, school personnel, the clergy, and all college and high school students." And colleges and universities did adopt *Loving Free* as required reading. Soon, even the media—press, radio, and television—began touting *Loving Free.* "It should be recommended to all young married persons or those contemplating marriage," said the *National Catholic Reporter. Publishers Weekly* called it ". . . a sincere and honest attempt from a married couple who try . . . they have something of substance to communicate to other couples."

Suddenly, that ordinary couple from next door with the four kids and the driveway full of rusty bikes became the nation's newest experts on marriage. Although we personally felt far from expert or qualified to talk about any marriage other than our own, instant experts we were labeled by many—like it or not. If success was somewhat of a mixed blessing, it did bring with it the unexpected opportunity to talk with countless other American men and women in major cities and small hamlets across the country: old and young; newlyweds; married forevers, and those who were trying the second time around; couples who were struggling to make their lives together smoother, and singles who had given up the effort but recalled the mistakes; on college campuses and in church groups and synagogues; before millions on the "Today Show," and with intimate handfuls at PTA meetings; in backyards, living rooms, hotel rooms, and convention halls on a face-to-face basis; on call in talk shows across America where the listener or viewer could express his or her honest feelings safely and anonymously. We talked with those countless other people and we listened. It was a unique, enriching experience.

Somehow, the fact that we were so much like they were, grappling—often inexpertly—with the same problems, made people feel comfortable with us. Somehow, the honesty and openness of *Loving Free* allowed others to be open and candid themselves. We became experts after all. In three years, we heard more about the problems and successes in other lives than most people hear in three lifetimes. We listened to the various ways others had found to solve their problems— or how they had failed and why. We heard the sad, the joyous, the tense, the trying, and the triumphant moments of living recounted by hopeful people, struggling people, people in pain. And we learned from all of them. Much of the sharing came from family and friends. More of it came from friendly strangers across America: housewives; career women; senior citizens; couples; singles; divorcés; parents and children; ministers and executives; reporters and mechanics; doctors, plumbers, and grandmothers. What emerged was the realization that we are all pretty much the same.

Most of us, whether we live in rural, urban, or suburban society today, face basically the same situations in our daily lives. There are in-laws who meddle, and husbands who come home late for dinner without calling. There are women who drive their husbands crazy by becoming Momaholics or PTA addicts, and men who drive their wives equally crazy by gluing themselves to TV sets for six hours of pro football each weekend. There are neighbors who gossip, and those who drop in unexpectedly and stay forever (or so it seems when you are busy). There is this year's teacher who picks on your child unfairly, or there is the child who suddenly, this year, hates spelling, or history, or school in general, and can't be motivated. And of course, there's always money, the snags and snarls caused by "never enough" and "who spent what"; the hassles when he wants to buy more insurance and she wants a vacation. Then there's the very human side of each individual to cope with: the husband who doesn't want his wife to return to work; the wife who exchanges the black lace negligée for a flannel nightgown. And for most of us, there are the children: those little tykes who toddle home from the playground innocently spouting newly learned four-letter words; the bigger ones who seem to possess only a one-word vocabulary—"Gross!"; the older ones who no longer seem to want our advice. So many of us in the midst of the child-rearing years ponder a barrage of new questions daily. How much allowance is too much? How strict should we be? How much pressure should we apply for good grades? How often should we let him have the car? How will we survive another rainy day with toddlers, another birthday party with five-year-olds? And of course, there is change—overwhelming, bewildering, and painful change—the pain of departure from traditions; the pain of living with mixed signals. If the Women's Movement claims unlimited potential for all women, what are the inner feelings of the individual woman when she can't shed her own past quickly enough to reach that promised potential?

Those are the fragments that make up much of our lives, whoever we are: learning to live with the people we love and in the changing world around us. How we cope with those individual bits and pieces, and what we think of ourselves as we watch others, who always seem to cope better, determine our guilt feelings. Through so many small segments of each day, we each quietly ask ourselves, "Am I doing it right? Are others doing it better? What will they think of me?" But how can we find answers when so many of the standards keep changing?

As the two of us traveled and listened, a new awareness began to form. Everywhere, the words being said sounded similar and faintly familiar. There were different voices, different accents perhaps; quiet whispers or strident shouts. But, as people shared, the messages were the same: "What I want is . . . If only I could . . ." In the people we met a common hunger existed to be more and to do more than they were, but something was holding them back. A persistent, insidious inhibitor existed. A tiny voice continually repeated *"no."*

It took us three years of listening before the click of recognition occurred: the inhibitor was guilt; and it was universal! Suddenly, all those words we had diligently saved, taped, jotted in notebooks, and on napkins, remembered and tucked away to ponder some day—all those words merged into a single pattern and made sense. "I'd like to . . . but *I'd feel guilty.*" Everybody did feel guilty—in some ways, at some times. A little part of every day was a downer, a guilt trip. We had heard the message from too many people to disbelieve it any longer. And the fragments had sounded familiar because those were the same words we had secretly whispered to ourselves at times. Yes, we had been there, too—often. The circumstances were sometimes different, but the feelings were the same. Each of us had felt the same guilts, wrestled with them, and won or lost a small battle according to the power of that particular guilt, or according to our own ability to deal with it at that moment. At each of those moments, we, like the thousands of Americans we met, thought we were alone.

This book is the sharing of a single truth, learned through that extraordinary listening experience. The truth is this: You are not alone. Guilt feelings exist and many others are also dealing with them daily. Because of the willingness of those others to share their feelings we personally have gained comfort and learned many means of coping with guilt. We now know what has worked for others, and we know what is working for us today. The experience of listening, and then compiling this encyclopedia of guilts—of funny, sad, and poignant little battles against guilt—has been freeing for us. We would now like to share all this with you in an effort to spread further that same comfort and freedom.

We have no illusions of grandeur about this book. It does not attempt to bump Freud's couch out of the room. Instead, it hopes only to provide that click of recognition. We know of no other book that speaks of guilt in the language of the people, and expresses their feelings in their own words. And like the people themselves, the feelings expressed here are warm and real, funny at times, inconsistent at others, but always honest. *Guilt-Free* was never written as a cure, only as a comfort. Think of it as you would think of Granny's feather bed: a warm refuge from those nagging self-doubts, bad feelings, and solitary thoughts that plague us all at times; a downy quilt filled with thousands of ways to recognize our guilt feelings as such and myriad ways to cope with them. We may not have talked with you in our travels, but we're sure you'll find parts of your own past and present here. And we hope the recognition will be as freeing for you as it has been for us.

1.

We're All from Whitefish Bay

You can't go home again.
THOMAS WOLFE

Home is where the heart is.

EVERYBODY FEELS GUILTY these days—with good reason. There's a tiny splinter of Whitefish Bay in all of us that causes acute discomfort. It's the mixture of past, present, and future we carry inside, and it pricks us at unexpected moments. Most of us recognize the feeling, even if we don't recognize it as guilt.

Whitefish Bay is a traditional Midwestern suburb. You may not have been here, but you know what it's like—tidy on the surface. The elm trees lining each street were saplings when Dick walked to school some thirty years ago. Today they tower and meet overhead to form tunnels as our four children walk the same streets toward the same schools. Whitefish Bay is older than most of us. It changes very slowly.

Some of Dick's old neighbors still reside in the houses they built some forty-odd years ago; some of his teachers are still around. The people who represent our pasts are here (even though I grew up a thousand miles away). We're here. And the future is here, growing up within our homes and beginning to buy the houses down the block. Here, as within each

1

one of us, the three generations reside, sometimes uneasily, side by side.

There are people who attend daily Mass; others who have never been churchgoers. Some of us formerly attended, then stopped for various reasons. There are women who give coffees for fun or to celebrate the arrival of new neighbors, proudly displaying silver tea services; but there are also younger neighbors now who would rather meditate or find their fun at a yoga class or consciousness-raising group. Some of the neighbors have known each other for fifty years. Others have never met.

There are men who spend hours each weekend manicuring already perfect lawns; others watch the Green Bay Packers instead, or let the lawn go to seed while they work for a political candidate; still others have torn up the grass to plant vegetable gardens. There are mothers who speak with pride about the new dough hook attachments for their Mix Masters; others rely on TV dinners to feed their families while they go back to school.

There are papas who have never poured a cup of coffee for themselves in thirty years of marriage; there are men who are learning in midlife to clean and cook (if only Campell's soups) because they've got a working wife—or perhaps no wife—these days. There is the woman who still feels most comfortable in hat and gloves when she attends bridge club or a luncheon; next door to her might live a hiking-booted environmentalist who works at the local nature center. Any given block in Whitefish Bay today might yield a mixture of intact families, single-parent homes, and blended families. In driveways or shopping center parking lots, you'll still see thousands of suburban station wagons, but they're beginning to mingle with the newcomers—jeeps, vans, and campers.

Change is occurring even in Whitefish Bay. It's easy to see where most of us came from just by glancing up and down our block. And it's easy to see where many of us are today. Where we are headed is a bit more difficult to know. That destination, and the comfort of the journey, depend to a great extent on our ability to cope with the Normal Craziness produced by change that resides in each of us.

What causes our guilt feelings? Webster defines guilt as "the act or state of having done a wrong or committed an offense; a painful feeling of self-reproach resulting from a belief that one has done something wrong or immoral." But this definition is far too easy, far too narrow. It takes too many of us off the hook and leaves us wondering why the hook still hurts. Let's define guilt in a broader sense—à la McDonald.

Guilt is having a crabby day; saying no; not doing things the way our mothers, fathers, or grandparents did them; not living up to other people's expectations; not living up to our own expectations. There is Bad Daddy guilt (not throwing the ball with Junior after work because the boss dressed you down) and Bad Mommy guilt ("If I see another flashcard I'll scream!"). Being selfish guilt (trying to look busy so I don't have to help you with your homework or the dishes—or hiding the last four Oreos to eat by myself). Envy, jealousy, or resentment guilt (wishing your sister would fall on her face just once because she's smarter, prettier, never had to wear braces, never had chipped nails and her husband makes more money). There is Bad Person guilt (a lack of compassion when you have the chicken pox and I have a headache, brought on by your chicken pox), and Bad Parent guilt (not wanting to be a Little League coach, not wanting to drive your kids to practice every week during "All in the Family," having to take a tranquilizer before accompanying a screaming bunch of Girl Scouts to the zoo). Static cling guilt (finding out after school that your son walked around all day with a sock stuck to the back of his shirt). I'm on the Pill (or my daughter, the coed, is on the Pill) guilt; I forgot your birthday guilt; I don't have shiny floors guilt; I can't stand two-year-olds—including my own—guilt; I'm not handsome, I'm not virile, I'm getting old guilt; why does she want another orgasm guilt; I think my teenager smokes pot guilt; I can't tell her my feelings guilt; I wonder if I'm a latent homosexual guilt; I forgot to call my mother guilt; I lost it in the stock market guilt; what do you mean buy a vibrator guilt; "nothin' says lovin' like something from the oven" guilt; my Guardian Angel is watching guilt; "I can't believe I ate the whole thing" guilt; I know the garage hasn't been cleaned but I want to watch the Olympics guilt.

Now don't these guilts sound more like you? Webster may have defined neurosis, but he never heard of Normal Craziness. It occurs when we feel that we're doing something wrong even though we're not.

The world has changed drastically since the lessons of our childhood were taught. We carry a multitude of obsolete rights and wrongs, blacks and whites, within us, but today we inhabit a world of grays—a bewildering diversity of values and ideas. Very little is as it was. Emily Post's admonitions not to eat chicken with your fingers have been replaced by a Colonel Sanders culture. Expectations of how people should live, behave, and feel are deeply ingrained in each of us. Often those expectations no longer apply, but when we try to abandon them, a stab of guilt occurs. You aren't a handyman like your father was and don't want to learn? Bad Husband. Your mother always made a hot breakfast for your father and the kids? You don't? Bad Mommy. No matter that your modern family loves Fruity Freakies and your husband would rather sleep ten minutes later and grab a donut at the office. You feel that twinge of guilt. It's inevitable. You are caught between three sets of generational expectations—your parents', your children's, and your own—and you can't expect to satisfy them all when they have such different values and norms.

Dick and I belong to the generation in the middle. Those older often frown on the changes we have made; those younger are impatient that we move too cautiously. It has never been easy to run the gauntlet between generations, but today, the space in which to maneuver has become distressingly narrow. We can barely squeak through. The days of comfort are gone for many of us. We're living future shock. Is it any wonder we feel guilty at times? It's become impossible to please everybody—or even most people. What your father taught may conflict with the new messages of our new culture. Dad said, "Save for a rainy day." The airlines now exhort us to "Fly now, pay later." How could we expect to be at ease in a world of double messages and mixed signals? Why do we expect to be comfortable straddling a fence that has already fallen down?

Departing from tradition makes us feel guilty. Not meeting the expectations of others makes us feel guilty. Being on the defensive makes us feel guilty. Having to explain ourselves makes us feel guilty. We make ourselves and each other feel guilty at every turn. No one likes to be out of step. We all want social approval—but whose? Our wives'? Our parents'? Our best friends'? Our co-workers'? Our neighbors'? They may all be different. The clash of change and tradition is a no-win conflict, especially when it occurs deep inside.

Today, so many of us have "fallen away" (a term that used to apply exclusively to religion) from the institutions and traditions of our youth: church, school, family, and the society that molded us. Today, we can be fallen away Jewish princesses, fallen away housewives, fallen away jocks, or fallen away male chauvinist pigs. What we're abandoning are our pasts, and each departure carries its own painful little sting of guilt. Not the guilt of doing wrong, but of doing differently. There are no moral, legal, or ethical questions involved. The questions instead are "What will they think of me?" and "What do I think of myself?"

Dick and I are part of the first generation to be reared by television, the modern molder of ideas. Howdy Doody was a gentle, if absurd, companion for many of us as children. Our own children are being molded by Gabe Kotter and the Sweathogs, or the Fonz, instead. It jars me to hear "Up your nose with a rubber hose" from the mouths of babes—my babes. We feel a vague sense of guilt as parents hearing our children use that expression; and yet, there's nothing really wrong with it. It's just change.

The simple act of taking a weekend nap while someone else is working shouldn't produce guilt feelings, but it does. What causes that little stab just below the breastbone when you do it? It's your gut reaction. Words and phrases from childhood come floating back: "slothful . . . idle hands . . . the early bird . . . make hay while the sun shines." Guilt is an emotion, not a thought process. Normal Craziness can't be dealt with or overcome by logic and reason. Sometimes it can only be conquered by laughter and sharing. And that's what this book is all about. If we can examine ourselves closely, like monkeys picking lice out of each other's coats, we might learn to laugh at ourselves and find some relief. We might discover where we've all come from and where we're headed; why we act and feel as we do; and why we couldn't possibly feel differently.

Not dealing with guilt slows us up. We feel cheated because we can't act as we'd like, speak our minds, be free. We often put the blame on others, building a core of anger, resentment, and bitterness. "Look what you're doing to me," we accuse. Never "Look what I'm doing to myself." Yet, we are, most often, our own worst enemies.

It's difficult for most of us to talk about guilt because it's scary to reveal weaknesses, insecurities, and human foolishness. We bottle up those feelings, believing that we're totally alone, probably crazy, certainly different. No one else has ever had these thoughts. No one else could understand. But it's not true. We're all there together.

Sometimes laughter and a nostalgia trip can be an expensive cure for guilt. While this book was never meant to be a therapy session, it has had some beneficial side effects for those of us involved. We'd like to think of the book as a giant consciousness-raising session. That's what the experience has been for us. And in the process, we and many of our friends have had some pleasant surprises: our guilt feelings are normal, universal, and far from crazy, despite the mixed signals. No one is alone in experiencing confusion or guilt today; everyone feels guilty! But most of us will manage to survive and to cope, with a little help from our friends. That's what this book is all about—coping.

When people share their guilt feelings, there's always much emotion—some tears, some hurt, but most often relief followed by a smile. Expect some pain and some uncomfortable moments. A page is turned, a mirror is held up, and the sudden recognition or the unexpected confrontation with the past can be momentarily overwhelming. But expect relief, too. It follows quickly.

This is definitely a book of mixed feelings: joy and sorrow; wistfulness and anger—but very little anger in the end, because when we begin to realize how we've been manipulated, we also discover we've manipulated others. The accusations quickly turn to chagrin. The finger stops pointing and hands join. "I'm not alone, and your story is worse (funnier, sadder) than mine."

Dick and I see this book as a celebration—not a dirge to man's ability to get himself hung up, but a tribute to his ability to identify with others and free himself in the process. We'd like to give back now all those thoughts gathered from friends and friendly strangers in a way that will make them smile, remember, and feel better. Let's discover Normal Craziness together. Surely you will find yourself here, and you'll find yourself among friends.

We might all feel better if we faced the scope of the changes affecting us and learned to live peacefully with them and with ourselves. We *are* all from Whitefish Bay. If only we could stop trying to live there twenty years ago.

2.

Before I Knew What Hit Me
(Guilt, Craziness, and Change)

One can resist the invasion of armies, but not the invasion of ideas.

VICTOR HUGO

America is the country where you buy a lifetime supply of aspirin for one dollar and use it up in two weeks.

JOHN BARRYMORE

SOMEHOW IT DOESN'T SEEM FAIR. We worked so hard to learn the ground rules as children. What we absorbed about the world then is permanently implanted in a corner of our minds. The twenty-five-year span from the heart of the Depression in 1933 until 1958 were the formative years for Dick and me. We sailed serenely into adulthood, confident that we could function as mature, married decision-makers. Within a few short years, confusion occurred over where the game was being played, let alone by what rules.

What happened?

While I was looking for a deal on diapers, "Let's Pretend" became *Hair*. Dick glanced away for a moment, and the penny candy store turned into a shopping center. We blinked and a heart was transplanted. Overnight, walk became drive. Doris Day turned into Linda Lovelace. We're not complaining; change is inevitable, and each of us has had to cope with it in his or her own way. But has it been as unsettling for you?

Somewhere between our youth and our middle age, the game rules changed. Quietly, one by one, our rela-

8

tives slipped away to different parts of the country, leaving the McDonalds a typical nuclear family. Gradually, the TV talk shows crept in to replace conversation over the kitchen table for the lonely housewife. At other times, the changes were noisy and abrupt. It was difficult to ignore the radicals of the sixties. With a raucous "Stifle it, Edith!" Archie Bunker replaced Ozzie Nelson as the father image for the 190 million American viewers. Values changed, people changed, we changed—or a part of us did. Another part can still be found wandering around a deserted ball park trying to play by the original rules.

The conflict is in determining if what was once supposed to be eternally true is still true; if what was once disgraceful can now be legitimately approved; if what was traditionally accepted can now be abandoned without discomfort. What happens when the formerly frowned-upon becomes healthy—and then gets out of hand? "Children should be seen and not heard" may not have been a valid child-rearing theory, but is the opposite extreme desirable? Should students occupy buildings and hold the dean hostage? When does enough become too much?

Culture is learned, and it seems we learned ours long ago in a far more innocent world. A noted anthropologist claims that we absorb more by the age of six (mostly without benefit of language) than we will learn for the rest of our lives. We watch; we listen; we pick up the "right" way to do things almost by osmosis. Our childhood creeds and conditionings are the hardest to unlearn. What once was correct should be correct forever, but time is never that kind. Habits, manners, prayers, and old truths return later to haunt us. "Now I lay me down to sleep" becomes "Are you running with me, Jesus?"—and it doesn't seem quite right, somehow.

In considering change, does it help to know that we've only been out of the cave for 150 lifetimes? That only during the last two has mankind used an electric motor of any kind? And that only we, the present generation, take television for granted? Does it help to know that in this lifetime both a knowledge explosion and a technology explosion have complicated our values? It doesn't help a bit when your children tell you they're bored by men walking on the moon. "Switch to Sonny and Cher, please."

To be comfortable, most of us need a sense of stability. We like to know what we can count on and to have some assurance that we're headed in the right direction. Anchors and landmarks are comforting in a choppy sea. We used to have many. Where have they gone? And what can we count on today to remain unchanged? Let's take a look.

Institutions were once among the most stable of our anchors. They were infallible, eternal, immovable, and often unapproachable. To question the doctor, the church, the authorities, or even Papa was unthinkable.

In medicine today, patients sue at the drop of a hat —or a scalpel. Good Samaritan laws are necessary to keep the bleeding body on the road from taking you to court later. Doctors strike and specialists supplement their incomes with best-selling exposés. The lab is quickly being replaced by the TV studio as a forum for medical debate. Courts decide who has the right to die.

It's been a long but rapidly traveled road from Bishop Sheen to Reverend Moon, and religious changes have occurred at express speed. Guitar Masses and balloons replace the somber Latin Mass for some Catholics. Gay deacons and female ministers are accepted by their congregations but rejected by the hierarchy in some Protestant sects; "Dig Christ" posters now adorn church walls, only a few feet away from statues of the saints. Parochial schools close, church attendance drops, and priests leave. Father James Groppi leads civil rights marches, and stirs the old "pay and pray" congregations to become socially aware and militant; and then he marries and ends up driving a city bus. "Accept without question" seems suddenly absurd and Catholic women join the millions who take the Pill. Clergymen criticize doctrine, each other, and the Pope. Splits occur in the Infallible and Eternal.

World War II veterans and Vietnam veterans brawl

with each other in the streets. "Uncle Sam Wants *You*" is no longer responded to with a sense of pride and patriotism. The Air Force advertises on television instead, promising travel and excitement. Recruits are shown playing tennis; not a weapon is in sight. The draft is abolished. Kent State and My Lai fill the public with outrage and shame. We wonder if God really is still on our side.

More details than we ever wanted to know about politics fill our TV screens. Law-and-order slogans elect politicians, then destroy them. Crime in the streets becomes crime in the White House. Congressmen are accused of sex orgies; a President is pardoned so he won't be sent to jail; and a Vice President charged with graft cops a plea. Riots occur, and violence for the sake of justice becomes a new way to gain attention. If you don't like it, burn it down! Clergymen pour blood into draft files. Monasteries are occupied by Indians. Cops become pigs, courtrooms are turned into circus rings, and everybody has a good excuse to avoid jury duty. A Washington secretary sues Angier St. George Biddle Duke for giving her VD—and wins $1.3 million in damages. Shameful becomes shrewd.

The nuclear family is struggling to stay afloat emotionally. Bewildered parents no longer call home to ask Gramma what to do about Junior; they call a crisis line instead. Gramma is in a nursing home anyway, or enjoying the sun in a retirement community. "Dear Abby" fills the void. Papa, as traditional head of the household, may have recently yielded to a liberated wife. Or perhaps Dad only has visitation rights today. Where once we felt a concern over mixed marriages, we now accept open marriages, serial marriages, or no marriages at all. Young people live together openly. Should they choose to marry, the services may be held while sky diving or scuba diving. What will that do to Gramma's heart condition? And what does she think about the divorces in the family?

We worry more about our young people today. They're so different. Depression parents try valiantly to communicate with Bomb Babies and often miss. The Protestant work ethic is no match for "Eat, drink and be merry, for tomorrow we die." This year's high school graduates have spent more time in front of a television set than in the classroom—and very little time talking to their parents. And why should they? They have an entire culture of their own, and different values. What was once a joyous hope-filled experience makes us apprehensive. What will happen to little Johnny when we send him off to college? Will he be a success? Follow in my footsteps? Or will he succumb to God knows what? Hippies? Flower children? Radicals? Dropouts? Drugs? It isn't corn silk the kids are smoking behind the barn these days, and panty raids have been replaced by no panties. Relax, Dad. It's out of your hands now. Sit back, watch the nightly news, and stop worrying. Oops! There goes Johnny . . . the streaker with the sneakers. Well, it could have been worse. He could have been holding the dean hostage.

The lines of our culture are blurred at times. When did our heroes change? When were Babe Ruth and Bob Hope replaced by Mick Jagger and Tiny Tim? How did Timothy Leary get to be a prophet? Abbie Hoffman a leader? Maybe they just slipped in along with acid rock when we weren't listening. We didn't sit up and take notice until Judy Garland's "Somewhere over the Rainbow" changed to Alice Cooper's "Dead Babies." We weren't concerned until the Beatles seemed innocent by comparison; until we realized we could no longer name the groups, identify with the costumes, or understand the words. But we couldn't ignore the music. The decibel count shattered our eardrums. And Grampa kept complaining that he couldn't tell the males without beards from the females.

When did our matinee idols cease to be fantasy figures, Cinderellas, and Prince Charmings? When Grace Kelly and Gene Kelly became Jane Fonda and Marlon Brando. Cinderella doesn't protest; Prince Charming doesn't criticize the kingdom. It all crept up on us. While we were out pulling dandelions, Ma Kettle turned into Maude; Henry Aldrich became Henry Winkler, the Fonz; Uncle Miltie grew dull. It's more exciting to watch Kojak screech his tires. Cher's navel is infinitely more intriguing than Perry Como's sweater ever was.

At some point, people stopped dancing cheek to cheek and began to jerk around the room alone in spasms. As the entertainment highlight of the year, *South Pacific* evolved into *The Exorcist*. When we were in college, *Catcher in the Rye* was considered questionable course material for young people. Today any kid can wander down to the corner drugstore and pick up a paperback copy of *The Happy Hooker* to share with the gang. And why not? Sex is no longer dirty; it's become a national obsession. A new breed of therapists is standing by to rid us of any remaining hangups. We've been freed by the Pill, Masters and Johnson, and legalized abortion. Men now speak casually about their vasectomies at cocktail parties. I once snickered along with the other twelve-year-olds when Dagmar's ample bustline first appeared on television. NBC "Saturday Night" recently showed movie footage using Raquel Welch's chest as a screen and our teenagers never even lifted an eyebrow. In high school, a few of us defied the Catholic Church's ban and snuck off to see *The Moon Is Blue,* feeling very daring and wicked. Today, we feel slightly out of it because we haven't seen *Deep Throat.* Are Dick and I the last remaining Americans who enjoy that distinction? So it seems at times. But status can now be maintained with the line, "If you've seen one X-rated movie, you've seen them all." We've experienced a sexual revolution followed quickly by a porn revolution. *Playboy* is passé and you're a square if you picket the massage parlor going up next door.

It's a new world symbolized by Maharaj-ji and Charlie the Tuna. Look around. We have contact lenses, CB radios, blow combs, cat food in forty-two flavors, and deodorized tampons (which don't even come in a plain brown wrapper). You may get mugged on the way to the health food store, but the organic vegetables will keep until you are released from the hospital and Blue Cross will pay the bills. We live in an era of contradictions, with convenience foods and gadgetry on the opposite sides of the coin. If your soy bean curd rots, if the electric can opener won't work, you can always go to Burger King for dinner. And everything has been computerized. For two years, Dick and I have been trying to stop *Time* magazine sending us double copies. The computer won't listen.

Football players use hair spray today. Women wear pants to work and kids wear jeans everywhere. Patched no longer means poor. Caroline Kennedy was named one of the world's worst-dressed women and probably enjoyed the distinction. Elton John was added to Mr. Blackwell's "Ten Worst-Dressed Women" list and used it as publicity. *Women's Wear Daily* has replaced Emily Post as the bible of the "correct," the "in," but it's still "do your own thing," whether that be braless, tieless, shoeless, or topless.

Crew cuts and duck tails vanished somewhere along the way with tinfoil balls and the hearty breakfast. Who hoards in a throwaway society? Who wants bacon and eggs and a high cholesterol count when there is Carnation Instant Breakfast? Victory stamps became trading stamps years ago. A chicken in every pot? Why not a three-car garage as our national dream instead?

In modern America, your friends are all armchair psychologists. When they aren't sailing, camping, or skiing, they are discussing meditation, astrology, the occult, or your hangups. Uri Geller, mysticism, and witchcraft are in. As the suburbs exploded, so did the craze for self-improvement: double your money, talk to your plants, and get your head straight quick. Use whatever expert is currently fashionable.

It's become a small world, made smaller by television. Now the experts come right into your home to solve your problems. But what's this confusion? Dr. Meyer Friedman says you should hang up your jogging suit—jogging is bad for your heart. Dr. Joyce Brothers says it's all right to have an affair, but Dr. Karl Menninger wants to bring back sin. Our multiple authority figures contradict each other on the daily talk shows. And if you feel you need advice, the priest who counseled you on your marriage problems last year may be having his own marriage problems this year.

But we accept it all. Our attitudes are broadening. We absorbed "Black is beautiful," "Ban the bomb," and "Save the whales" in less than a decade. Good for us. In a decade, we learned to live with both nuclear destruction and nuclear disarmament. In short succession, we grew accustomed to war, apathy, radicalism, and assassination. Look how quickly we took the first Catholic President into our hearts. How rapidly we accepted the first black mayors. How easy it was to sit back and watch Billie Jean King beat Bobby Riggs. We're really something. In less than a lifetime, we've gone from the farm to the moon, from simple to complex, with hardly a flutter. Adaptable, that's us. Almost.

Women's Lib, Gay Lib, and pop-top cans. Black studies, busing, and freeze-dried onions. A runaway divorce rate, the Peace Corps, and prostitutes writing bestsellers. Who'd have thought it?

We've watched the decline of the Ma and Pa grocery store and other small family businesses like it. Acquisitions and mergers are the thing. Big is better, whether for farmers or manufacturers. We've coined new clichés: "the corporate image," "the corporate dollar," "the corporate man." Because of our growing inability to deal effectively as individuals with the "corporate entity," new professionals have emerged: the consumer advocate and the union negotiator. We realize the futility of fighting a computer or a conglomerate alone. We need Ralph Nader. We need the unions, even though they, too, frustrate us at times. A single voice today is barely heard and hardly heeded. And what are we fighting for? Good service, product reliability, our money's worth—expectations once taken for granted. But who will back up the product assembled by a hundred men instead of one? And whom can you put the finger on when the faces on your color TV set blur and turn purple? Only recently, the American economy became a service economy and it doesn't work well. The Maytag repairman might well be the busiest man in town, and your Gremlin has a thunk in the motor. Pride of workmanship declined when bigger became better, and who can blame the bored assembly-line workers? Get the job done, the hell with overtime, and get off with the camper for the weekend.

So much has happened so rapidly, is it any wonder that awe and innocence occasionally turn to cynicism? We sat in our living rooms and watched a President speak directly to men standing on the surface of the moon—a moment of intense national pride. We later watched the same President resign in disgrace. At that moment my chest ached and something inside twisted itself into a knot. We took our children to Disney World last year. This year, CBS television presented American families with the opportunity to stay at home and watch a reenactment of the Manson murders in their own living rooms. Chappaquiddick is barely remembered. There are new headlines to think about. New York teeters on the brink of bankruptcy and the U.S. Postal Service seems to be going down the chute as we celebrate the Bicentennial. A young man consults "Dear Abby" with his problem: he wants to sue his parents for $100,000 because they had him circumcised as a baby. What's this world coming to, we wonder at times. What's become of our heroes and heroines? A former First Lady, tragic but aristocratic in her grief, captures the nation's heart. We want to keep her a widow forever. After all, we own her. But she refuses to play our game and later appears braless, barefoot, and remarried! Frank Sinatra punches people and Princess Margaret vacations with her boyfriend. So much for the anchors of stability.

No wonder the kids are cynical. No wonder they walk around wearing T-shirts that read "Up Yours." How do we explain the world to them when we're disillusioned ourselves and more than a little bewildered? "We didn't make things this way," we say, but we're not quite sure who did. Could it really all have happened while we were looking the other way?

The changes seem to affect us more deeply and more personally than they do our children. We are being asked to adapt and accept, while simultaneously abandoning tradition and the teachings and absolutes of the past. It frightens us to let go of so many familiar lifelines at once. There's a potential mistake inherent in every choice, and we seem to have far too many new choices. Where is our guidance? The past no longer seems to apply. The future is up for grabs. We're expected to substitute guesswork for certainties. Where will we make our mistakes, we wonder—with our children, our marriages, our jobs? And will they be big ones?

These are schizophrenic times when everyone feels a little unhinged, but most of us cover up well. We're swept along, speeding off to who knows where while trying to put it all together on the run. Once in a while, we feel a wistful yearning for the old safe game rules and the comfort of knowing exactly what is what—and a vague sense of guilt for plunging on alone in the dark. Occasionally, we glance over our shoulders to see if anyone is back there frowning at us. Is that Gramma standing on the shore shouting, "God'll getcha for that!" It well might be.

3.

The Splintered Suburbanite

When in Rome, do as the Romans.

*The truly free man is he who knows how to decline
a dinner invitation without giving an excuse.*

JULES RENARD

"I DREAMED I met the Welcome Wagon Lady as I
was riding my Toro lawn mower and sipping Metrecal
in my Maidenform bra." That could have been the
slogan for suburbs across the nation in the fifties and
early sixties.

It all started innocently enough. We were in love
with the idea of the suburbs and the warm, fuzzy feeling of belonging. Suburbia was the American Dream
come true.

If you recall high school and college students in the
fifties, the description that comes to mind is placid.
We were teddy bears. Rebellion to us meant the Boston
Tea Party or *Mutiny on the Bounty*. We certainly
didn't rebel against the lifestyle of our parents; we
craved it. Not only did we yearn to pick up where
they left off, but to better them. We couldn't wait to
marry, build a nest, and fulfill those idyllic dreams of
togetherness. How else could I become Donna Reed;
Dick, Robert Young? As quickly as we could scrape
together the down payment, it was out of the apartment and into the little white house with the picket

18

fence. Suburbia was where it was at and we couldn't get there fast enough. Buck the establishment? Heck, we were dying to become the establishment!

When Dick and I bought our first suburban home in 1961, we were part of a nationwide trend. Soulmates all over America were flocking to the suburbs to put down roots. Almost thirty-five million people have moved into or been born in the suburbs since 1950. Today America is the only nation on earth where suburbia is the plurality lifestyle. We helped make that happen.

Why the mad rush, the craving for a little piece of earth all our own? Why not? It sounded like the ideal lifestyle. Suburbanites were uniformly young in the late fifties. Everybody was married; everybody had children. Like birds of a feather, we were eager to join up with the flock. Magazines and television had been promoting the image for almost ten years: Saturday-night backyard barbecues with friends; neighbors sharing freshly baked coffee cakes; a wide sidewalk for little Timmy to ride his tricycle. The perfect life, and most of us wanted it.

But there were other reasons. The nuclear family was beginning to prevail, even though we didn't call it that yet. We only knew that for many of us, Mom, Dad, and the clan were far away. Industry was beginning to move young men like Dick around. It was no longer likely that you would be born, married, and live out your life in the same city or town. For the first time, some of us found ourselves alone in strange places. We missed our families and friends, and we had that most natural of human desires—the longing to belong. Suburbia offered the answer for the newly mobile family—intimacy, a peer group, jolly good fellowship, and the coziness of calling people by their first names. There was ready acceptance and quick rooting for the couple willing to abide by a few simple rules.

It seemed a fair exchange. If we wanted suburbia to substitute for the larger families we were leaving behind, rules were a small price to pay for acceptance and warmth. Besides, our generation was accustomed to playing by the rules. If the lady next door was to become a substitute aunt, sister, or mother, she was entitled to the privileges of such. After all, expectations and the need for approval went hand in hand with any family. The trade-off was acceptable to most would-be suburbanites, and, en masse, we rushed into our new nests proudly displaying the passports: strollers, second-hand lawn mowers, and time-payment booklets. It was easy enough to get through the gates.

Once settled, pictures hung, our few pieces of furniture in place, there was time for the important things. Dick and I met the neighbors, I coffee-klatched, and we both sniffed the wind to learn exactly what was expected of us. It was amazingly simple: we discovered that the suburbs were really tribes. But instead of the ethnic or religious tribes most of us had known previously, these were based on economics: blue collar, white collar, button-down collar. Like all tribes, each had its own rigidly prescribed set of taboos, rules, and rituals. Discipline was swift, and there was one punishment for all crimes—isolation. Flub the rules and no one would invite you back. You could find yourself lonely and undesirable overnight.

As demographer Ben Wattenberg accurately described us, "They wanted deeply to associate with their own kind." We really did, and eighty million of us decided the price was worth it.

Dick and I made the instantaneous changes necessary to blend in as proper suburbanites. Overnight I went from being a carefree stewardess who had rarely cleaned her apartment or cooked (other than to reheat leftover airline food) to a fastidious suburban homemaker whose main concerns were germ-free toilet bowls, sparkling laundry, and 101 ways to fix ground beef. Dick made the quick transition from nonchalant bachelor, whose only previous culinary skill had been prying open cans of Franco-American spaghetti, to diligent backyard chef with garlic salt in one hand, marinade in the other. Two lighthearted singles in Dallas who had hidden the dirty laundry behind the couch whenever we had a big date turned into Milwaukee's Mr. and Mrs. Clean with amazing speed. And it wasn't that difficult. All the little tape recordings our parents had been plugging in since childhood began their instant replays the moment we walked through our own mortgaged front door. Onion dip, bank loans, place settings for eight, crabgrass cures—they all came back in a rush of *déjà vu*. To my mother's utter amazement, I remembered how to clean a bathroom. Dick's father almost suffered a minor seizure the first time he saw Dick spreading fertilizer. But we enjoyed doing these things—for a while.

What about the other tribal rules and expectations? On the surface, they, too, seemed simple, direct, and easily met: "Get along . . . get involved . . . get ahead." Those three basics covered everything. "Keeping up with the Joneses" was another way of stating those same rules, but the implications didn't daunt us for a moment. We wanted to play, and plunged eagerly into the sea of expectations, whooping, "Love us! Love our kids!" It didn't take long for two bright and willing students to learn what this conformity really entailed.

The primary expectation in the "get along" category was neighborliness. "As you were greeted, so shall you greet." We were welcomed with homemade cakes, casseroles of spaghetti, and coffees. We welcomed others in the same fashion, and then proceeded to learn everything about their lives and their children. As soon as the moving vans pulled away, we settled into the serious business of sharing: children's clothes; lawn equipment; manual labor in the yards; gossip; recipes and household hints. We dutifully divided clumps of our best perennials and passed them around. Wives passed husbands around to help with heavy lifting, furniture moving, or digging. The sharing expectation was so strong that little remained sacred. I once asked a neighbor for a cherished family recipe and was almost refused because her mother had made her promise not to give it out. She eventually gave me the recipe despite her mother, for I had the status of *neighbor!* Any good dessert, hors d'oeuvre, or casserole recipe made the rounds so rapidly that it soon became community property. It was best to maintain contact with a friend or two from other parts of town so that different suburbs could be tapped occasionally for fresh ideas.

Neighborliness included the children. It was acceptable to criticize their behavior behind their parents' backs, but never to correct them yourself. Only the crabby lady on each block could exercise that privilege because she was already ostracized. You could politely ask a child to stop trampling down your petunias, but you couldn't kick him out of your garden; and you rarely told his mother because that might alienate her. We all believed we had perfect children.

Social behavior was also governed by "get along" standards. Dick and I dutifully returned invitations even when we couldn't stand the people. In another era, we might have cheerfully ignored half the couples we met, but at that time, a party attended meant a party given—and parties had their own sets of rules. I made stroganoff until I began to taste it in my dreams, and soon my only ambition in life was to become the Hot Hors d'Oeuvres Queen of Whitefish Bay. Many a night was spent packing the freezer with tiny clam or cheese canapés for the weekend festivities.

Dick, who doesn't drink himself and never learned to mix a decent martini, dropped sharply on the social scale for both transgressions. To be the only cold-sober soul in a room was offense enough; not to roll, shake, or stir the martini pitcher with loving care was almost unpardonable. To regain his status, he went through a period of "more is better, stronger is best." Suddenly, our parties ended with a thud. Dead bodies littered the living room floor and dying ones hung draped across our germ-free toilet. A substitute uncle finally set Dick straight one night after his wife plugged our plumbing with her expensive wig. We switched to Hueblein's—not as acceptable as mix-your-own-perfect-martini, but safe.

Parties were segregated by sex. Men were allowed sports, politics, business, and lawn care as topics of conversation, but had to discuss them standing in clumps at the far end of the room or gathered around the outdoor grill. Women were allowed to sit (except at large cocktail parties) around the chips and dips, and their topics were child care, home care, and cleaning products, with an occasional mother-in-law or antique sale thrown in for spice. We maintained our status by comparing potty-training, thumb-sucking, and first-tooth stories. I only transgressed once. While passing a tray of blue cheese puffs one winter night, I lingered too long at the edge of the men's clump and had the audacity to remember the name of a Chicago Bears' linebacker when no one else could. It took months to regain my former status on the other side of the room. Poor Dick managed to err at almost every party by wandering off to a corner with another female to discuss marriage and child-rearing problems. He not only crossed lines, he was "heavy," a serious suburban sin. And he didn't *mingle!* It was an added burden on me to keep him from slipping off the social ladder entirely, but as long as we kept inviting, I knew they had to invite back.

Opinions were uniformly bland; it was another suburban sin to upset anyone. Even though we knew the safe subjects and stayed within the boundaries, problems invariably occurred at the table. Seating was always arranged in a male/female/male/female pattern, which forced everyone to cross-talk so the men could continue with their subjects and the women with theirs. It became a suburban fine art to pick out your thread of conversation from the babble of voices. An alternative was gossip about neighbors or friends who weren't present, and everyone was allowed to participate in that game simultaneously. Maybe that's how it got to be so popular.

All of our friends were required to blend together like vanilla pudding. The players had to be interchangeable so as not to spoil the symmetry of larger parties. An added suburban burden was being held personally responsible for one friend's behavior to another. If you brought Suzie as a substitute to bridge club and she made a social error, it was your fault. (A friend once invited a sub who picked a toenail while playing cards. Obviously, she didn't know that fingernail picking was acceptable, but toenails didn't exist in suburbia.) Or if one of our guests had a little too much to drink and insulted another, we, as hosts, were the villains. We should have chosen better. It was all right to pass out at a party, but not to become belligerent. For years, there were no raised voices in the suburbs.

The first time an incident occurred at our home, I was devastated. Two old friends from Dick's bachelor days lurched in unexpectedly one night to join a dinner party already in progress. (This in itself revealed them as nonsuburbanites, but they were old friends.) They proceeded to crunch the toes of our other guests by debating the religions of some and the politics of others, just as we had all done in college. Conversation grew heated. People were actually arguing at our table. As host and hostess, we were temporarily at a loss but finally handled it in the finest suburban superstar tradition. I shoved another miniature egg roll into everyone's mouth while Dick poured another drink down their throats. How quickly we had become uncomfortable with controversy.

The second stage of blending required involvement. "Get involved" was a tribal rule not to be taken lightly. Next to child-centered interests, clubs were the hub of activity in suburbia: bridge, Mah-Jongg, poker, tennis, golf, garden, Newcomers. For every interest, there was an organized way to pursue it. You might belong to a bowling league or a gourmet dinner club, but you belonged to something. And as surely as the property taxes came due once a year, the human urge to play one-upmanship grew with the clubs. What began simply as potato chips and pretzels at the first bridge game inevitably became a flaming dessert a year later. As the suburbs grew, the number of related activities increased along with them. A woman could keep busy every day of the week; a man, every night.

For women, the primary daytime involvement centered around the children and their schools. The good mother planned her child's activities, managed his social life from the toddler stage on, and maintained his popularity by throwing better birthday parties than the mother next door. Part of our adult status rested on our children's ability to adjust and be sociable.

"Keeping up with the Joneses" meant keeping up with the Jones kid, too.

My friends and I dutifully organized play schools for our youngsters as soon as they could walk. If there were not enough children on the block of the right age, we imported them once or twice a week from blocks away. There was a vague unhealthy aura attached to the child who played with another child of a different age, so we enrolled them in little clubs of their own called nursery school and creative dance. Like their parents, it was important for children to learn to get along with their own kind. Gone were the days when the entire neighborhood gang played together, and the littlest child was chosen last when teams picked sides. Gone were the days when you prayed for someone to have a younger brother or sister to take your place at the bottom of the heap. There was no bottom of the heap for suburban kids—only a vast middle. Everything had to be fair and uniform. And everybody got to play. It was a mother's job to see that it was so.

Another part of a mother's responsibility toward her children concerned enrichment. Chauffeuring mothers and the need for a second car began with the craze to better our children. We bombarded those poor tykes with lessons, bored them with Kinder-concerts, and dragged them on field trips to any establishment that would allow a mother and four runny noses through the door. We took them everywhere with us. Our children knew more about the inside workings of a supermarket at three than I did at twenty. Thanks to TV and being pushed in a grocery cart from the first moment they were able to sit slumped over their own navels, most children could identify brand names long before they could read. Temper tantrums in the aisles were inevitable, but, nevertheless, embarrassing. "Gimme Fizzies," Eric would scream each week. I would pluck an unwashed carrot from my basket and shove it, pesticides and all, into his mouth instead.

Since the suburbs had neighborhood schools, mothers were expected to be heavily involved there, and "keep in close touch" became our motto. PTA's blossomed all over America, and the number of committees and school-related activities mushroomed. As quickly as we built and completed the schools, we mothers created new jobs for ourselves. Room mothers invented themselves to help teachers organize the parties that were fast becoming standard practice for each holiday. Costumes for plays and Hawaiian Punch were hauled to the classroom by the carload. As children, we were once grateful that a holiday meant time off. Now youngsters expected a suitable celebration to mark George Washington's birthday or that of another six-year-old. Organizing the menus and the field trips for the year became a full-time job. And like the birthday parties and dinner parties at home, one-upmanship crept into the classroom. Mothers kept expanding the children's expectations: little home-baked, heart-shaped cookies for Valentine's Day; little bunny-shaped cupcakes with jelly-bean eyes for Easter. The ability to bake in different shapes was elevated to a high art during those years and remains one to this day. Secretly to tap the local bakery when your own creativity ran out was a cardinal suburban sin that a good mother never admitted.

Although fathers were at work all day, they were not excused from a high degree of evening and week-end involvement with the children. While mothers were fostering enrichment, dads were developing the competitive spirit. Scouts, Little League, Indian Guides —all required paternal encouragement and involvement. How many badges could you help your son earn? How many Pine Box Derbies could you help him win? Start throwing the ball with Junior as soon as he's old enough to hold it. Stand at poolside and clock him as soon as he joins swim club. Encourage him . . . buy him equipment . . . build the teams of the future. If the suburbs were tribes, a father's responsibility was to sire and ready the young warriors who would later do battle on the playing fields against other tribes and bring us all honor. (A long-standing rivalry between Whitefish Bay and a neighboring suburb actually revolves around a "Glory Cup" that passes to the winning football team each fall.)

If fathers built the teams, both parents were responsible for supporting the youthful gladiators once they reached junior high or high school. Parents sold or bought pizzas to send the band to Florida, peddled light bulbs so that the debate team could compete in Washington, and hawked soft drinks and popcorn at games to support the teams. And what was a season without a banquet to end it? The rituals of competition grew from team uniforms and equipment to one hundred pom-pom girls and a half-time show with fireworks and cannons—all backed by the equivalent of the Mormon Tabernacle Choir singing on the sidelines. The Romans marching off to war had less elaborate rituals. And we parents cheered from the stands after setting it all in motion.

Children were merely one facet of the across-the-board involvement required of suburbanites. Community life was another. The volunteer invented herself in those early years of suburbia. Women collecting for charitable drives pushed the stroller with one hand and clutched the envelope with the other. Men collected for candidates, political parties, and church fund-raisers. Good citizens ran for the village board, the town board, or the school board. The rest of us held coffees for the candidates. Local elections began to take on the flavor of national and state elections, with lawn signs, slogans, and debates. In 1975, community involvement went big time in Whitefish Bay when this little village hired a professional lobbyist to defeat a bill before the state legislature.

When businessmen caught on to the flight to suburbia they followed us erecting shopping centers and restaurants. Then came the churches and synagogues. Thus in suburbia, religion was brought to our doorsteps, and it, too, offered opportunities for involvement. You could belong to the sisterhood, the altar society, be an usher, teach Sunday school, or sing in the choir. Most of us did something; it was another facet of belonging, and it was expected. Within a few short years of our move to the suburbs, involvement in the many facets of community life became a total commitment. One could live a full, but ever-narrowing, life without ever leaving the suburb.

The final expectation for suburbanites was "get ahead," and that required two things—acquiring and keeping up appearances. The two went hand in hand. Acquiring was clear-cut and simple. It meant "power" this and "ten-speed" that, as rapidly as your budget would allow. Trucks and station wagons rolled through suburban streets delivering the new necessities of life: blenders, dishwashers, Lazy-Boy recliners, and Weber grills. But more on that later.

Keeping up appearances was more complicated. We suburbanites had our own subtle dress code. "What are you wearing?" became the ritual end-of-the-week question. Not that this was difficult to guess, because everyone shopped at the same stores (which had the added bonus of making everyone aware of what everyone else paid for their clothes). A quick look around the room any Saturday night would reveal exactly how well you were keeping up with the Joneses. Occasionally, someone pulled off a daring shopping coup while vacationing out of town and caused a flurry of confusion for weeks.

Besides your kids, your marriage (which also had to appear perfect on the outside), and your clothes, suburban appearances included your home—inside and out. Clean up, paint up, fix up, redecorate, remodel—something had to be redone constantly to keep up with neighborhood standards. Forget to weed the garden and you'd hear about it quickly enough. Allow your teenager to park his jalopy out front and you'd hear about that, too. Your house was no longer a home; it was a status symbol. Your property was, in reality, community property, and one bad apple could downgrade the appearance of an entire block.

As with every other aspect of suburbia, we organized to keep up appearances. Leaf rakings and lawn clippings were deposited at the curb in tidy piles to be scooped up by the Great Green Leaf Eater that rumbled through the streets on Mondays and Thursdays. Children could not play in the piles because the Leaf Eater didn't pick up scattered strays. (How sad that an entire generation of children grew up without ever knowing the smell of burning leaves in the fall.) Garbage cans were hidden inconspicuously behind little enclosures built for that purpose and painted to match the trim on the house. Dogs were leashed or fenced. If you saw a dachshund out for its evening stroll, it was sure to be followed by a man or woman carrying a pooper-scooper.

As suburbia grew, so grew the restrictions. "We've got a nice little community here—let's keep it that way." Suddenly there were numerous things you couldn't do to your little piece of earth. Permits and approvals were needed for additions, fences, and pools in some suburbs. How high, how wide, and what color might well be decided by popular opinion. In 1973, a suburban Milwaukee housewife living in the village of Wauwatosa planted a vegetable garden in her front yard because she claimed the back yard was too shady. The offending garden was quickly referred to the village's Public and Municipal Affairs Committee. Alderman Marvin Stach argued that "If you don't stop it, front-yard gardens are going to pop up all over." He was quoted as saying that the proper Wauwatosa front yard had "a nice lawn, a few shrubs, and maybe a few flowers—something you can be proud of." Wauwatosa quickly passed an ordinance prohibiting front-yard vegetable gardens. In Columbia, Maryland, a resident now needs the approval of an architectural committee to plant any bush more than two feet high, and Fido's doghouse must be stained to match his master's house. If you move to Reston, Virginia, you'll be required to paint the children's swing set gray-brown to blend with the environment. In Westlake Village, California, hanging a clothesline that your neighbors can see is forbidden.

What occurs inside your home may also be subject to community approval. Several years ago, two couples decided to share a single-family home in the Milwaukee suburb of Shorewood. This was no budding commune or sex club invading innocent suburbia; two compatible families simply wanted to share the responsibilities of child rearing and household duties and the financial burden of owning a house. They bothered no one, but the village quickly took issue, and the couples had to take their case to federal court to win the right to pursue a personalized lifestyle.

No more little gnomes or Bambis on the front lawns, in many suburbs. No more deviance. When we flocked to suburbia seeking an extended family, we never dreamed we were creating a Big Brother for ourselves. Once every American happily thought of himself or herself as a rugged individualist. In the suburbs, we sacrificed that individuality in order to belong—and who's to fault us? We got exactly what we came for, and we loved it—we really did—for a while. Suburban life glowed until the picture window began to develop cracks.

As the suburbs grew, so did the demands on suburbanites. The number of drives increased; there were more teams to support; more activities to attend; more requests for time; and so many more subtribes to pledge allegiance to. Any single involvement, whether PTA, Scouts, or soccer, could magically expand itself into a full-time commitment. There were more children, more expectations, and more restrictions than many people felt comfortable with. The possibility of disappointing someone became inevitable. Many of us had no time left, but we had created an insatiable monster and it was to demand more of us. But how to say "no"? We had become habitual rule-followers and approval-seekers. Besides, we had been so busy for so long, most of us never realized we were no longer doing the things we wanted.

A few members of this substitute family began to rebel. We still loved the family, but felt strangled by its rules, its intrusions on our privacy and time. We still enjoyed the feeling of belonging, but, like adolescents, longed to test our wings alone again. Fifteen years was a long time to be dutiful, and the family ties were beginning to bind. We craved a little space to move around, a little breathing room.

Someone finally held up a mirror. Occasionally, it was a newly settled mobile family who arrived tired. They had made so many moves that each time it seemed easier to put down fewer roots. More and more frequently we heard the statements: "I'm going

to take a year off this time before I get involved . . .
I'm going to pick and choose this time." A few families were actually beginning to hedge about the rules.

The young adults from the postwar baby boom
brought the most interesting, challenging, and disturbing comparisons to traditional suburbia. Many of these
young couples had been influenced by the radicalism
of the sixties. They weren't seeking a tribe or community to belong to, but simply a house and a decent
school system. Their activities were centered elsewhere, their interests were vastly different, and they
had no intention of getting involved in recipe swapping
or the perfect martini. If they didn't like the school
system, they'd work to change it, but without joining
the PTA. They had challenged systems before and had
already rebelled against much of what we had come
to suburbia for. This was the first crack in the picture
window.

The effect on the typical suburbanite was stunning.
People actually showed up at the supermarket and the
school board meeting in T-shirts—and they weren't
always polite. They debated the tried and true and
broke the norms without flinching. Invite this couple
to a neighborhood gathering and they might show up
in jeans, claim to know nothing about bridge, say
"Bullshit!" and circulate a petition among your other
guests calling for amnesty for draft resisters. If, *if* they
invited you back, they might seat you on the floor,
serve wine and cheese on paper plates instead of bourbon and beef, and light up a joint while they discussed
backpacking the baby through Yellowstone. How could
the average suburbanite cope with that? It may have
been a short jump from shirtwaists into pants suits, but
it's a long step into jeans.

Other comparisons were internal. It's difficult to
keep people from growing. The very activities that
were approved by suburban standards created new
interests that were not. The adult enrichment classes
offered by the local high schools had always been acceptable. Gourmet cooking, home decorating, furniture refinishing, Great Books—all were designed to
increase suburban superstar status. I diligently worked

my way through the offerings of two local high schools until I eventually stumbled across one course that tweaked more than a passing interest—pottery. From high school classes, the interest took me back to college courses. Eventually a hobby grew into a business, and that took time. Dick's years of involvement in local organizations and campaigns led naturally to deeper involvement in politics. Once an interest grows serious, it requires time, and for us, the time had to be stolen from an already full life. Thus we faced our first conflict with suburban involvement and a choice had to be made.

When adult enrichment classes became college courses, another comparison occurred: the fifties child met the sixties child. Teddy Bear met Long Hair, and it was a stimulating exchange. Few of the young people were radicals, but they were involved in a totally different world—one that made the sheltered concerns of our past fifteen years seem shallow and self-centered. Waking up your wood paneling with Pledge was no match for saving the woods. Knowing the batting averages of the Cincinnati Reds suddenly seemed less important than knowing how to contact your congressman on environmental protection. The Greening of America was occurring simultaneously on campus and on the talk shows. A larger, more diversified world was coming into view. Whether it frightened or excited us, we could not avoid comparisons. Men began to ask themselves a few quiet questions; women did the same. The most common was "Is this all there is— crabgrass, bunny cakes, and Little League?" Every medium was telling us there was more, and the word "involvement" took on an entirely different meaning. Groupthink began to splinter.

Some of the faithful didn't rebel. They just collapsed in exhaustion. Finally, it had grown too much even for them. "Enough is enough" was the cry we heard from men and women who had dutifully put in their time for years and now wanted someone else to do it. Most of us had entered suburbia with small children, and they were now teens or young adults. They, too, held up mirrors. They no longer wanted to be perfect kids or play our games. If we were "doing it for them," much of it suddenly seemed unnecessary. Another natural life-cycle shift occurred simultaneously. As our children and affluence grew, family interests changed. The vacation homes, camping, skiing, and snowmobiling we could now afford took us out of the community. Another crack in the picture window.

But mostly, it was the feeling of "too much" that broke the bonds. We've heard dozens of variations of one former volunteer's theme over the past few years: "If I'm going to do all this work, I might as well do it for pay." And she did. Children grew up, the Women's Movement created an impact, and women went back to work by the millions all over America. And everyone knows a working wife can't be a good suburbanite.

When people began to take a closer look at their lives, another logical question was asked: "Is this really the healthiest environment for my children?" Not all could answer "yes." We're now witnessing a minor migration to the country or back to the rims of the cities. Some mobile families discovered a new anonymity when they moved to the southeastern and western regions of the U.S. and liked it. A Jewish couple from the Bronx, overwhelmed by family demands and ethnic neighborhood narrowness, moved to the Southwest to escape. As they describe it, "We wanted to be by ourselves for once and have no norms." They've lived on the same block for three years and have made no effort to meet the neighbors. They are typical of the many couples in Los Angeles, Dallas, and Atlanta who now state with pride, "I love the neighbors. I've never laid eyes on them."

Other couples who moved used the move to change lifestyles that had become too constricting. As a lifelong friend and resident of Milwaukee wrote after her move to Phoenix, "We pick and choose now because we don't want to get sucked in as we were before. No more playing 'we owe them.' No more 'can you top this' with tenderloin. It's a poolside hamburger for guests now or a trip to the deli, maybe followed by a movie. We're more discriminating in our social life, with fewer friends and fewer obligations. We like it that way, and we've filtered enough couples to find the few who enjoy the same relaxed lifestyle. I could never go back!" Nor could many others.

But it's not that simple to walk away from anything that has been an integral part of your life. Though the suburban expectations grow to overwhelming proportions, the alternatives are neither free nor easy. If suburban bonds are painfully tight, there's also pain when they're cut, whether one flees physically or emotionally. It's the pain of guilt—the guilt of abandonment. It's hard to leave part of your life behind. Those who fled physically may not miss the obligations, but they surely miss the feeling of belonging. Never meeting the neighbors is just as bad as having the neighbors constantly on your doorstep. Being part of a community takes away some of your freedom in exchange for the warmth of acceptance, but being without a community takes away warmth.

Those who moved forward into another stage of life, whether back to work or on to new interests, also feel twinges of guilt. We feel a little selfish each time we say "no" to a drive, to a bake sale, to the chauffeuring. We're not accustomed to saying "no," and making time for yourself does seem selfish when you've never done it before. And we genuinely miss a few of the things that once overwhelmed us. It is nice to know a neighbor will step in to look after the kids in an emergency. It's nice to know a neighbor's name. We miss the warmth and we miss part of what we left behind. It wasn't all bad. It wasn't even mostly bad. It was just too much.

It was pleasant standing around on a Saturday afternoon swapping crabgrass stories—as long as the neighbors didn't follow you back into the house when you wanted to do something else. It's great knowing the milkman and the mailman for years. They leave milk even when you forget to mark the card and deliver the letter with postage due even when you're not home. It's a good feeling walking down a street or into a store and hearing people call you by name—as long as they don't call out all your business, too. I love wandering out on the first warm day of spring and discovering that the rest of the block is still alive and well—as long as I can wander away again when I'm ready. That easy freedom may not be possible for many of us yet. Our guilt feelings get in the way.

We created suburbia and then elevated it to the status of an institution. When we did that we forfeited our right to criticize or change it without guilt.

Suburbia isn't the best of all possible worlds, but what is? As often as our close friends have heard me complain about suburban norms over the past few years, we haven't moved. As with the institution of the family, we can't find a better alternative at this stage in our lives, not out to the country for more chauffeuring, not closer to the city for a higher crime rate. But staying doesn't mean we think nothing needs changing.

The problem is "to have your cake and eat it, too" —bunny-shaped or not. We want to live right here, but now we want to do it our way, and that's hard because Dick and I were raised to walk in suburban shoes, not to be rugged individualists. More diverse interests have replaced many of our old activities, but we'll never be totally comfortable as fallen-away suburbanites living in the old neighborhood because we don't *do* what we once did. Our own recent past comes back to haunt us. I know I no longer live up to everybody's expectations—I don't even try to—but I haven't grown accustomed to the disapproval yet, and there are many who disapprove. Which one of my tribe will be disappointed in me today?

But others are experiencing the same pulls and tugs. There are many splintered suburbanites who have been cut up a bit as the picture window finally cracked apart. Even though all the houses and front yards may still look the same from the sidewalk, there's a rich mixture inside many of those homes today. Numerous individuals are having second thoughts, quietly testing unused wings, and experiencing the guilt feelings that go along with change and a taste of freedom. There is a support group waiting for the recently fallen away, though some of us don't realize they're waiting because we've never asked. We've been accustomed to polite conversation for too long.

4.

Blood Is Thicker than Water, but It Clots (Mom, Pop, and Auntie Minnie Guilt)

I may be frequently wrong but I am never in doubt.
EVERYBODY'S FATHER

I am only trying to help.
EVERYBODY'S MOTHER

WHO CAN MAKE YOU FEEL GUILTY faster than anyone in the world? Probably your mother . . . followed closely by your father, Aunt Minnie, your sisters and brothers, grandparents, and any other assorted relatives you may have scattered around. Parents definitely have the edge, though, when it comes to making the average adult child feel guilty. They hardly have to try. "Why don't you call more often? . . . You haven't written lately . . . We never see you . . . Aunt Martha says she hasn't received a thank-you note from you yet . . . What about Thanksgiving? . . . Christmas? . . . Hanukkah? . . . I hope you appreciate what I'm doing for you . . . I waited for a call from you today . . . Your father has been worried about you . . . We're all expecting you to be there . . . Come and give Gramma a hug—Lord *knows* when we'll see you again." It's lucky parentally-induced guilts don't pop out like boils. Most of us would be unable to sit down.

If you think *your* parents make you feel guilty, they may be minor-league players compared to some others. Our candidate for the most notable one-line squelch from a mother to her married daughter on keeping in touch is: "It's hard for me to write when I have nothing to respond to." The most colossal single guilt trip experienced by an adult male probably occurred when a twenty-four-year-old Jewish son from New York, taking his first trip through the Southwest, forgot to call home one day. His elderly parents frantically notified the Arizona Highway Patrol, begging them to look for a black Volkswagen that surely must have crashed. What else could have kept him from calling? Oh, the guilt.

How do they do it? How can they make us feel guilty so easily? It's simple: they are parents, and no matter how old we are, we are always their children. They are accustomed to telling us what to do, and we're accustomed to responding. As a sixty-three-year-old man told us last winter, "When my eighty-six-year-old mother comes for Sunday dinner, she still reminds me to put on my rubbers before I go outside—and I do it."

Most of us have been operating on auto-parent as long as we can remember. At times, it's helpful. For example, we probably operate on auto-parent for the first hour each morning without realizing it. We lurch from the bed and recordings of our mothers' voices begin to play in our heads. "Brush your teeth, Harold . . . Change your underwear, Harold . . . Wear warm socks . . . Eat a hot breakfast, Harold—it's going to be cold today . . . Drive carefully, the roads are slippery." No thinking on our part is necessary to get from the pillow to the office because Mom is still guiding us every step of the way.

At other times, we resent the auto-parent response because it makes us feel guilty unnecessarily. That little-kid "Did I do something wrong?" reflex can come back in a flash whether we are twenty, thirty, or forty years old. All it takes is a pair of pursed lips or one raised eyebrow to signal disapproval. Your mother asks, "Have you returned Cousin Harriet's casserole dish yet?" You haven't and instantly feel a stab of guilt. Your dad says, "Are those sideburns you're growing?" and at thirty-eight, you automatically find yourself on the defensive. The two people who once had the right to govern every aspect of our lives find it a difficult change to relinquish the authority when we reach adulthood. How many parents have innocently opened a conversation with the line "I don't want to meddle in your business, but . . ." Then they plunge right in and meddle. It shouldn't surprise us. What makes us think it's easy for them to let go after all those years of wiping noses.

Are parents being selfish when they make demands? Is it loneliness and too much time on their hands that makes them meddle? Are they deliberately looking for ways to make us feel guilty? Some are, of course (there are always a few mean, ornery parents who go out of their way to make life miserable for their children), but most have no intention of interfering or making us feel guilty. They don't even realize they're doing it. It's the problem of expectations—theirs and ours. They expect more from us than we can possibly live up to, but we keep trying anyway. We've never learned to ignore the raised eyebrow. And besides, "Look how much they've done for us." The more we love our parents, the more guilt we feel when we disappoint them. And disappoint them we will; it's inevitable that somewhere, sometime, somehow, we will let them down. We grow up, we marry, and our allegiances are split. Now there are two sets of backgrounds, two sets of traditions, and two sets of parents to please. Where can we have Thanksgiving dinner without hurting someone's feelings?

I don't know anyone who doesn't experience lightning flashes of parentally-induced guilt. "Oh my God, I promised to call Mother tonight and forgot!" It's one in the morning—too late—and you know no matter how much you apologize later that day, she'll still feel hurt. Don't you care about her? Don't you think about her? Don't you love her enough to remember to make one lousy phone call? Just try to fall peacefully asleep with those thoughts running through your mind. Have you ever forgotten a Mother's Day, Father's Day, birthday, or anniversary because you were

busy and it just slipped past you? Dick manages to
miss at least one family milestone each year. No matter how good his excuse, he feels like a rat, a crumb,
an ungrateful child. And if he doesn't have a good
excuse, it's worse. One of the guiltiest moments in our
lives happened the night of his father's last birthday.
The rest of Dick's family lives in Tucson, and they
were throwing a birthday party for Grampa there. We
knew about it and planned to call during the party.
But because of the two-hour time difference, we became involved in our own activities and forgot. We
didn't even have the excuse of company; I was reading, Dick was watching television. At midnight, the
phone rang. It was Dick's sister reminding us and
covering up for us. She told Grampa *we* had called
and then put him on the phone. The happier and more
excited he sounded, the more I felt like a worm. Dick
still cringes. It was *his* father.

Most guilt feelings regarding parents aren't that
simple, straightforward, or deserved. More often they
involve a lifestyle or change that fails their expectations, even though these areas are no longer any of
their affair. Still, we've disappointed them and they
find ways to let us know. Fathers pressure sons to
follow them into the family business or into their own
profession. If Dad is a doctor, it's difficult for a son
to choose art, police work, or teaching without feeling
he's letting Dad down. Eighteen years ago, a friend
of ours married an intelligent, creative, but untidy
wife. Each time his parents have visited, he has felt
their reproach because the house is always a mess:
a frown at the sneakers under the couch, a roll of the
eyes at the clutter in the hall, a sniff in the kitchen.
He's happy with the way they live, his wife is
happy, but Mom and Pop aren't. She has never measured up to his parents' standards, and that's a reflection on him. At least those parents expressed their
disapproval subtly, unlike one mother we know who
cleaned her daughter's apartment before she brought
friends over to visit.

Few parents give their grown children the gift of
freedom from expectations and judgments that Dick's

mother has had the unique ability to do. More typical
is the proverbial "Jewish mother" stereotype (who
could just as easily be an Episcopalian father). What
pleases most parents—their form of expression, their
friends' opinions, their traditions, values, and priorities
—are the right ones, the only ones. They seldom consider what's right for you. Deviate from their norms
and you may discover a judgment lurking behind every frown. Your father drops in and wonders why you
are unshaven on a Sunday afternoon. Haven't you
been to church? Or he calls and states that your
mother isn't feeling well. The implication is you should
drop everything and come right over. And if he calls
your office and wants to chat for a half-hour, you
can't say you're busy because it implies he's not, or
that you're too busy for him—and how could you be
too busy for your own father? If a Jewish boy marries a Gentile girl, you can bet it will be discussed
at length by all members of both families. Although
prejudice is lessening, it is still likely that a Baptist
may encounter some family problems in marrying a
Catholic and an Italian-American in marrying a Wasp.
And anyone who marries "beneath" him or herself
risks disappointing the entire clan.

Often it is the most loving parents who induce the
most guilt because it's difficult to rebel against an en-
veloping fog. These parents never express their disapproval openly. Still, you know it exists. A young
friend is currently fighting a desperate internal battle
against being eased into her parents' lifestyle. They've
led an uneventful, sheltered, suburban, middle-class
existence without making ripples. Their daughter wants
to make waves. She longs for involvement, adventure,
and an interesting career. She does not plan to marry.
Although her parents have never opposed her directly,
she senses their worry, their disappointment, and their
unspoken disapproval. Why does she want to live so
far from home? Why doesn't she settle down and give
them grandchildren like her brother has? Where have
they failed? Those silent accusations make her escape
almost impossible. In a recent letter, she wrote,
"Mother is coming to visit this Tuesday for several

days. She can't wait to see my apartment and get 'a glimpse' of my life. I wish I was glad she's coming, but I'm so uncomfortable being alone with her these days. I told her I have to work, but she assured me all she wants to do is cook, clean, and watch TV. So I should go about my business. How does one do that?" With a giant case of guilt.

Many of us who live in isolated nuclear families feel a vague sense of guilt and failure because we do not resemble the Waltons. American families probably never did. Parents and children drift apart naturally with distance. My own family has been scattered across the country for sixteen years, and it's difficult to remain close to a brother and sister who live thousands of miles away, and whose lives and interests have taken different directions. My mother, like all mothers, maintains the fiction that we are still a tightly knit clan, and that she is its nerve center. She works diligently to keep us all in touch, but the truth is, we are not in touch. We haven't been for years. Still, I frequently feel a pang of guilt for contributing to the drift. No matter that my sister and brother don't write or phone any more often than I do. I have my own conscience to deal with each time I call home and receive the family news second hand.

It's a little different with Dick's family. We are the only family branch separated by distance. While we realize it's impossible to stay as close as the others can, we still feel guilty that we can't keep up with everything that happens, and when Dick's father plays nerve center, the guilt feelings pop out. "Why don't you drop Barb a line? After all, you are her only brother. And don't forget your niece's graduation next month." Those gentle reminders and admonitions cause an aching sense of guilt, an out-of-step-with-the-family feeling. Logically, we know it's not our fault we are two thousand miles away, but then whose fault is it?

So many parents struggle to maintain the Walton illusion. A friend of ours dreads his occasional business trips to New York where his relatives still live. His parents can't understand why he isn't interested in touching base with each family member and each old family friend. The truth is they have little in common anymore, and what's of daily interest to them has long ceased to be of any interest to him. "Come out and see Aunt Sophie's new couch" brings an inward groan. How can he see his own friends and avoid Sophie, Maude, and Uncle Mortimer when his mother lines up family dinners for every night of his visit? How can he avoid being stuffed with strudel when he's on a diet? How can he say "no" and shatter the myth his parents still hold dear? It's hard to pick up where you left off ten years earlier, and as he stated wistfully, "They don't realize I can get better conversation in a Greyhound bus depot than I can in Aunt Sophie's living room." But we all keep trying because we blame ourselves for the lack of closeness. And we wind up sneaking in and out of the old hometown and feel even guiltier.

It's often difficult for parents to realize that a business trip that brings you home isn't a vacation. Another friend recently spent a week working in New York and stayed at a midtown hotel for convenience. He visited his parents in the Bronx on Monday and worked for the rest of the week. When he phoned on Friday to say goodbye, his father said, "How come you didn't keep in touch all week? You could have called collect." "But Pop, I'm here in town." "That's what I mean. I would have loaned you a dime." Ouch! Jerry quickly rearranged his schedule to squeeze in lunch with his father, called back, and his father informed him that *he* was busy for lunch. Ouch again! Jerry went home a guilty and chastened man.

Why don't parents let go of us? Why don't they realize that our lives, our families, and our interests have changed? Because parents don't let go easily. It's not their style.

Some couples welcome a move away to gain a little breathing room. The first guilt-producing question is "Why are you leaving? Are you so unhappy here?" The second guilt trip occurs when the relatives come to visit. Distant cousins passing through town carry a message from home—and your mother's expectation that you will put them up. Some friends of ours finally ended that game by asking a cousin who called from the airport, "Where are you staying?" They knew that word about their inhospitality would quickly travel back, but they were tired of disrupting their lives on the spur of the moment for relatives they hardly remembered. Now all they have to do is learn to live with the knowledge that Mom and Dad think they are selfish and inconsiderate.

It's a little more complicated when Mom and Dad come to visit themselves. The short vacation can be handled, even at inconvenient times; the long stay can be a continual guilt trip. Some friends in California complain that their parents visit for eight weeks each winter, and while the older couple rent their own condominium nearby, they have no friends of their own to relieve the pressure on the younger family to entertain them. For two months, it's expected that their friends will be at beck and call and will spend every available moment with their parents. Any normal continuation of their own lives is taken as an insult. "Why are we out here," asks the mother, "if you don't want to be with us?" There is no guilt-free answer to that question.

Other couples who have moved away to break the family hold on them panic when Mom and Dad retire and speak of moving closer to their grandchildren. One friend wailed, "How can I tell them we moved to get away from them?" She can't, and may instead have to rely on the guilty methods of another woman who has been making her Southwestern city sound like Calcutta since she first heard of her parents' retirement plans. "I've told them about the traffic, the high cost of living, the crime rate, the rattlesnakes, the duststorms, the scorpions, and the flash floods," she said. "If none of that discourages them, I'll start on the diseases."

One of the most uncomfortable guilt experiences involves being caught between the expectations of grandparents and the actions of grandchildren. We, as parents, are responsible for our children; we rear them. When they don't measure up, it makes for a giant case of guilt. Grampa thinks Johnny's hair is too long and his jeans are falling apart. How can Grampa take him out to dinner looking like that? "Why isn't the boy out for football? And how can you allow Suzie to go braless? It's shameful the way she sits around all day watching television with her boyfriend —practically on his lap. And no growing child should be a vegetarian. She'll ruin her health. Doesn't she ever put on a skirt?" The world of our children has changed drastically from that of our parents; we're bound to be caught in the middle at times—and feel responsible. There is a marvelous Yiddish word —*shonda*—that describes the guilt feelings when your children don't measure up. It means "a shame," "a family disgrace." It's a *shonda* for a Jewish boy to be on welfare. Even though he may feel it's his civil right today, Gramma and Grampa will be devastated. It's a *shonda* if your daughter abandons the flute and takes up the guitar—"Tsk . . . to waste such talent." And God forbid they should become hippies, dropouts, or start living together!

There are thousands of little *shondas* that tweak the average parent. The innocent admonitions of grandparents make us feel as though we have fallen down on the job. "Carrie looks pale . . . Timmy is getting so thin . . . Shouldn't the girls have some music lessons? . . . Billy is such a shy little boy . . . Why don't you ask the children to write more often? . . . That child never eats enough—and he has such dark circles under his eyes . . . Do you really think swim club is a good idea? I read in *Reader's Digest* that swimming can do damage to a child's heart." The statements imply our failure as parents, and we take them all personally, whether they were intended that way or not. Perhaps part of the reason contemporary parents push their children so hard is they feel guilty not giving the grandparents something to brag about.

Probably the most difficult responsibility for a parent is getting the grandchildren to write or visit as often as the grandparents would wish. It's hard to corral a busy child and immobilize him or her long enough to write a letter. For openers, they never know what to say. Dick and I have finally resorted to making the letter writing part of our children's monthly chores, and that relieves some of the guilt. But even I forget to remind them at times and that makes me feel doubly guilty. A middle-aged father of two teenagers complains that his mother constantly makes the children feel guilty by asking why they don't come to visit "poor sick Granny" more often. Granny is neither poor nor sick, and when the children do stop in to see her, she's never home.

Grandparents don't understand the lifestyle of their grandchildren and the impossibility of their expectations. Grampa comes to visit and after four days, Timmy wants to sleep overnight at a friend's house. "You mean you would rather go out than be here with Grampa? I came three thousand miles to see you." There's an old Mel Brooks routine that sums up that grandfather's attitude perfectly: "I don't want to talk to you. I don't want to play with you. I just want to look." It's a natural conflict: Grampa is sixty-eight; your son is ten. He has other things he would rather do than be looked at. Nevertheless, it makes *you* feel guilty. Why didn't you rear a son who could sit quietly for a week, play checkers, and listen to stories about relatives he has never seen? The same problem occurs when the children visit their grandparents. Often there's little for them to do, and the older they get, the more they balk at the visits. As a teenage girl remarked to her parents after the last trip to see her grandfather, "How will I feel when he's dead? I feel so guilty already."

If your children don't measure up to the accomplishments or behavior of the other grandchildren, there's more implied guilt. One grandmother constantly compares a set of unusually docile grandchildren to the normally active family of another daughter. "When Nancy's kids come over to visit, I just sit back and relax. They're so quiet and well behaved." As the angry mother told me later, "If I hear her say that one more time, I'll scream! Those kids have probably been beaten into submission by their Nazi father." Still, the comparison hurt.

It's also distressing to hear comparisons between

ourselves and our own sisters and brothers. The least successful members of a family are bound to feel guilty when they hear parents boast of a sibling's success. "Catherine has such a beautiful home" implies that you do not. Whether our parents intend the comparisons innocently or not, we line ourselves up with our siblings all our lives and measure carefully to see how well we stand. In our own eyes, if we don't compare favorably, we feel guilty. Who is more beautiful, more handsome, more active, has more friends, more money, better cars? Who can afford more exotic vacations or more for their children? Who sews more creatively, keeps a cleaner house, is a better cook? Who tends a neater yard, can rewire Dad's lamp when it breaks, and can buy bigger and better gifts? The comparisons are there within our heads, and we make them constantly. Whenever we think we have missed the mark, we feel a twinge of guilt and resentment. Since parents who lived through the Depression are often impressed by money and status, the comparisons are not always in our minds, but real. Little do we dream, however, that those relatives momentarily ahead feel just as guilty being used for the comparisons.

Who is the most dutiful family member? Does a sister visit the folks more often? Does she keep up the family traditions better than we do? Does she write more frequently and remember birthdays more consistently? Why are Mom and Dad going to *their* house for the holidays? Who usually entertains the elderly aunts and uncles? Who keeps in closest touch? Family obligations and traditions are a constant source of comparison and they cause us to lay impossible burdens on ourselves at times. We feel a responsibility toward each member of the family, and their failures or problems are, in part, our own guilty failures. When a sister divorces, we question ourselves, "Surely, there must have been something more I could have done?" When a brother's business fails, we wonder how much difference we could have made if we had not been so busy with our own lives. "If only I had been there," a friend said after her sister's marriage fell apart.

There was nothing she could have done, but she still feels guilty for living hundreds of miles away during a crisis—too far to be a "good" sister.

There is another type of guilt inherent in departing from family traditions. As we assimilate more into the American culture, some ethnic traditions lose meaning or become impractical. But if your parents still practice them, you're bound to feel guilty when you change. A generation ago, Jewish families frowned on drinking. Many modern Jewish couples have difficulty explaining to their parents that casual social drinking has become a part of their lifestyle. The same problem occurred with a friend from a strict Lutheran background. She is in her mid-thirties and her parents still have no idea that she smokes and drinks—and has been doing so for fifteen years. When she visits her family, both "vices" cease for the duration of the visit. If you come from a frugal German family, you may have difficulty explaining your modern spending habits to an old-fashioned father. Being a conspicuous consumer and credit-oriented may be the American way, but try justifying that to Papa.

Despite all the bad jokes that have been made about Jewish mothers, a word does have to be said about Jewish family traditions. Do Jewish sons and daughters experience more guilt feelings in relation to their families than the rest of us, or does it just seem that way to them? Certainly, for many of our Jewish friends, family expectations have been higher. As one man told us recently, "You're aware at a much earlier age of your responsibilities as a Jew, what you owe the Jewish community, what you owe your family—for example, to a brother who isn't making it or to an aunt who has lost her husband. If you 'have,' everybody in the family is entitled to a part of it. Even though it never really works that way, the tradition of being family-oriented is deeply entrenched. If you break away, the guilt is a lot stronger."

Three sets of friends from three different regions of the country and three different economic backgrounds described identical Jewish family expectations. Bringing disgrace to the family was the cardinal sin. Jewish mother jokes may first have started as an attempt to laugh off the impossible expectation of never disappointing. Typically, said Isabele Appell, a friend raised in New York, "the good Jewish mother is said to follow her son into the bedroom on his wedding night to make sure his underwear is off the floor so she won't be embarrassed." But another close friend commented more seriously on a Jewish jewel thief caught recently in Phoenix. "I hope the poor man's mother never finds out," he said. "That would be a *shonda!*"

Another expectation was to remain close to the Jewish community, which encompassed home, relatives, and the synagogue, and even entailed patronizing other Jewish professionals—doctors, lawyers, insurance men. Moving outside the community for either friendship or interests caused raised eyebrows, which, in turn, brought embarrassment to parents and guilt to the errant child.

The third and greatest expectation was honor thy parents—no matter what. Tied in with what one of our friends describes as the Jewish fascination with death, that one can produce a monumental guilt trip. He claims his father started threatening to die soon after he was born. "Someday I'll be dead and you'll be sorry for all the fighting and yelling you're doing now. Someday you'll cry bitter tears when you remember the way you treated me (or your mother)." How could this Jewish son not feel guilty—even if his father lived to be a hundred and ten—and how could he even consider putting his mother in a nursing home?

But the rest of us suffer, too. Christian or Jew, we get caught, not only by parental expectations, but by in-law problems as well. Did you know that two-thirds of the world's societies set some kind of limit on contact with mothers-in-law? Americans try to be more civilized than that, but from the number of times Dick and I have heard the statement "She's never setting foot in this house again!" perhaps we should take a hint from the less civilized. As one forty-year-old husband described his in-laws, "What I have with Joan's parents is not a love-hate relationship, it's a hate-hate. Next time they come, I'm leaving."

Getting caught in the middle of an in-law fight is a no-win predicament. When you referee, no one is likely to thank you or love you for it. If your wife isn't getting along with her mother, of course, you'll support your wife. But be prepared to have everyone turn on you as the instigator and the outsider. You may suddenly find yourself blamed for every family problem. "If she hadn't married that no-good bum, she wouldn't have the nerve to treat her own mother this way." "If Harold wasn't so selfish and demanding, he would encourage her to spend more time with her own parents." The best husbands and wives can do under those circumstances is to continue to support their own spouse and let the family abuse fall where it may. Fighting back does no good, and feeling guilty when they make you the scapegoat does no good either. You probably did nothing worse than exist in the wrong place at the wrong time.

The opposite side of that coin is the perfect son- or daughter-in-law. You can bet it isn't you being discussed in those terms. As some grandparents swap exaggerations about their grandchildren, others do so about their sons- and daughters-in-law. They probably don't even believe their own praise, but it causes horrendous guilt feelings in the poor flesh-and-blood newcomer to the family, who then tries valiantly to measure up. One mother-in-law, speaking to her son's wife over coffee: "Marcia Marvelous is such a daughter-in-law. You wouldn't believe what a saint that girl is. She takes Mrs. Schultz shopping at least twice a week and even came over and helped her clean out the storage room. Last week, while her mother-in-law was away, she surprised her by shampooing the carpet. Such a sweet girl." And from Poppa: "Arnold has such a son-in-law. He calls Arnold every day, and takes him to lunch twice a week, regularly. The kid is doing so well he just bought an airplane, but you know he never makes a move without consulting his father-in-law." Don't listen! You can never measure up to either Marcia or Marvin Marvelous, and you'll only feel guilty and ghastly trying.

It's often seemed to us that people suffer less guilt in rebelling against a hateful parent than in trying to live up to the small, impossible, day-to-day expectations of a loving one. Those friends who truly have been hurt by a parent or relative disagree, however. "You're supposed to love your mother," they tell us, "no matter how much she resembles Vampira." Perhaps—but do you have to *like* her? We've met numerous people who have truly manipulative, rotten parents. They know it and are aware that the healthiest thing they could do is flee. But they don't. They keep going back for more and continue to be bloodied. When we ask why, they explain that they feel it must be their own fault. Somehow, they should be able to find a way to make it work one of these days, if only they keep trying. Everyone else has a sweet, lovable, kindly mother or father. It must be some personal sin that causes their parent to be hateful.

How much less guilt-producing it would be to face the fact that not all mothers are lovable, not all fathers are warm and helpful, not all sisters are sweet and loving. As a matter of fact, some of them are horrible, and if they weren't related to you by blood, you'd probably never go near them. If that's the case, why not admit that you may have a parent like Maude's, who was described as "an outpatient at the Boston Clinic for the totally wrong," and end the guilt trip? Mother doesn't always know best or deserve the impossible attempts to please. But few people can admit that to themselves, and hardly any can admit it to others. A close friend recently told me how embarrassed she was when a neighbor asked why her parents never visited. "I couldn't say, 'Because I can't stand them.' I just couldn't admit it out loud."

Still, few parents are viciously manipulative; most simply overwhelm us with goodwill, love, their expectations, and their demands that we remain good children. When times change and families change, when we grow at different rates and drift apart, we're bound to fall short of those expectations and feel guilty.

But maybe we should feel guilty for a different reason: for not leveling with our parents, for continuing to pretend to be what we were years ago, to be what we think they want. Instead, we go through the motions of trying to please them in ways that may no longer be valid for us, but do we tell them that? Probably not. They don't know we're not the Waltons anymore. Yet we wait impatiently for them to catch on and feel angry, resentful, and guilty when they don't. We keep waiting for *them* to change. Is that a fair expectation —at their ages—when we give them no clues? Perhaps our expectations of them are as unrealistically high as theirs are of us. Did we really expect them to raise us and then be able to let go easily after all those years?

5.

I'm Okay, You're Not Okay
(Guilt and Religion)

Amazing Grace
How sweet the sound
That saved a wretch like me. . . .
PROTESTANT HYMN

Jesus died for somebody's sins but not mine.
PATTI SMITH

God'll getch ya for that!

MAUDE

WHO CAN MAKE YOU FEEL GUILTY faster than your parents? Only God . . . or the childhood images of Him most of us learned from parents, the clergy, the nuns, and our Sunday school teachers. We were taught God had immense power over our lives, and immense expectations. But as children, we couldn't seem to be that good, that holy, that perfect, and most of us were doomed to failure and guilt before we ever finished memorizing the rules. It may be that the only adults free of religious guilt today are those who grew up as atheists. But even they experience a smidgen of fear at times, a trace of uncertainty. As an old friend confided years ago, "I often wonder if everyone else is right and I'm wrong. But I won't know until I die." Unfortunately, neither will the rest of us.

The orthodox religions of our youth cloaked us in sin and an almost claustrophobic sense of inadequacy. We were born in sin, we would die in sin, and there were so many mistakes we could make in between.

As a graduate student of Catholic background described his religious upbringing at a recent seminar, "Religion scared the daylights out of me as a child. I felt guilty because the whole human race was constantly downgraded and portrayed as evil. And I was part of that deplorable race. 'Man is inherently wicked' . . . 'original sin' . . . 'the sins of the flesh' . . . all of it. And they were right! Sure enough, every time I turned around, I committed another sin, starting with being born. Questioning made you a doubter, if not a heretic, because if you were virtuous enough, God would give you the gift of faith, and you'd never doubt. That made doubting a failing or a shortcoming in itself. And disagreement was unheard of. I guess it still is in many places. Remember just a few years ago when some cardinal in Boston wouldn't allow any priest in his diocese to baptize some woman's baby because she had publicly taken a pro-abortion stand? Punish the sinners! That was the church of my youth. It was like a big, angry parent. There were the rule-givers—the clergy—and the rest of us were followers —the sheep—and we walked around scared out of our wits most of the time. Humility and humiliation were the same thing as far as the Church was concerned. How low could you bend? And if you didn't measure up, when and how would the punishment strike? I spent half my life committing ridiculous unimportant sins and the other half waiting to get clobbered."

Dick and I know the feeling well. There is a wall hanging above my desk that reads "OH, GOD, DON'T CLOBBER ME!" People who see it laugh, and then glance quickly over their shoulder. So do we . . . after all these years.

The orthodox religions did little to foster personal growth or self-esteem. As a rabbi recently told us, "The Jewish faith never gave anyone the opportunity to have an opinion years ago. Everything was structured in black and white, good and evil. Every little detail of life had its corresponding rule." A middle-aged Baptist woman echoes those thoughts: "It was my church's attitude that the ministers alone had the right answers

—always. We were brainwashed!" Dr. Nathaniel Brandon, writing in *The Psychology of Self-Esteem,* agrees:

> . . . one of the common strategies employed in "brainwashing" is that of inculcating or provoking some form of guilt in the victim—on the premise that a guilt-ridden mind is less inclined to critical, independent judgment. . . . Guilt subdues self-assertiveness. The principle involved is not a new discovery. Religion has been utilizing it for many, many centuries.

If Baptist, Episcopalian, Lutheran, and Methodist authorities brainwashed their church members, the Catholic hierarchy probably taught them how. Dick and I always felt guilty as little Catholics. There was so much one could do wrong, so many rules and laws to break or forget. We lived in perpetual fear of what we might do next, and in perpetual mourning for past sins. That's a heavy burden for a ten-year-old to carry, but as Catholics we reached the "age of reason" at seven and were thereafter responsible for our own "sins."

Catholicism was a religion of blood and gore. Children attending Catholic grade schools twenty-five years ago didn't need violence on television; they got it in the classroom. Everywhere there were pictures and statues: the bleeding Sacred Heart, the crown of thorns, whippings and scourgings, weeping women, a nail pounded mercilessly through gentle hands, a sword through the heart. These were climaxed by a glorious crucifixion scene. Gentle Jesus had a rough life and no one was allowed to forget it. If God would let that happen to His "only Beloved Son" who was sinless, what would He do the next time He caught me making a face behind my mother's back?

Catholicism prior to Vatican II could hardly be considered a joyful experience for children. There was little celebration of God's glories; instead we sacrificed and made retribution for mankind's general failings, and our own particular ones, during Lent, Advent, and meatless Fridays. We were continually striving to become worthy enough to celebrate, but we never quite made it. Nor did we see others reach that level of worthiness, for the older people grew, the more they seemed to mourn, fear, and atone. But that pattern fit the general teachings of the Church: the payoff for all this sacrifice would come later, in another life. Upon death we would receive our rewards—or our punishments.

As children, Dick and I never really believed it was possible for us to get to heaven. Others might make it perhaps, but not us. I was far too naughty, too careless, too slovenly, too forgetful to be saved. My stomach always growled before Communion, and I once broke my brother's collarbone by accident. Dick daydreamed during Mass, forgot his morning prayers when he was late for school, and hiccuped during Benediction. When I was nine, I memorized the entire catechism, but still couldn't stand Winifrid Slately—or my own sister. And no matter how many times I turned the other cheek, Billy Lanner still teased me. I finally beat him up. How could God be anything but disappointed in us? We were convinced He had long since given up on us, but nevertheless, the nuns said He watched constantly. God was everywhere. And when He was busy elsewhere, our own personal Guardian Angels kept Him filled in.

Trying to keep the Angels from running back with bad news, little Dick and little Paula (a thousand miles apart) worked their little tails off. We collected holy cards, had everything we owned blessed (including our parents' cars), went to confession every Saturday, and wore our scapulars until they rotted around our necks. We did not wash off our ashes on Ash Wednesday evening. We wore them for days until they smudged away. For half of each year, it seemed, we dined on macaroni and cheese, or tuna casserole, trying to atone. We wore out rosaries, repeating the Hail Marys, said grace before each meal, and crammed in every short prayer we could remember in between. "Mary, Queen of Peace" murmured two hundred times might cancel out a small sin like talking out of turn or calling your brother a jerk. Three hundred repetitions of

"Jesus, Mary, and Joseph, pray for me" were guaranteed to rescue a soul from purgatory—or knock thirty days off our own sentence when we arrived there. We not only had the obligation to save ourselves, but also those others who had died before us. If they were roasting in purgatory, only we the living could release them. A nursing instructor at a local university recalls trying to keep herself awake all night as a child on All Souls' Day each year in order to say enough prayers to rescue her dead relatives.

We were also admonished to save the living. The girls competed with the boys in the classroom to see who could "ransom" the most pagan babies. These were the poor unenlightened waifs in faraway lands whom our missionary priests were trying earnestly to convert. Five dollars would "ransom" a child, educate him or her in a missionary school, and give that child our name. There must be dozens of adults running around Africa and India today named Paula Palangi and Dick McDonald. Our fathers shelled out a fortune in five-dollar bills through the years, as did others. Competition was stiff. Each classroom displayed a poster with the picture of a large green tree. For every girl who "ransomed" a pagan baby, a yellow flower was pasted on the tree; for each boy a red one. We (and thousands of other kids across America) spent our milk money and our lunch money and every other nickel we could scrounge to buy those flowers—and felt guilty when our parents asked why we were always hungry. But we felt doubly guilty when the boys beat the girls or vice versa. Then there were gold stars for every daily Mass attended during Lent. In sixth grade, Dick captured the gold star award, winning a rosary blessed by the Pope. It wasn't easy. He had to get up at 5:30 each morning and attend three Masses per day.

We worried constantly. In those days, you couldn't eat or drink anything after midnight if you were planning to receive Communion the next morning. What if a drop of water rolled down our throats while brushing our teeth before going to Communion? We couldn't receive then, and what would others think if we were the only ones to remain kneeling in the pew? What sin would they think we had committed? And how many other Catholic children carried a brown-bag breakfast to school each morning consisting of cold hard-boiled eggs? We worried that our minds would drift during the droning Latin Masses. That Sister would creep up from behind and find us daydreaming in church. Or that Father would find us lacking in the classroom when he reviewed the catechism lessons of the day. Out of sheer terror we often forgot what we had so diligently memorized the night before—the fourth Beatitude, the third Commandment, the fifth Deadly Sin. We lived in fear that we would fail to measure up.

We paid for Masses for the dead, lit candles, and worried whether it would be enough. The best thing that could happen to a Catholic kid in the forties was to be run over by a delivery truck immediately after leaving the confessional. Then, we hoped, someone would pray us out of purgatory.

If Catholic youngsters worried, others did too. Protestants worried they would forget their Bible passages before Sunday school. Jewish teenagers were uneasy about the bacon, lettuce, and tomato sandwich they had eaten at the drive-in after the dance. Some Baptist teenagers were taught dancing was sinful. Smoking and drinking were forbidden to many Methodist youngsters. Gambling was considered sinful by several Protestant sects (we Catholics could enjoy bingo games in the church basement every Tuesday night). Any expression of fun or frivolity was considered immoral by several of the fundamentalist Protestant denominations. "Would Gentle Jesus, meek and mild, have done that?" many of us asked ourselves. Some of us answered, "yes," some "no," and some didn't know who Gentle Jesus was. If a triple dose of sin for Catholic teenagers consisted of staying out late necking on Saturday night, over-sleeping and missing Mass on Sunday, and then lying to your mother about where you had been, a triple guilt trip for Jewish teens was eating shrimp fried rice at the Chinese restaurant across the street from the temple on a High Holy Day. It's too bad we didn't know each other at the time. We could have shared guilty experiences.

Many of us were kept isolated. I never had any non-Catholic friends until I entered college. A Jewish friend from the Bronx remembers that as a child he never met a goy (Christian), though he knew what one was: a goy was the person called in on Friday nights to turn on the synagogue lights because Jews couldn't do physical labor on the Sabbath. Baptists worried about contact with Catholics; fear of papist influence made them keep their distance. A Baptist roommate of Dick's was astounded to learn that Dick's life was not totally controlled by Rome. Few of us mingled or formed close friendships until we were adults. As a result, few of us learned that others suffered separate but equal guilts. We were admonished to convert each other should we ever have the opportunity; we seldom got that close.

One of the fears that kept us apart was mixed marriage. If we should meet and become friends, we might fall in love. Then what? One of my closest friends, Margie Meldman, relates her strongest Jewish guilt feelings as a teenager: "My God! What if I should fall in love with a Gentile boy? That would really be a *shonda* for my parents, friends, and neighbors." For Catholics, dating, becoming serious about or marrying a non-Catholic was not a *shonda* but a sin—or an "occasion of sin." At thirteen, Dick accidentally fell in love with the Jewish girl down the street. The nuns at school heard about it and squelched the harmless adolescent romance by making him feel guilty and sinful. Did he take his faith so lightly that he was willing to jeopardize it at such an early age? In college, he seriously dated a Methodist girl whose mother was strongly anti-Catholic. She effectively put an end to that budding romance by her outright hostility. Burt Meldman wryly claims that Jewish boys in the fifties only dated Gentile girls for what they could get: "Jewish girls didn't put out for Jewish boys until after marriage."

Deep, lasting friendships among the three basic groups—Protestants, Catholics, and Jews—were rare for young people. Too much inherent prejudice and mistrust had been instilled in us. Our Jewish friends today inform us that they were warned about Gentiles: "As soon as you make a mistake, they're going to call you a dirty Jew and turn their backs on you." The reverse of that warning to Christians was equally lacking in subtlety: "If you ever have dealings with a Jew, hang on to your wallet." Those were hardly attitudes to encourage friendship or understanding.

Because of mobility, education, and assimilation into one culture, those attitudes are rapidly changing. Mixed marriages are accepted by most parents today, even though grandparents may still express dismay. Although young people are breaking down the prejudices, some problems remain. A mixed marriage between two people of strong faiths may falter when children enter the picture. This letter from a twenty-five-year-old Denver man typifies the problem:

> My fiancée and I are close to marriage. I'm Catholic, she's Lutheran, and we're both stout believers. We respect each other's faith, but find it impossible to reconcile one major problem. When it comes to children, we each want them raised in our own faith. The marriage plans have come to a standstill over this issue. Neither of us wants to face a divorce later because we can't work it out.

That much has not changed. Nor has the problem of reconciling basic beliefs. A forty-year-old Memphis man of Protestant background expressed a common dilemma of the seventies:

> I am in love with a Catholic woman and would like to marry her, but she can't get a dispensation from her church even though her husband walked out and left her with their four children. She would like to remarry, but is afraid to oppose her church's teaching on divorce.

Afraid with good reason. If a slice of bologna on Friday would doom a Catholic child, what would happen to the adult who deliberately defied the Church on a major ruling? Considering the indoctrination, how many Catholics can choose divorce and remarriage without traces of guilt and fear?

No adult walks away from orthodox religious background without some remnants of guilt. Fragments of the children we once were remain in all of us. In 1971, only 27 percent of the American people expressed confidence in organized religion. According to a 1975 Harris survey, fully 40 percent of Americans believed organized religion was mostly out of touch with the people. Still, many of us hedge our bets. We may have fallen away from our churches, but we are not comfortable allowing our children to do the same. "Why do we have to go to Sunday school?" asked the children of a friend in San Diego. "Because I did," answers their mother who no longer attends church services herself. Some Jewish friends claim they send their children to Hebrew school to ensure they will "learn the traditions and heritage they sure aren't learning at home." A Jewish woman of forty was embarrassed recently when she heard her teenage son ask a Gentile friend to stay for dinner. "Have you ever had good Jewish cooking?" the boy asked. They were having ham for dinner!

We know of agnostics who faithfully drop their children off at church services each Sunday. Jews who haven't set foot in a temple for years have their sons bar-mitzvahed and their daughters bas-mitzvahed when the time comes. As one Phoenix couple stated, "We should have just handed the kid a thousand dollars. It would have been less hypocritical." They aren't alone. Catholics who have long since disengaged from the institutional church have their children baptized and see that they receive the sacraments of First Communion and possibly Confirmation. Former Methodists, Episcopalians, Presbyterians, and Lutherans often search for a less stringent Protestant sect to join during their children's formative years. "Just something with a few hymns and a church atmosphere so that the kids can get a taste of it," they say.

Why go through the effort and the hypocrisy if you no longer believe? Because the conditioning was powerful. We have to cushion our own nagging doubts. "I'm playing it both ways just to make sure," said one friend. A more accurate reason might be our inability to break with the past completely. Parents feel the necessity of giving their children "something" in the way of religious training, even if it's only something they can reject later. It's impossible for many of us to imagine our children taking responsibility for their own beliefs, for forming a value system for themselves. And we have little confidence in the moral structure set forth in our own homes; example doesn't seem enough. Lastly, it's virtually impossible for many of us to imagine raising children without using God as the ultimate authority. "How will we control them?" many ask. How indeed? We have no frame of reference for guiltless religious freedom from our own pasts . . . and no guarantee that today's more rational approach to morality won't get us clobbered on Judgment Day. While many are willing to take that risk for ourselves, we hesitate to take it for our children.

If we worry about God's expectations, we also concern ourselves with the expectations of others. "We started going to church again," said one suburban Methodist father, "because the kids wanted to know why everyone else on the block was going and we weren't." A Jewish suburbanite first stopped attending Friday temple services because they bored her and she was tired of trying to keep up with the weekly fashion show: "You could die of a heat stroke dressed in boots and furs during Indian summer." Eventually, she ceased to attend High Holy Day services, too, because she felt hypocritical, as many Christians do who only visit their churches at Christmas and Easter. Her husband continued to attend so as not to disappoint his parents. Only when they moved to another city did he, too, stop going to temple. Similarly, our family stopped attending weekly Mass shortly after Dick's parents retired to Tucson. Sometimes it seems easier to deal with God's judgments than with those of our fellow men.

As children, Dick and I were expected to attend a three-hour service from noon until 3:00 P.M. on Good Friday, one of the most solemn days of the

Christian year. In our youth, offices closed, the streets were deserted, and not a child was to be seen during those three hours. Today it seems strange to hear the sounds of our children's laughter as they play outside on Good Friday afternoon. I'm not hypocritical enough to force them to stay indoors, but I'm not totally comfortable with the change either. It's difficult to forget the years of mourning and atonement. Some Jewish friends recently made their eighth-grade daughter stay home on Yom Kippur, the solemn Jewish Day of Atonement. They did not make her attend temple services, but kept her out of school for fear they would be criticized as bad Jews. Many teenagers go through a natural period of questioning and disbelief. We did too, but it's difficult for many parents today to cope with the increased openness of their own children. We may have had the same doubts, but we kept our mouths shut out of fear. They have little fear. It's particularly difficult for Dick to hear our teenage son calmly discuss his current agnostic views. Dick respects his right to them; he admires Eric's courage and the questioning process; he just can't listen without some guilty twinges as Eric expresses his lack of faith in front of others.

If the faithful haven't changed, their religions may have. Jews now have the choice of being Orthodox, Conservative, or Reformed. But if you were raised in a strict kosher home, will you ever feel totally comfortable using one set of dishes? How do the millions raised with the belief theirs was the one true religion deal with ecumenism? Once we were urged to convert the infidels before they perished in flames and their own ignorance. Today we welcome them and attend services in which ministers of different faiths officiate side by side. When my only brother was married in a Methodist church ten years ago, I, as a conscientious Catholic, was forbidden to participate in his wedding under pain of sin. I was sad and felt more than a little guilty not being able to take part in the wedding of two people I loved, and who loved each other. How could it be wrong? Since then, the Catholic Church has changed its ban on participation in mixed marriages, and I feel more than a little resentful that my "Infallible Church" couldn't get its act together sooner. The opportunity is lost forever. Dick and his family could not attend a younger sister's marriage outside the Church fifteen years ago. We all may have had doubts about the Catholic Church's ruling at the time, but at the time, it was sinful to doubt.

The thinking adult today is often torn by doubt. Is it really *sinful* for some to drink, smoke, dance, gamble, or use the Pill, but not for others? It doesn't seem logical, but can we buy some of the religious package without buying all of it? Not without guilt and doubt. A full 83 percent of Catholics approve of artificial birth control today, but until the Church changes its ruling, many will still carry tendrils of guilt to the Communion railing—if they receive at all. Given our staggering divorce rate, remarriage seems a logical and sinless act to many today. To condemn those millions from broken marriages to a life of loneliness seems barbarian—but guilt is a strong deterrent to happiness.

Many of today's societal norms conflict with earlier childhood religious teachings. "Turn the other cheek" hardly seems feasible in a nation currently mindful of civil rights, women's rights, and assertiveness. How many times will we let the parking lot attendant shortchange us, or the mechanic overcharge us, before we forget the teachings and fight back? Our current desire for self-esteem conflicts with the self-image of an undeserving sinner carried over from our youth. And we were taught to judge others, often harshly, as ourselves. As a thoughtful friend wondered recently, "Maybe I've become too nonjudgmental now. I can understand and sympathize with almost everyone, and I find it harder and harder to condemn people for what I might well do in the same situation." That's too much of a departure for his comfort.

Clergymen were especially aloof in our youth. They hardly seemed human. And a major part of the sexual inhibitions many of us have experienced can be laid directly on the doorsteps of our churches. Ministers and priests either exhorted us to "avoid the sins of the flesh" or treated sex with loathing and disdain. Even within marriage, sex for Catholics was subtly disapproved. Celibacy was God's highest calling, and if you couldn't meet that standard, well, second best was having lots of babies to make up for your human weakness. If you had to "do it," you had better produce something for God in the process. Before marriage, we were inundated with catalogs of sexual sins and sexual warnings. Impure thoughts, impure deeds, impure actions were ticked off in classrooms and Sunday schools until it seemed that no action, no thought, was completely pure. Ignorance and fear replaced an adequate sex education for many of us and they could not easily be converted to sexual joy and fulfillment after marriage. But as a former Methodist schoolteacher who now teaches sex education in high school has told us, "At least sex existed for you; even if it was dirty or sinful, it was real. For me there was nothing. It was never mentioned at home, in the pulpit, or at Sunday school. Imagine the fear and guilt growing up, watching and wondering as your body changed, and never being able to ask."

Once we believed our clergy to be above our own sexual needs, weaknesses, and failings. Today more of us understand the clergy's humanness and their natural frailties—as we do our own. They, too, have sexual needs. They, too, become alcoholics, and they have marital problems. They, too, are as stingy, self-centered, ill-tempered, wasteful, insecure, sexually tempted, and human as the rest of us. But they never let us know that when we were growing up, for as the rule-givers, they had to appear above reproach to their flocks. How else could they have urged us toward perfection? They were the representatives of God Himself, the ultimate perfection. What a terrible burden for us and for them. How many were shattered trying to maintain the illusion?

The great number of defecting clergymen and religious in the past few years has alarmed many people. "What do they know that I don't know?" the bewildered flock wonders. The departures may be reassuring and may lessen the guilt for those of us who have already fallen away ourselves, but for others, the sudden depletion of the ranks is unnerving. It's difficult to condemn any priest or nun for wanting to put an end to loneliness, for desiring sexual fulfillment, a family, or companionship; it's equally difficult not to wonder how soon the Rock will crumble completely. We see too many chips lying about today. Many of the remaining clergy are changing faster than their flocks can tolerate. In the midst of the new liturgy, the vernacular Mass, and the recent involvement by ministers, priests, and nuns in social actions, the traditional Catholic often feels abandoned. Frances Noel Barber stated in a recent letter to *Time* magazine, "My friends and I did not 'leave' the church; we were driven away by guitar strumming, Protestantizing ecumenists." To look for another Rock? Where will he find one?

Women, who for so long were considered not only inferior but unclean by many faiths, refuse to accept that stigma today. We're appalled by the label "daughters of Eve," and reject the traditional belief that we caused the world's woes or original sin. Every major religion has been controlled by men since its inception, and religions have played a strong part in shaping the societies around them. Much of our society's attitude toward women stems directly from religious influences. Orthodox Jews are still separated at their religious services; men and women are forbidden to worship together. The Episcopalians are currently undergoing a civil war over the ordination of eleven women priests. The Catholic Church refuses even to consider ordaining women, and allows them no voice in the hierarchy of the "Universal Church." Thirty years ago, the worst punishment a boy in a Catholic classroom might be forced to suffer was being banished to sit with the girls. Is it any wonder the male conviction that women are inferior is so deeply ingrained and difficult to change? We learned it from a basic source—our religions.

Most American women refuse to be scapegoats any longer or accept responsibility for evil. Whoever passed that stupid apple around, it wasn't me, or my mother, or my grandmother. And to be considered unclean for a natural act is an outrage. After the birth of our third child, fourteen years ago, a special ceremony was held for me following Randy's Baptism. It was called being "churched" and involved a short, simple blessing by the attending priest. I had no idea at the time that it symbolized my return to grace after the unclean act of bearing a child. Today I couldn't be dragged to an altar to participate in such an indignity. But I, and millions of other women, meekly and ignorantly accepted the insult for centuries.

There was so much we didn't know. Church history was often revised to anesthetize the faithful. I attended three Catholic grade schools and one high school, and did not discover until college that the glorious crusades had in reality been mercenary bloodbaths. The horrors of the Inquisition and the fact that at one time the Catholic Church had two simultaneous Popes were carefully left out of Dick's Catholic history books. So was the fact that Christianity built its towering cathedrals with bounty from the dead as it spread its message around the globe. We learned about the Christians and the lions in school, because in Nero's Rome it was our side that was being persecuted. Not a word was breathed about the persecution of others by us. What a guilty shock it was later to learn how many the Rock had crushed in the name of Gentle Jesus.

Our generation was trained in absolute obedience and discouraged from questioning dogma. But the clergy are no longer the only educated segment of society as they once were, or the only teachers. Today's educated flock cannot be so easily influenced or led. Our churches once professed to have all the answers; today clergymen themselves confess to doubt. Nationwide, church attendance has dropped 40 percent overall in a thirteen-year decline. Only one in three Catholic adults now attends weekly Mass; less than a third believe in papal infallibility. While little Catholics like Dick and Paula were made to feel guilty twenty-five years ago because they didn't have a religious vocation, today only a third of Catholic parents say they would be pleased if their son became a priest. A lot has changed. Sins that once would have condemned us to hell no longer exist. Forms of worship, rules, symbols, and acts that were once a major part of our lives now seem irrelevant or have disappeared entirely. The institutional church has lost much of its authority. How will it recover in a changed society? As a former clergyman told us, "I felt more of a true religious experience reading *Jonathan Livingston Seagull* than I did in church."

And yet religious guilts die slowly. Those of us who were raised with the church or synagogue as ultimate authority have a difficult time making a clean break. It's terrifying to assume responsibility for your own life when others have always done it for you. It's difficult to begin a direct relationship with God when you are used to an intermediary. In our uncertainty, we search for supporters who reaffirm our new beliefs, who soothe our consciences. Because Dick and I publicly declared in our last book, *Loving Free,* that we had broken with the Catholic Church's stand on birth control, we are frequently asked about our current standing with the Church. "Do you still belong to a parish?" people wonder. "Do you go to Mass? How do you handle religious training for your children? How has the Catholic Church reacted to you?" People want to know, not because of idle curiosity, but because they want support for their own actions, reassurance for their own doubts. While the true believers have their security to fall back on, the rest of us need comfort, too. "If you haven't been struck by lightning, perhaps we won't be either," seem to be the unspoken words behind the questions.

Most of us still want something to believe in. There's a void without belief that quickly fills with guilt. It took strong authority figures to instill guilt, but he who gave can often take away. Some clergymen are beginning to realize this, and work toward undoing the past. They are more open about their own shortcomings. They are trying to be more human, more identifiable as one of the flock. They are trying to present God less as an angry parent and more as a loving father.

"God can accept you the way you are," some of them are saying, and, with relief, some of us are tentatively beginning to believe it.

Over the past ten years, I have moved from childhood indoctrination to confusion to resentment to a semi-guilt-free peace with a selection of truths that I can believe in. So has Dick. If we still envisioned God as an avenging deity, we would never have been able to drop the shackles of guilt and fear. Fortunately, we've found a more comforting vision: a God in sympathy with mankind, amused by what we do to ourselves and often saddened by what we have allowed others to do to us; a God who created human beings and is proud of His work, not disappointed; who occasionally shakes His head wistfully and says, "I never meant it to be so complicated."

And yet . . . when the car skids suddenly on a slippery road, my heart thumps wildly and in those brief seconds a flashback inevitably occurs. I begin an automatic "Hail Mary" and cross myself instinctively. And later, alone in the dark, like so many others, I wonder, "What if they were right all along and I'm wrong?"

6.

And Now a Word from Our Sponsor (Guilt and Television)

Advertising may be described as the science of arresting the human intelligence long enough to get money from it.

STEPHEN BUTLER LEACOCK

The impact of television on our culture is just indescribable. There's a certain sense in which it is nearly as important as the invention of printing.

CARL SANDBURG

Nothin' says lovin' like something from the oven, and Pillsbury says it best.

UNTIL LAST WEEK, I never realized what a flop I was. I lay helpless in bed with the flu watching television, unable to defend myself from hundreds of comparisons. Weak with guilt, I finally crept back to my desk two days later, convinced I was an abysmal failure as woman, wife, mother, and person. Never once had I checked the potency expiration dates on my children's vitamins or returned the free sample of toothpaste to the mailman because our children got good checkups with the old brand. My skin doesn't glow; our dishwasher leaves spots; my hands don't look as though I have a maid; and our dog cheerfully eats whatever nutritionally unbalanced slop the kids toss into her dish (she is particularly fond of pizza, sandwich crusts, and brown bananas). No one has ever seen a face reflected in our dishes; and with two smokers and four children who love bacon, the house has a perpetual case of house-a-tosis. During my periodic bouts of blondness, I have not had more fun. As a matter of fact, in thirty-eight years, my hair has never been long and silky, bouncy, shiny, or manageable. Even when I was a baby, it wasn't baby soft. Generally speaking, the closer he gets, the worse I look. One of our teen-agers has a pimple, and whenever I call my family or old friends long distance to have a meaningful chat, they are not at home.

The only consolation of my two-day marathon tele-vision orgy was discovering that Dick doesn't measure up either. He never throws his arms around the chil-dren when they burst into a meeting at his office to tell Daddy they only have one cavity; and he looks far from jaunty spreading fertilizer. When he stands upright, there is a tiny bulge around his middle that keeps his Haggar slacks from hanging straight. When he sits down, they tend to wrinkle in the crotch. His jeans are always baggy; frisky European cars are too small for him; and an Arnold Palmer golf shirt did not improve his game. He has occasionally been known to sweat after using both a sticky roll-on and a dry deodorant. Even the Dry Look doesn't help his cow-lick from poking out to one side. His teeth do not resemble those of a twenty-three-year-old tennis pro, and he's too cowardly to have his hand tattooed like the Marlboro Man. His life is sadly lacking in gusto, and Thorpe Finance probably wouldn't give him a loan. Neither one of us ever has as much fun as the Pepsi People. Do you?

Advertising has changed the way Americans buy. Television is changing the way we think, feel, act, and live. Combine the two, and a gigantic guilt migraine begins to throb in many American heads. Consider television as our newest institution, with the same au-thority, authenticity, and impact accorded our estab-lished institutions. Indeed, television is all-pervasive. It intrudes upon us, persuades, and compels us as no other institution ever has, while innocently masquer-ading as entertainment. The man from Missouri said, "Show me," and television did—lifestyles, products, and expectations we never had before.

Ninety-eight percent of the households in America have at least one television set; 64 percent have two. That great a percentage of our population neither completes a high school education nor actively practices a religion. But we do watch TV, and as a nation, consider it our most believable medium—more so than newspapers, magazines, and radio combined. That's quite an impact for something that has frequently been referred to as the "Boob Tube" or "chewing gum for the eyes." According to a 1975 Roper poll, Americans rate TV stations higher in credibility than other community institutions such as schools, local government, newspapers, the churches, and the police. That's not surprising; we are on more intimate terms with our television sets than we are with our other institutions. The average American adult spends three hours and two minutes per day watching TV (a fact that many of us vehemently deny). That is more time than the same average American spends reading, pursuing a hobby, maintaining friendships, eating, or talking to a spouse. *"I* don't watch much television," we repeat over and over. "I can take it or leave it." But it's rarely true. As media critic Ben H. Bagdikian stated, "Never before in human experience have so many people in so many different places been marshalled before a vivid instrument to have precisely the same idea inserted into their brains at precisely the same moment." There are women who spend more time with Johnny Carson and Mike Douglas than with their own husbands. And we may not know the name of our congressman, but we all know who the Jolly Green Giant is.

The average family is exposed to 1650 separate advertisements a day. The average homemaker is bombarded by a billion dollars' worth of ads each month. Fully thirty-six minutes of our three-hour daily viewing time is concentrated sales pitches. That is four minutes more than Americans currently spend reading their daily newspapers. Some of the nation's most creative minds have been employed to convince us in thirty seconds that we cannot live another moment without something we may never have heard of before.

Is it any wonder we all rush from table top to toilet to tile, wiping, swishing, spraying, and swabbing?

And our children watch far more television than we do. According to a recent University of Texas study, they strongly identify with various TV characters—on commercials and in programs. It isn't difficult to understand, then, why they crave products that didn't even exist two years ago, and how they have absorbed a new culture without even noticing. By the time he graduates from high school, the average American child will have spent more time sitting in front of a TV set than in a classroom. The National Association for Better Broadcasting estimates that the same child between the ages of five and fifteen will have witnessed more than eighteen thousand violent deaths under the guise of entertainment. Innocence in a walnut-paneled box, television is not. A Boob Tube? Don't underestimate it for a minute.

No other institution has captured our minds as rapidly or as painlessly. The spread of Christianity took centuries; television hooked us in thirty years. In 1946, there were only ten thousand TV sets in the entire nation. Eight years later, there were thirty-four million. By 1956, two out of three families owned a set, and as a high school senior growing up on the East Coast, I could no longer remember what life had been like before television. In 1960, 115 million people watched at least one Kennedy-Nixon debate; television had become the reporter, the mouthpiece of the nation. Three years later, almost every American watched and then rewatched numerous video replays as Jack Ruby shot Lee Harvey Oswald. Without doubt, television has changed the course of our culture and probably our history. But what has television done to you personally?

For one thing, it's made you aware that it is a terrible sin to have a hemorrhoid in America. It's made you want more goods than you can possibly afford or need. It's probably made you more self-conscious about your body and more insecure about your appearance and the appearance of your home, as well as your role and your lifestyle. It may frequently make you feel inadequate, as the gorgeous blondes in hair-care commercials often do to me. Most likely, it makes you feel guilty at times because you can't do, buy, or be all that you see. And what you see today is virtually the whole world.

Let's talk about advertising first—everyone's least favorite subject. One of the earliest examples of be-havior modification through advertising was an ad campaign launched in the twenties by a cigarette man-ufacturer. The company wanted to increase sales by encouraging the women of America to smoke, a trend that had just begun. But it was afraid to show a woman actually smoking. Instead, the ads depicted a slim, elegantly dressed female leaning toward her handsome escort. "Blow the smoke my way," read the copy. It worked, and with that successful campaign behind them, manufacturers next directed their ads at over-weight females, encouraging them to smoke rather than eat.

In general, advertising persuades us to buy through fear, guilt, and a sense of inadequacy. If the nice man tells us bad breath will drive away our friends, we will eagerly buy his mouthwash. Who wants to be friend-less? If the nice lady makes us believe a combination of lavender paste and black goop will give us Cover Girl eyes, and that Cover Girl eyes will catch or keep a man, we rush off to our drugstores. Who wants to be lonely? And if Madison Avenue can convince us our children will adore us for putting tiny cans of pudding into their lunch boxes, we will probably buy canned pudding (or feel guilty informing the children it is too expensive). Who doesn't wish to be adored? Television didn't invent manipulative advertising. It simply ele-vated it to a high art form.

Large advertising agencies often employ psycholo-gists and motivational researchers to study the mind of the consumer. Together, they have learned to manipu-late our snobberies, secret desires, fantasies, and anxie-ties to make us buy. And it works. Remember the aristocratic man with the black eye patch? He sold a lot of shirts for Hathaway. Snob appeal. Have you ever sipped white wine on a deserted island beach as the sun slipped softly into the sea? Not many of us have, but we'd like to. That's how Lancer's creates a market for its new white wine.

These images are based on our fantasies. But how many products have we purchased because of insecurity or anxiety? We've been manipulated by experts into believing that if our feet smell; if the grease stains won't come out of our clothes; if our shower curtains grow mold; or if a flake of dandruff drops on our shoulders, the world will sneer and our friends will abandon us.

Anxiety sells other things besides deodorant, feminine hygiene sprays, and denture creams. It also sells cars to impress the neighborhood, the boss, or our in-laws. It sells insurance to keep our families secure and put an adequate new roof over our heads in case a tornado knocks the house down. And it sells credit—loans for items we probably can't afford. But most often anxiety sells an incredible array of beauty and grooming aids. We've become a quivering mass of guilt attempting to look and feel like the slim blond god and goddess we see advertising the products. We don't measure up, but as soon as we buy, our problems will be solved—wrinkles, unpopularity, drabness, and gas pains will instantly disappear. "Hate that gray? Wash it away." "Jock itch?" "How's your love life?" "Tired blood?" "Ban takes the worry out of being close." "Shake up your mouth." "Irregularity?" "Aren't you glad you use Dial?" "I'd like to have a word with you about diarrhea." And if trying to become perfect makes us tense and headachy, Anacin "calms anxiety and lifts depression."

Advertising frequently fosters in us a double expectation. Now you not only have to clean it, you have to enjoy doing it. Do you really know any woman who dances around and sings while she dusts? Or one who smiles serenely when her children smear pizza across the sofa cushions? Or who laughingly claims she will "Shout it out" when her husband sticks the elbow of his best shirt into a bucket of tar? I personally become rather upset when those things happen—and wonder why I am less serene than the "average" woman. And how many men have you seen smiling gaily in the ninety-five-degree sun as they ride their "weekend freedom machines" around a half-acre of lawn while grass clippings and pollen blow into their noses and stick to every sweaty surface? Ridiculous as it seems, advertisers not only promise to solve our problems, but ask us to believe we will love doing the nastiest of chores with the help of their products. If you don't enjoy sticking one arm in your toilet or unplugging sinks clogged with grease and hair, there must be something wrong with you. Well, perhaps there is, but then I am no judge. I have never lain in bed chortling while my oven cleaned itself, and the only friend we know who giggled in bed about Mr. Muscle had a difficult time explaining it to her husband.

Advertising also creates extravagant lifestyle expectations. "Pepsi adds sparkle to any get-together" they promised in 1960. "Enjoy life with Miller High Life" was the theme in 1962. "Get your party off the ground with Smirnoff" said a 1963 *Life* magazine ad. "Where there's life, there's Bud." "It's the Pepsi Generation." "Things go better with Coke." But do they really? Hot dogs might, but how about life itself? And that is the implied promise: "Coke adds life" they tell us. "Join the Pepsi People." We would like to but we can't find them. Where are those towns where old and young celebrate together, and have fun each weekend cleaning up vacant lots and holding mini-Olympics? It isn't happening in our town, but perhaps that is our fault. Our teenage daughter Kelly remarked at the beginning of the last school year that summer had been a disappointment. We were surprised because her summer had been filled with sailing, swimming, and waterskiing and with many friends. "But," she said, "I never seem to have as much fun as the people on the Pepsi commercials." Neither do we, sweetheart. And like you, we occasionally watch and wish we could climb through the television screen to join those imaginary people. A doctor was recently describing his feelings while watching one soft-drink commercial during which a little boy rolled joyously around with a litter of adorable puppies at his grandmother's house. For a moment, he longed for that kind of spontaneous rapture until he remembered how much work it had been when his own St. Bernard had twelve puppies during final exam week in medical school. But how many little boys and girls watch and wish they had that kind of grandmother? And wonder why they don't have that much fun?

How many men enjoy a life filled with gusto and adventure? We know few who can manage more than the daily routine of earning a living spiced by an occasional handball, softball, or golf game. But liquor, beer, and even chewing-gum and breath-mint manufacturers now subtly promise gaiety, camaraderie, and adventure if we use their products. Canadian Club whisky promises spine-tingling adventure in sports that practically no one has the money or physical stamina to pursue—wind surfing at Moorea, hang gliding, water-balloon walking down the Thames, desert sailing on the snowy sands of Baja at sixty miles per hour. No wonder Dick's life lacks gusto—he doesn't drink liquor. Will chewing a particular brand of gum double your fun as promised? Will it make you young, beautiful, and comfortable on a cantering horse? And would it have made you fight less with your sister as a teenager?

Promises, promises. They continue to hook us because we would like to be all that we see. I continue to buy Hamm's beer, not because it tastes better, but because I'm hooked on the lovable Hamm's bear and the lifestyle he represents—woods, water, camaraderie. Even though our family spends summers in the same part of the forest as the shambling bear and his rugged master, our life is not quite as adventurous. Still, I keep sipping Hamm's and hoping. Advertising leads us to expect instant happiness. When that doesn't occur, the fault must be our own, not that of the product.

Rationally, we know no product could possibly deliver all it promises, but frequently we are taken in anyway. It has been said that a saturation campaign on television can sell anything—a product, a personality, or an idea—that is not inordinately repulsive. It's probably true. After months of watching a stun-

ning creature sporting a new electric-blue facial mask
on TV, I hauled my own thirty-eight-year-old face to
the corner drugstore seeking repairs. I should know
better. Still, if it could make her look that beautiful
with the mask on, think what it might do for me. Naturally, I got the one box in five million without directions, but plunged ahead anyway. For two hours, I
sat waiting for my itchy electric-blue glue to dry,
while the family howled, rolled on the floor, and
dragged in numerous neighborhood kids to see my
funny face. When the moment to peel and reveal
finally arrived, the damn thing wouldn't budge. My
eyebrows and fuzzy facial hair were stuck tight. I am
still trying to grow them back.

If want, want, want, buy, buy, buy has persuaded
us, reasonably intelligent adults, it has turned our children into insatiable consumers and guilt-producers.
They also want, want, want; parents can't always buy,
buy, buy. Big Wheels, Barbie dolls, and G.I. Joes
become obsessions to the child who sees them paraded
across his television screen daily. How can Daddy and
Mommy say "no" to everything when there is so much
to want? And the product knowledge our children
absorb along with the advertising makes it doubly hard
to say "no" without feeling guilty. Their arguments
are too good, too glib. Recently our eleven-year-old
son was badgering Dick for a kitten. We are not a cat
family, and Dick used the standard approach of most
dog lovers: cats need litterboxes; litterboxes smell.
Mike calmly informed his father that deodorized kitty
litter was now available, and if that didn't work, the
litter box could be sprinkled with a box of Arm and
Hammer baking soda. "It eliminates odors, too, you
know." Eleven years old and a walking commercial!
When all logical arguments were destroyed, Dick had
to admit, "I don't like cats," and accept the Mean
Daddy image.

Television advertising exerts tremendous pressure
on us to buy our children items we know are not good
for them. I wish Ann Blyth and her TV friends would
stop implying that I don't love my children because I
won't feed them preservative-filled balls of fluff and

sugar between meals. But, "You can't skimp when it comes to your kids," she says. If the Twinkies ads are not blatantly designed to sell via guilt, I don't know a better example. Except possibly M & M's. Why do they promise that my little tykes will love me more if I rot their teeth; that they will gaze adoringly at me and say, "Thanks, Mom," if I hand them another bag of M & M's? And during the last commercial break, only ten minutes ago, that nice white-haired man selling toothpaste cautioned me to avoid between-meal treats. Are they out to drive me crazy?

When conflicts between stars and authority figures arise, whom does one choose? Lorne Greene tells us that 100 percent meat is best for our dog, even though it's expensive as hell. A pretty girl, on the other hand —and our veterinarian—inform us that a "speck of cereal" is healthier. Nevertheless, we still feel guilty reaching for the bag instead of the can. Doesn't our dog deserve the very best, the very tastiest, the same as Lorne Greene's dog? Some conflicts are even more confusing. I have personally withdrawn from the orange juice battle. Let astronaut Jim Lovell and Anita Bryant fight it out without me. Tang versus the Florida Sunshine Tree? It's easier to buy grape juice than decide.

Although advertising has engendered equally impossible expectations for both men and women concerning lifestyle, beauty, and sex appeal, it has done some particularly wicked things to wives and mothers. From the first moment I saw the 1965 Campbell's Soup ad—"They always eat better when you remember the soup"—I have felt a twinge of guilt on cold days, even though my children prefer peanut butter and jelly sandwiches for lunch. But that's minor-league guilt. Two candidates for the slyest, most underhanded guilt-producing ads ever written are a 1965 Quaker Oatmeal ad in *Life* magazine and the 1976 Wisk detergent commercial shown on television. The full-page Quaker ad showed a sleepy, tousled tyke in pajamas looking unbearably sad and forlorn. The copy read, "Out of a nice warm bed into a bowl of cold cereal? Poor k-k-k-kid." It's been twelve years, and I still walk around with vestiges of hot-breakfast guilt every morning, even though Quaker itself has long since climbed on the cold-cereal bandwagon. And with Quaker 100% Natural Cereal of all things! Which can be eaten dry as a snack! Between meals! Without milk! I hope *they* feel guilty. Our teenage son has not eaten breakfast in months. I can understand the stage he's going through where nothing is appealing for dinner except pizza, hamburgers, and tacos, but no breakfast? Not even a cold one? That's too much for a guilt-ridden mother conditioned by television and instant oatmeal.

The Wisk commercial induces paranoia. A wife is shown playing charades or driving through toll gates with her husband (who never showers, it seems). People around them suddenly cease all normal activity and begin to point, stare, and whisper. "Ring around the collar," they sneer, while she hangs her head in shame. It's all her fault, of course. Why, I wonder, doesn't that woman turn to her husband and hiss, "Wash your neck more often, you slob!" But they wouldn't sell Wisk if they couldn't make us feel guilty.

Men have had to bear an equal share of guilt-producing advertising from locker room macho to lawn care. None, however, has raised a more unfair and unrealistic standard of Good Fatherhood than a 1961 bank advertisement displayed in *Life* magazine. It showed a lonely wife and child sitting on the floor of a new home amidst cartons and moving crates. The caption read, "How long will they be strangers in town?" The copy laid that burden squarely on Daddy's shoulders. "You, the man of the house, can help them hasten the getting-acquainted process by quickly re-establishing your reputation for dependability and character." Poor Dick. We had just moved from Dallas to Milwaukee when that ad ran. If his young wife and baby were not happy in their new home, it was certainly going to be his fault. Perhaps we need a word with Ralph Nader or the Surgeon General. Each guilt-producing ad should be required to carry a warning: "Caution: This advertisement may be dangerous to your mental health."

But enough of advertising and what we can't buy for

ourselves or each other. Television programming has exerted a more subtle influence through its role models. Until quite recently, the "typical middle-class families" of the sit-coms were impossibly unrealistic. Lovable Ozzie Nelson never worked, it seemed. All he did was lounge around the house waiting for a problem to arise so he could solve it. Would David find a date for the dance? What father couldn't remain calm if that was the greatest crisis he ever encountered? Didn't Ozzie ever drive home after losing the big account and find David had smashed the fender of Harriet's car? Didn't he ever have a headache and shout, "Stop bouncing that goddamn basketball in the house!" Not that we ever saw.

The situation comedies of the fifties, which Dick and I grew up with, uniformly depicted American middle-class family life as bland, happy, and problem-free. Why weren't our homes like that? Television children didn't fight or squabble. Teenagers were neither sullen, argumentative, nor temperamental. They didn't barricade themselves in bedrooms for months playing music or grumble when asked to do the dishes. Instead, they sat around the living room playing checkers with a lovable and loving sister or brother, serenely waiting for the next family conference to be called. Together they would all solve Little Beaver's or John Boy's problem. And when the conference was called, they didn't moan, "I've got a date in ten minutes—and as far as I'm concerned, you can put my stupid sister in a foster home. All she does is hog the bathroom!" Many of us grew up believing these scenes were being enacted in other households and that our own was out of step with American reality—the only home that didn't have a perpetually beautiful and calm mother; a perpetually handsome and wise father; courteous teens with clear complexions and sparkling smiles. Fortunately, programming is changing. We are, thanks to Norman Lear and a few others, now seeing some horrible, harried, bigoted, and infinitely more normal mothers and fathers—and children. Rhoda's mother, Archie Bunker, Maude, and George Jefferson may not be real either, but the images are more familiar. We don't have to live up to them.

While television programming deals with more controversial and realistic family situations and subject matter today, there is still one major difference between those lives on the screen and our own, one more impossible norm: everything and anything can be solved in a half-hour or an hour on television. What kind of expectations of us does that create in our children? Homosexuality, venereal disease, drug problems, alcoholism, marital distress, even the family trauma of a sexchange operation can be deftly handled between 8 and 9 P.M. in living color—and they can do it night after night without having a nervous breakdown. So why can't you solve a minor annoyance such as a money problem or Johnny's poor grades and lack of motivation in a week?

And why are Marcus Welby, Ben Casey, Dr. Kildare, and Dr. Gavin all much more concerned about their patients than our doctors seem to be about us? Of course, both Gavin and Welby are unmarried, so they rarely leave the hospital or office, never sleep, and only handle one or two patients a week. This allows them to become deeply and emotionally involved in the lives of each patient. Nevertheless, I hope my own doctor feels a twinge of guilt for falling down on the job. He never takes me out for coffee, and sometimes it takes weeks just to get an appointment.

The entire concept of work is unrealistic as portrayed on television. Even Mary Tyler Moore, America's sweetheart, evokes a subtle guilt trip. She depicts the typical working woman in a warm, friendly cocoon of love. Why aren't the rest of us surrounded at the office or plant by people who really care about us, who socialize with us, and who willingly step in to solve our away-from-the-office problems? Bob Newhart's associates create the same atmosphere of wholehearted involvement. Are the rest of us, who hold down boring jobs in drab offices, surrounded by semistrangers, to believe the cocoon only forms in newsrooms or psychologists' offices? Or are we the ones who are lacking?

The soap operas, which dealt with real-life problems

long before regular programming did, provoke their own peculiar forms of expectations. Judy Kloman, a friend who had never watched a soap opera before, commented on one segment of "Days of Our Lives." "Julie's son is lost and presumed drowned," she said. "If she, in the face of monumental disaster and heartbreak can look that gorgeous and be that soothed by Gramma's stupid platitudes, why am I so irrational when someone breaks a finger? And why do I look ugly when I cry? Of course, they're not real, but I'll bet some viewers are fooled." Indeed. A soap-opera villainess who appeared with us on a talk show in Houston last year claimed that people yell and call her names on the street and in restaurants. She was slapped once and spat upon. "How could you take poor Claudia's husband when you know she has to have a hysterectomy, you bitch!" Persuasive? Television intrudes upon our defenses. What we see, we believe.

While regular dramatic programming and the situation comedies were reinforcing unrealistic middle-class goals, the talk shows began to offer the opposite expectation. Beginning in 1954 with Steve Allen's original version of the "Tonight Show," we could sit in our living rooms and watch a parade of the zany, the weird, the mad, and the beautiful. The more oddball their ideas or personalities, the higher the Nielsen ratings. Many of them became national celebrities by rejecting middle-class values. If one watched enough talk shows, the outer fringes began to seem like a new norm. If we couldn't measure up to The Brady Bunch, perhaps we could toss it all aside—like Timothy Leary or Alice Cooper. But it wasn't quite as easy as it looked. Lots of kids tried it and found upset parents, angry school administrators, or jail awaiting them instead of a new normless society. Jane Fonda might be allowed to knock God, motherhood, and the flag on network television, but don't you try it in suburbia. Mia Farrow and Goldie Hawn may have their babies out of wedlock and apparently escape repercussions from society, but that doesn't mean your own father won't kill you if you come home pregnant. The talk shows made nonconformity seem too easy and painless.

Many of us are concerned about the effects of television on our children. In ten years, we have progressed from innocence to horror. Any sane parent realizes that so much violence can't be healthy. Even so much immobility can't be healthy. We'd like our children to participate more in their own real lives—to play, to spend more time with friends, to read—and yet, television is the best baby-sitter ever invented. When there is office work to be finished at home, a floor to be scrubbed, a party being given, we compromise, don't we? We let them watch whatever's on and feel a little guilty about our lack of consistency. The very convenience of television has made it too easy to give in. A child whines, and the alternative is as simple as a flick of the knob.

Television is changing the way most of us live, and although we may not like what's happening to us, we rarely stop to analyze it. It's affecting our marriages and our family communications. Few of us would deny that. We don't talk as much anymore; instead, we sit side by side watching others talk and later feel guilty about the loss of closeness in the American family. We don't do as much together or alone—and feel vaguely guilty about that. Television has made spectators of us instead of participants, and no one more graphically illustrates this than the average American male. Just try arranging a meeting, a family outing, or a bridge game on Monday night during the football season. Or on Saturday afternoon, or Sunday afternoon, or during the Olympics, the NBA playoffs, the World Series, the hockey match, the golf tournament. Men suffer the triple guilt of knowing they have become passive watchers, knowing they are stealing the time from their families, and knowing it will cause discord in their homes every weekend. The worst guilt comes from knowing they won't change.

New conflicts occur within families because of television: which program to switch on when Mom and Dad want to watch one show and the kids prefer another. Or when Mom and Dad disagree. It's difficult to stick to Junior's bedtime when a "great" show is only half over. It's difficult to stay at the dinner table when a "great" show is about to begin—even if Mom did slave over the pot roast. Dick even finds himself fibbing occasionally in order to finish watching a show, as do many of us. The phone rings and he tells a friend, "I'll call you back in twenty minutes. I'm tied up right now." Why doesn't he tell the truth? Why doesn't he just say, "At this moment, I prefer a television program to you"? Because he doesn't like himself much at that moment—and he feels guilty. But how many of us are equally annoyed when an engrossing program is interrupted by friends, relatives, or even a news bulletin?

What we have allowed television to do to our personal lives and to our families causes deserved guilt, and it can be fought. We can make ourselves and our families aware that programs are illusions, nothing more: words, deeds, and situations portrayed by actors and actresses who are no more or less perfect than we are, who, off-camera, snap at their children, keep untidy houses, find themselves overdrawn at the bank, and occasionally fail to measure up—even to us. We can remember that people love us, not because we wear Old Spice or one-sixteenth of an ounce of blue grease on our eyelids, but because we wear our hearts on our sleeves at times, and laugh, cry, and act much as they do. We can remember that the thirty-two-year-old impostor whose Ivory Liquid hands won't give her away dragon breath in the morning. And if all else fails, if we still feel guilty, we can look that screen right in its glaring eye and say, "Up yours, Wisk . . . Quaker . . . Brut . . . ! Stick it in your ear, Clairol . . . Alpo . . . Clearasil! I've got your number now."

7.

Sex Is Dirty, Save It for the One You Love (Guilt, Sex, and the Sexual Revolution)

Help! The Sexual Revolution is passing me by.
ARIZONA STATE UNIVERSITY SOPHOMORE

"EVERYBODY ELSE IS DOING IT. What's wrong with me?" Millions of Americans have been quietly asking themselves that disturbing question for the past several years. We are all supposedly sexually liberated now, but despite the Sexual Revolution, don't you still feel just a little squeamish using the word "penis" in public? Or the word "sex" in front of your aging mother? How rapidly we expected ourselves to change, and how hard it has been to do so. Ten years ago, a married couple might have felt guilty if they enjoyed oral sex. Today a married couple might feel guilty if they don't. Ten years ago, most of us believed we were sexually normal; anyone—or any act—deviating from our ingrained standard of proper sexual behavior was considered perverted. Today a couple might be considered peculiar for preferring the missionary position. There is suddenly a whole new spectrum of sexual norms and behavior to measure up to. Many of us were once brainwashed into believing sex was dirty. Well, they have done it again. But this time they have brainwashed us into believing everyone else is sexually normal and we are subnormal. We've been caught in a time warp.

It's difficult to believe it was only 1969 when *The Sensuous Woman* appeared and changed the reading and discussion habits of a nation and less than ten years since the Sexual Revolution became a household phrase. Stories about swinging, swapping, *The Joy of Sex,* Masters and Johnson, multiple orgasms, *Open Marriage,* legalized abortion, Linda Lovelace, Gay Lib, topless dancers, and massage parlors poured forth from the media down upon our parched Puritan souls. We, the American public, suddenly experienced an orgy of new guilts reading about what seemed to be happening to everyone but us. The artillery of the Sexual Revolution was exploding everywhere—except in our own bedrooms. Valiantly struggling to shed the teachings of the past—"Sex is dirty" . . . "Homosexuals are sick" . . . "Women don't enjoy sex" . . . "God created sex for the purpose of procreation only"—we began to get the disturbing message that something might be drastically wrong with us. We were out of sync because we still had hangups. The whole world was doing it all—and we were not. Homosexuals were "coming out" and marrying; our neighbors were having multiple orgasms, or orgies, or providing their teenage daughters with the Pill; everyone else had been to a topless bar; and virginity had become an unwelcome burden for the young, to be dumped as quickly as possible. How did we suddenly get so far behind? The Sexual Revolution was passing us by! Or, as a distraught University of Ohio student moaned, "Where is it? I can't find it." Across the board, our sexual expectations changed and increased. We hobbled frantically along trying to catch up, while still dragging our Puritan pasts like unwieldy sacks of garbage. In our haste to measure up to an overwhelming new set of norms, to become liberated (or at least broadminded), we forgot we were still the same little parched souls inside, listening to the internal voices of our parents, our churches, our schools, and the society of the forties and fifties, all saying "If it feels good, it must be a sin."

Too much too fast? Of course. We tried to wipe out centuries of repression with a ten-year Sexual Revolution that occurred mostly in the pages of popular magazines or on talk shows. Even if it was all true, how could we expect to absorb so much so quickly and feel comfortable? Or guiltless? A lesbian complained to me last year that she has been unable to have an orgasm since "coming out" as a lesbian. I wanted to shake her and scream, "How could you expect an orgasm so soon? I'm paralyzed by far smaller changes than that! I can't even watch my husband do the dinner dishes without feeling guilty!"

We have a new image of ourselves to live up to today: the Sexually Liberated Person with the Absolutely Perfect Sex Life and No Residual Hangups. In ten years, we have managed to exchange one set of hangups for another, and with our new expectations we are experiencing distressing new guilts. We can now make ourselves feel guilty by admitting, even in a tiny dark corner of our minds:

1. *I can't do it.* (What? Take your pick: make love with the lights on, tell your children *you* had premarital sex, or invite your boss and his wife to an X-rated movie.)

2. *I can do some of it, but not all of it.* (How about using the Water Pik Shower Massage to masturbate? And how about discussing it intelligently with your husband afterward?)

3. *I can do most of it, but there is no one to talk to who wouldn't disapprove.* (Except the Sensuous Man or the Sensuous Woman. Go ahead, just try to find them in Whitefish Bay—those happily, openly, sexually comfortable people.)

Masters and Johnson speak of the "invisible spectator" who watches from the corner of the bedroom as impotent males, premature ejaculators, or nonorgasmic females try unsuccessfully to perform. The very thought of a critical or disapproving imaginary presence makes comfortable performance impossible. Catholics were taught that each child was assigned a Guardian Angel at birth who stood behind our right shoulder and guided us through life. We used to tease and sit down quickly, trying to trap the Angel before he could get out of the way. Is he still there watching today, as Catholic adults creep into adult book stores to purchase their first vibrators? And then take them home to try to enjoy them without guilt? As guiltlessly as we practice artificial birth control?

Perhaps the "invisible spectator" is a parent, or Sister Mary Claire, or the sixth-grade gym teacher, Miss Gleason, who was assigned the uncomfortable task of showing the film on menstruation, or Coach Spencer, who warned us sex would drain our vitality and stamina. Despite the Sexual Revolution, those disapproving voices, those frowning faces from our past, still appear as specters to haunt many of us. As a fifty-year-old Cleveland homemaker said, "I was born in an era when you weren't allowed to talk about sex or ask questions . . . but we knew it was wrong somehow." A forty-year-old Miami newscaster accurately described how "It wasn't that parents or society ever came right out and said sex was dirty. They *implied* it in a thousand ways instead. It started in the cradle with the way the mother handled the child; the way the mother let the child wash and touch himself; the way parents treated each other and talked to each other in front of the children; the way they never touched; the closed doors; the 'Sh-sh-sh.' There were so many subconscious ways children picked up the message there was something a little sinful, evil, dirty, about going to bed with a member of the opposite sex. But no one ever really explained what it was. It was left up to the kid to figure out for himself why he should feel guilty." We got the message. We got so many messages. The mother of one of our friends often asked her as a young adolescent, "How does a big girl like you manage to get grass stains on the back of your sweatshirt?"

Once we worried about sexual sins. Today we worry ourselves sick about sexual liberation. For years, we measured every sexual act trying to avoid damnation, and were happily ignorant of the sexual performance of others. But once magazines, newspapers, and television began to report on the Sexual Revolution, we started to compare ourselves with others—not with their hangups, but with their performances. If Morton Hunt reports that the average American married male between the ages of thirty-five and forty-four had sexual intercourse 102 times last year, the forty-year-old male doesn't say, "I'm doing pretty well. I made it ninety-nine times." He worries about the three times he missed . . . and suddenly realizes there are actual numbers to be measured against in every category. If we learn today that 65 percent of our white-collar workers under thirty-five agree that homosexuality should be legalized, what does the blue-collar worker or the man over thirty-five worry about? He fears he isn't liberated enough because homosexuals still scare him to death—and he secretly worries that the reason they scare him is that he may be a latent homosexual himself. His wife today reads *Cosmopolitan* or *The Joy of Sex,* and secretly wonders why she isn't enjoying sex as much as other women; or why she can't even discuss with her husband varying their sex life with lotions, artificial stimulators, and the fifty-six illustrated positions without both of them getting uptight. How much, how often, where, how, with whom, and with what have become troubling new statistics. But everybody else seems to be handling the new data and managing quite well—even *Reader's Digest* has climbed on the sexual bandwagon. What's wrong with us?

"Normal" has become a new no-win game. We suddenly crave reassurance, as do the writers of these letters from around the country.

From an eighteen-year-old Duluth mechanic: *"I want sex every night. Is this normal?"*

From a Florida homemaker: *"We have been married for two years. Please tell us what is physically normal for married people. What is the husband's responsibility to his wife in bed? What is the wife's role in bed?"*

And from a Memphis man: *"Exactly what does being oversexed or undersexed mean?"*

From a sixteen-year-old boy: *"I'm worried that I might be abnormal physically. I am very tall for my age, but built too small. So I am embarrassed to go all the way with a girl. Is there some way to help me develop better?"*

From a Boston mother of two: *"How can one get over childhood sexual taboos and get more into the swing of things?"*

From a college student in Texas: *"Please tell me what's a normal age for male virginity. I'm twenty-three and still haven't made it. I'm really getting hung up."*

Aren't we all? But with whom can we discuss our worries? Masters and Johnson are lofty, and besides, they have no branch clinic in Whitefish Bay. Nor can you talk back to a magazine article if it implies that you don't measure up.

Let's take a closer look at that Sexually Liberated, Utterly Broadminded, Absolutely Un-hung-up New American. Does such a person really exist? If he or she does, Dick and I have not yet met this person, nor do we measure up to that standard ourselves. No one we know can state unequivocally, "I can handle it all without flinching." But the many thousands of people we've talked to in the past three years are worrying about that impossible goal. Here are some of the new concerns that now make many of them feel guilty.

Broadmindedness. Most of us can be broadminded about a situation that applies to someone else. But as soon as a threatening sexual issue strikes close to home, we freeze. We tense up and wheel around looking for the Angel in the corner. Take extramarital affairs. We can be very calm about the latest statistics. If the majority of the men and women in America want to have an affair today, that's their business. We've even become more tolerant of the people around us who are having affairs. Joe at the office may be playing around with Mary from the insurance company on the floor below. "But they aren't hurting anybody," we shrug. Now bring it a little closer to home. Your best friend is having an affair? You'll probably make allowances there, too. "He's such a brute. No wonder she found someone else." Or, "She's such a bitch, she deserves it." But discover that your best friend's husband or wife is the one having the affair and the broadmindedness diminishes. "That rat! How can he do it to her?" You agonize over whether to tell or not, decide you are incapable of playing God (or too cowardly to meddle), and wind up feeling guilty about your silence. Now bring the extramarital affair all the way home. The liberal sexual attitudes vanish. There is no broadmindedness left in the average American home when one partner discovers the other has been unfaithful. There is only hurt, anger, and shattered trust. Tolerance? Understanding? If we don't tear the marriage apart, we torture ourselves with questions for years: "Was she better than I am?" "Was he bigger?" And if you are the one having the affair, you know how impossible it is to completely silence that squeaking conscience. The fear of being caught resides just below the surface, while the fear of God remains buried in a far corner of the mind. We can tell ourselves we are cool and liberated, but we're not. We are human, and our transgressions continue to worry us. We would like to alleviate our guilt, but can't.

A married South Carolina woman perhaps typifies the problem. "My husband is not well," she wrote. "He has had a stroke, even though he is only forty-six. I am forty-one. We used to have an excellent sex life. Now I can't sleep at night. How does a woman like me have sex with another man without getting involved or without feeling guilty?" She doesn't—not without guilt. While some may claim that the concept of one penis belonging to one vagina for life is obsolete, we are too rooted in our own pasts to practice such a startling departure from conventional morality without guilt. We were taught that promiscuity is wrong, and we can't shuck off a lifetime of conditioning just by reading an article or a report in *Playboy* or *Ms.* magazine.

Guilt and the loyalty to one penis or one vagina may continue even after the death of a spouse. One fifty-nine-year-old Houston woman, widowed for eleven years, told us she has been frigid since the death of her husband, even though she has tried to pursue an active sex life for the past several years. Desire is not always enough to overcome guilt. She can tell herself it is permissible; her conscience seems to be clear. She can repeat over and over that she is harming no one, but the fact remains: she can't *do* it. Nor can a sixty-year-old Santa Fe widow who also wanted an active sex life, along with companionship. She was dropped by a seventy-three-year-old widower after their first date because he wanted (and needed) oral sex in order to gain an erection. She had never performed oral sex before—and she simply could not begin at sixty. Why did she feel guilty afterward? Not because she had lost a man, but because she was unable to change herself that rapidly.

Once upon a time (not long ago) an unmarried woman felt guilty for going to bed with any man; today she may be made to feel guilty if she dates him and doesn't go to bed with him. Or doesn't enjoy every partner every time. Or can't perform adequately each time. We have a young single friend of Methodist background who thought she was unable to have an orgasm without a deep commitment to one lover. To prove to herself she was truly liberated from that archaic notion, she picked up a man in a bar one night and went to bed with him—strictly as an experiment. "It worked," she told us later with mixed feelings. "He didn't even know my name. But I felt shitty afterward." And why not? Nice girls don't sleep around, remember? We may read that every other nice girl is leaping merrily from bed to bed, but that means little in our own bed. While the words, the articles, the books, may be enlightening or encouraging, the actions are bound to be painful at first. There's too much we want to abandon at once, and no one is willing to settle for baby steps.

No matter how many million copies of *Open Marriage* are sold, few people, married or single, can handle the sexually open relationship yet. We personally know of only one couple who seem to be managing that extraordinary burial of normal jealousy, possessiveness, and insecurity. The rest of us wonder what it must be like to sit calmly across the breakfast table and talk about last night's fling over the orange juice. "Was John a good lay, dear?" It's an inconceivable question for most of us. And we wonder how others grew to be so secure. Doesn't she ever have a bad day with the children and say, "I wish you wouldn't sleep with Marsha tonight; I'm feeling a little depressed and I need you here"? Doesn't he ever come home from a gruesome day at the plant to find her gone and resent it when she rushes in tousled and flushed from another man? "I went ahead and made my own dinner, Mary, because I know how much you enjoy giving Stanley a blow job." Ah, c'mon. We not only can't do it; we can't even imagine it. But we've been told others are more liberated, so what's wrong with us?

I personally feel terrified by an actual confrontation with mate swapping. So does Dick. If close friends pressured us, caught us with our defenses down, how would we escape? And how would we face each other and them the next day if we didn't manage to escape? Or what if one of us wanted to experiment and the other didn't? That seems to be a far more common worry. A highly sophisticated reporter for an Atlanta newspaper recently found herself confronted by her own forgotten hangups. She was assigned to an undercover story on wife-swapping in the suburbs, and thought it would be an interesting experience. Her husband agreed to accompany her while she attended some social, nonsexual functions with a group of swappers. But after two weeks, his curiosity was tweaked. He suggested trying an actual swap—in the interests of journalism, of course. In the interests of their marriage and her sanity, she quickly withdrew from the story— and told us with regret that she should have been able to handle it. Should? The superreporter simply couldn't face being human.

Some friends of ours recently had house guests who insisted on swimming in the nude in their pool. These normally liberal friends felt guilty and foolish because they couldn't bring themselves to join the other couple, and felt even sillier sitting around with their clothes on. They were further horrified when the guests practiced oral sex in the back seat of their car while being driven to the airport. What does one do in that situation? Keep up the cheerful chatter about TWA from the front seat? Pretend it's an everyday occurrence in your liberal world? The main thing one does is avoid the rear-view mirror.

We are so hard on ourselves. Because there has been an infant Sexual Revolution, we suddenly expect to shed, as easily as a reptile skin, a lifetime of now unwanted conditioning. We should be able to discuss openly any aspect of sex with our partners today, right? Masturbation, wet dreams, fantasies, curiosities, past lovers, present performance. If we are not repressed, it's supposed to be easy, right? Well, it's not. The most difficult thing in the world to discuss is your own sex life with your own partner. And while some can handle a little and others a lot, nobody can handle it all—not all the time. You may have become relaxed about discussing masturbation, but when a bout of temporary impotence strikes, the topic becomes dangerous, and the vibrator suddenly becomes a threat instead of a toy. Your masturbation is a symbol of his failure. And when that passes, a new problem may replace it. If talking about your Robert Redford or Raquel Welch fantasies was fun and easy last year, why do you suddenly find yourself avoiding the subject of fantasies now that they star your teenage son's or daughter's friends? Those fantasies are not quite as simple to admit to a middle-aged husband or wife, are they? But we expected that once we climbed over the first hill, we could coast the rest of the way. It's too long a journey from never talking about sex to talking easily about every aspect of it. And there are uncharted potholes in the road.

We expect too much of ourselves. If we believe today that sex is normal and natural, we also unfairly expect ourselves to be able to handle every aspect of it comfortably. We should be able to grow old and not worry about what our children think if we are still openly and joyfully sexually active. But we do worry. The Dirty Old Man image haunts us, or others remind us of it. We've heard older women speak with disdain of widowers in their sixties and seventies who have taken up with young hussies in their fifties—"for obvious reasons." Masters and Johnson and the McDonalds may applaud you for a long and healthy sex life; your friends may find you disgusting.

Sex is fun, and the enjoyment of it is not sinful. We should be able to do it all, anything, everything—and comfortably. Then why can't we take our wives to a massage parlor; ask our husbands to accompany us to see a male go-go dancer perform; experiment with bondage; hang from the ceiling; buy a projector and watch blue movies together at home; turn on the music and do a striptease for each other; make love on the Ping-Pong table while our children watch television in the next room; or walk around comfortably nude in front of them? Because some of those things make us feel silly, some embarrass us, and others frighten us. Even the suggestion of a new act, a new position, a new technique, or a new level of sexual freedom causes a churning fear in many of us. What will our mates think if we suggest pornography, for example, as an educational tool for the two of us—or a turn-on? We worry that they might scream "Pervert!" —and how would we cope with that? It hardly soothes our internal fears to know that according to Cody Wilson of Adelphi's School of Social Work, more than ten million married Americans lowered their anxieties and inhibitions, and improved their sexual communication, as a result of looking at, or reading, pornography together. But those were ten million anonymous strangers. What about us personally? How will our own wives or husbands react if we bring home copies of *Latent Image* and *Hustler?* With disgust? Will they accuse us of being sick? Many of us are afraid to find out. And because we're unable to talk, it's too much of a risk to act. There is an interesting paradox that showed up in a 1973 Purdue University study: the more authoritarian the marriage, the more both spouses were sexually aroused by pornography—and the more sternly disapproving they were. In other words, the bigger the no-no's, the more they turn us on . . . and the harder it is for us to admit it, to ourselves, to our spouses, to the world.

Other liberated theories and actions frighten us for different reasons: they make us doubt ourselves. Homosexuality is a perfect example. To be called a fag is one of the worst insults, and most terrifying stigmas, for a man or boy. Many men harbor an intense fear of having the faintest tinge of homosexuality rub off on them. Perhaps that is why we calmly accept our daughters as tomboys, but still worry if our sons seem sissyish, play with girls, dolls, mother's clothes, or cosmetics. While many of us today can calmly and rationally view the struggle for Gay Liberation from afar, or can even comfortably have homosexual friends, male or female, we immediately revert to the hidden terrors when homosexuality strikes closer to home. Homosexual tendencies in their own teenage son are not something most fathers and mothers handle calmly, even though they may be quite at ease with a homosexual co-worker at the office.

For years, I believed that only men harbored an intense fear of latent homosexuality; the problem didn't apply to women. I discovered last winter how wrong I was. A friend of mine declared her bisexuality to me and to the world in a burst of exuberance. That was fine. I have had other bisexual acquaintances in the past and they never made me feel personally threatened—but they had never attempted to seduce me personally. This friend did, and it rocked me to the core. It brought out every fear, every question, every doubt that any man has ever felt. This was not a casual, one-time sexual pass, but a concentrated effort to convert me. "You're not truly liberated sexually until you've had a bisexual experience," she would say. "How can you be sure you aren't bisexual until you've tried it? True friendship and true love between any two people can only be expressed ultimately in a physical relationship." Because of my recent liberal self-image, those arguments became increasingly difficult to counter. "But I'm not bisexual," I would say. "How do you know?" I couldn't answer that satisfactorily. "But I don't want to have a bisexual experience" seemed a feeble response under the barrage. "Why?" was always the final question. It took months to realize she was deliberately making me feel guilty in order to wear me down. One day, at a workshop on human sexuality, I took the chairman of the local Gay Liberation chapter aside and described my problem. The solution she offered was incredibly simple and logical. "If a male friend put the make on you that hard, Paula, and if you didn't want to go to bed with him, how long would it take you to tell him to drop dead?" "About five seconds" was the obvious answer. "Well, what's the difference?" she asked. The difference had been my own confusion, my own fears, my own broadminded image of myself. I couldn't look at the situation objectively because it was too close. It's one thing to view two lesbians or two homosexuals making love on a movie screen. It's an entirely different matter when the celluloid becomes flesh and wants you. Most of us run like hell.

Our self-doubts take many forms, and frequently leave us incapable of performing or handling innocent sexual acts with ease. We sometimes fear that should we ever fully break down the sexual barriers, crash through, and begin to enjoy ourselves with abandon, our bodies might take over and run away with us. Sister Mary Claire would be proven correct. We might revert to animals—or worse. Some friends were telling Dick and me last year that they sometimes take Polaroid pictures of each other posed nude. They mentioned it was stimulating for them as a couple, and it added another dimension to their sex life. Dick and I thought about it later but never pursued the idea. Dick seemed to have no hangups about it or strong feelings one way or the other—"unless," he said, "it got out of hand." "What's out of hand?" I asked. "If it became an obsessive part of our sex life—a perversion—or if there was heavy use of the pictures afterward to masturbate," he answered. It's interesting to note how each of us draws the line at what constitutes perversion in a different place. For my part, I have no strong feelings about another couple using a camera, or about the morality of two people taking sug-

gestive pictures of each other. I don't think it's wrong
—but *I don't want to do it!* Instead of perverted, I
would feel silly. I enjoy my body, but evidently, don't
have a strong enough streak of exhibitionism to overcome the hangup. (And notice I used the word *hangup*. If it isn't wrong, but I still can't—or don't want
to—do it, then it must be a hangup, right? How silly
we all are.)

I was delighted to learn last fall that a woman
Dick and I strongly admire still has a few hangups
left herself. Professor Florence Schmitt, an expert in
the field of human sexuality who teaches at the
University of Wisconsin in Milwaukee and does private counseling, admitted that she is unable to handle
sadomasochism—on any level. When those who enjoy
that form of sexual expression come to her for professional help, she refers them to another counselor.
Whips and chains turn Flo off. Well, bravo! In this
age of enlightenment, we have been led to believe
nothing turns off the sexually broadminded person. We
should be able to handle the entire spectrum with
ease—and a little training. The reality is that we are
human, and certain things may always turn us off.

As smugly liberal as I often pretend to myself I am,
I cannot comfortably look at the male nude centerfolds
of *Playgirl* magazine on an airplane while sitting next
to an elderly grandmother who is reading the latest
issue of *Good Housekeeping*. Now why—if nude males
no longer are a hangup? If I can read *Playgirl* comfortably in my own living room without feeling guilty,
why can't I do it there? Any man who ever sat lovingly
gazing at the *Playboy* centerfold on a plane can easily
answer that question. When the stewardess asks, "Dinner now?" you jump a foot. The "invisible spectator"
becomes a real one who has caught you looking at
"dirty" pictures. A Chicago mother with six athletic
sons comfortably hung their jock straps on the clothesline to dry for years—until her own mother mentioned
during a visit that she thought they made a distasteful
display. The woman still hangs the jock straps out, but
is no longer totally comfortable. Each time she wonders how many other "invisible spectators" around

the neighborhood also think jock straps are "dirty."

Many couples can practice oral or anal sex, but cannot comfortably admit it because of religious tradition, the law, and fear of their friends' disapproval. If it is considered illegal or immoral (as both those acts still are in many states and within many religions), there is an inherent guilt attached to the admission— no matter how silly and archaic those laws may now seem. Far more than 50 percent of all married couples now regularly enjoy oral sex, but we never know which side of the percentage line we are talking to, do we? And we are concerned about our images.

Even that which we were once able to do easily may become distressingly uncomfortable when we assume a new image—married, mother, father, or old. A young woman who had posed as a nude model in college with no inhibitions now has difficulty handling the same situation after marriage. She is horrified because her husband would like to carry pictures of her in his wallet and hang them inside his locker at work. "But I'm a mother now. What would the children think when they grow up if they ever found out?" Nudity within our own homes should be comfortably acceptable. Learning to like our own bodies instead of feeling ashamed of them seems a step in the right direction. And yet, so many couples who comfortably bathed with their toddlers, who walked to and from the shower undressed when there were three-, four-, and five-year-olds around, suddenly stop when those toddlers turn into teenagers. We just can't do it anymore. One snicker, one flash of embarrassment from an adolescent son or daughter, and we're through. We feel irrationally guilty, not only for things we have done in the past, but for the things that we have sensibly stopped doing temporarily.

Anything tried once sexually automatically becomes a new norm. If I give Dick a total body massage and don't offer to do it again for months, there's always the unspoken question, "Was it unpleasant? Didn't she enjoy doing it?" I may have forgotten about it or simply not been in that same mood again for months, but the void remains in his mind, if not mine. Fortunately, Dick and I are able to talk openly about those hanging questions, but many people can't. Couples try oral sex once, a vibrator once, and genuinely don't enjoy it, or cannot relax enough the first time to let themselves enjoy it. The act is not repeated, but the expectation remains in the other person's mind, and the unspoken guilty questions hang between two people. "Did I smell bad? . . . Didn't I do it right? . . . Did she hate it? . . . . What does he think of me now for suggesting it?" Perhaps you made love once in the woods, or in a car, with the children nearby in the house, but the lack of total privacy, and the fear of being discovered, made it an uncomfortable experience. You don't want to repeat it, but never directly state that and never explain why. And he never asks. Each person is left with his/her own guilty questions. "Wasn't it good?" he wonders. "Why am I hung up?" she asks herself. "Am I cheating him of something he enjoys because I can't do it?" The desire for sexual privacy is deeply ingrained. It doesn't disappear with one roll in the moss. Nor does talking to each other about sexual problems or wonderments become easier just because someone now says it should be. As one woman on a late-night radio talk show told Dick, "I can only talk to you because you can't see me." But what a magnificent baby step. Some of us don't realize how far we've already come. We only look to the end of the road and say, "I'm nowhere yet."

Most of us can talk comfortably about sex only when we believe we're safe, when we know those around us have similar attitudes and feelings, and will not disapprove or attack us. We don't always know that about our own husbands and wives. And yet, there is only one way to find out how others feel, and that is by revealing ourselves first. It's never totally safe, and often we're afraid to take the risk. People do take the risk, however, in order to grow. Several students in the nursing school at the University of Wisconsin in Milwaukee told us how difficult it is to carry the attitudes about sex they are learning in their Human Sexuality classes out into the larger world and remain comfortable. Within the safe atmosphere of the classroom, attitudes can be freely explored, films viewed, and anything comfortably discussed. Outside the supportive group, however, the students often feel awkward, embarrassed, and guilty. A textbook like *Sexual Deviance in History* raises eyebrows when toted around the office, home, or the local hamburger stand. "What are they doing over there, teaching you to screw better?" is the frequent snide question, not only from friends, strangers, and co-workers, but from husbands and wives who feel threatened by sexual change or growth in their partners. We have a Victorian tradition concerning sex: if you can't handle it, snicker at it. Ridicule the other person to cover up your own insecurity. What does that attitude do to the person who is genuinely trying to improve his attitudes and grow sexually? It makes him feel different, perverse, and often guilty.

Some of the most poignant guilt feelings take place within marriages. A new marital expectation of the Sexual Revolution is to have the Perfect Sex Life. But what does that mean? Sweat, passion, ecstasy, and multiple orgasms every night? If we stop to think it through rationally, we realize no two people could meet that standard for a lifetime. But we rarely stop to analyze our expectations. The Sensuous Woman, Hugh Hefner, and Linda Lovelace seem to live and breathe sex all the time. They exude an aura of blatant sexuality the rest of us seem to lack, but do they really do it every night . . . and is it always *great,* with firecrackers, skyrockets, express trains, and fields of daisies? That's as absurd as the image of the totally secure and comfortable wife-swapping couple. It is as absurd as believing the perfect actors and actresses on television commercials who try to sell us products that will never make the rest of us look like they do. The Sensuous Woman must have occasional gas pains and not feel up to sex. And wait until Linda has three children and tries to make passionate love after spending the day chaperoning forty screaming Cub Scouts at the Museum of Science and Industry. Even Hugh is human. He runs a multimillion-dollar organization, and like any executive (or assembly-line worker), must have periods of overwork and tension that keep him from performing well. But if he ever suffers a bout of temporary impotence like other men, we never hear about it. The impossible images remain intact. Most of us keep trying to live up to them and wonder why we can't. We're still human, even if they are not, and that upsets us.

We doubt there is a man over the age of twenty-five who hasn't found himself—at least once—in the awkward, embarrassing, and devastating position of being unable to get it up. A recent letter from an old friend sums up the panicky feelings: "I think I'm entering the male climacteric. Bouts of impotence at just the *wrong* times; no way to explain it. Cold sweat, hot sweat, anguish! Jeez! Peter Pan had it made." Bouts of temporary impotence are becoming increasingly common, not only for the harried executive, but also for the blue-collar worker whose wife has been reading the women's magazines and suddenly expects new performance standards on his part that take her needs into consideration for a change. And impotence is increasing in eighteen- to twenty-five-year-old single males as they confront the newly liberated female in bed, the woman who knows what she wants and isn't afraid to ask for or demand it. In a 1970 *Psychology Today* survey, one third of the male respondents had had difficulty in achieving an erection. Is it any wonder, considering that men are being confronted for the first time by knowledgeable and assertive women, women who are initiating sex, making the moves, and examining their performance? It must be a shock for any man suddenly to be viewed as a sex object. The anxiety of measuring up to that norm is one most women are already painfully familiar with.

Temporary impotence is probably as common as the common cold, but when it occurs in marriage, both husband and wife feel guilty. "What's wrong with me?" we each ask ourselves. "Am I losing my appeal? Is there another woman?" the woman secretly wonders. And the man tortures himself: "My God, what's happening to me? How long will it last?" Instead of discussing it, reassuring each other, most of us retreat with the unspoken fears and blame ourselves. The worst anxiety and the worst guilt occur when couples get into bed night after night without talking about it.

It's equally common for women to experience temporary impotence, but we don't call it that. We call it a "headache" or Johnny Carson, because we can't admit that at times we are unstimulated, too tired, too tense, or simply not in the mood to make love. The noisy Girl Scouts, the new baby, the new job or extra work at the old job, the chairmanship of the committee or an argument with our mother may be getting us down, and it's bound to have an effect on our total life and our sex drive. It's no more unusual for women to be a fraction off balance than it is for men, but neither side of a couple can comfortably acknowledge being less than the ideal sex partner. When the frequency of intercourse drops, for whatever reason; when we genuinely aren't in the mood (or are in the mood for quiet sex rather than passionate sex); when we aren't up to the full portion of oomph, or the full measure of variety and stimulation; when it's late and we really would like to go to sleep, we blame ourselves for being human and feel guilty for cheating someone we love. For the past several months, while Dick and I have been working on this book, we have stolen nights, weekends, and every available free moment of time for writing. This book is affecting our sex life because it's impossible to overtax body and mind and not feel the toll. But even though it has happened to us before (while working on the last book, to be specific), even though we expected it this time and were not surprised, we still find ourselves apologizing to each other and worrying. "Is it my fault?" "Am I letting you down?"

Women have eternally had one sexual advantage over men: we can fake it, and a recent *Redbook* survey shows that two out of three women have. Why? For the obvious guilty reasons: we're ashamed to admit we don't have orgasms; didn't have one tonight; or don't feel like one right now. If we have never experienced an orgasm, we blame ourselves and look, not to the past where the cause may lie, but at ourselves in the present. We are deficient—at this moment, in this bed. Possibly it is our husbands who are deficient, but few women are courageous enough to risk shattering what we have been led to believe is the fragile male ego. Though he may well be to blame because of ignorance or poor technique, very few of us have the ability to tell a man that difficult truth, and then attempt to educate him—assuming we would know where to begin ourselves. We're frightened by the new problems such honesty might create, so we fake it instead and feel guilty for our lack of courage. But what about the happily married orgasmic woman who occasionally fakes it? Why does she do it? Tired, angry, or disinterested, she may fake it so that he won't consider himself lacking—and because it's faster. Faster than explaining; faster than having him try harder; faster than any possible discussion afterward. She's convinced it's her fault, she doesn't want to give the impression it's his fault, and because she feels guilty about her lack of response and the deception, she wants it over with and forgotten as quickly as possible.

It is only in the last five years that Dick and I have begun to accept the fact that dips, highs, lows, changes in frequency and desire are no one's fault. They are common occurrences for any two people who have other facets to their lives besides sex. Those facets occasionally drain away energy and even the awareness of sex temporarily. But what could be more natural? On some days, we're hungrier than on others; at times, we become engrossed in what we are doing and forget to eat. We never alarm ourselves about that. Why should changing sexual appetites over the course of a lifetime be less natural? They aren't, but two people must truly believe that before he can stop worrying about a dip in desire and she can stop faking it. At that point, we can say to each other, without guilt, "I'm not up to it tonight, but I'll be happy to do whatever I can for you."

Orgasms, positions, variety, all impose their individual guilts when we are attempting to attain the Perfect Sex Life. What if you've tried all the positions and decide you really enjoy the missionary position best? Why keep giving each other charley horses when you know what you both like and what works?

Because variety is a new norm. If you once had three orgasms in three minutes, that becomes another norm. Simultaneous orgasm, achieved once or twice accidentally, becomes an impossible new standard. Who has theirs first, and using what method, becomes the criterion for all future experiences. Clitoral, vaginal, manual stimulation, the vibrator—it's an endless orgasmic guilt game if we allow it to be. We know of many couples who feel unnecessary guilt because the wife cannot achieve orgasm without manual stimulation. There are thousands, perhaps millions, of women who need manual, oral, or some stimulation other than thrusts of the penis to reach orgasm, but is that perverse? Does it signify a deficiency in them or in their husbands? ("Isn't my penis good enough, big enough, long enough, thick enough?") If the end result is achieved for two people—by whatever means—why can't we relax and enjoy it? Instead of patting ourselves on the back for solving a problem, we concern ourselves with the method. In sex, Dick and I are convinced there are no norms—no right ways, wrong ways, better or worse ways. Satisfaction for two people, whatever that means to them individually, is the only important goal. If we could all truly believe that, we might get on with the real Sexual Revolution, the one that occurs in each individual bedroom.

I don't fantasize often, and when I do, I have relatively tame fantasies compared to what I now read is common for other women—few orgies, no homosexuality, no brutality, and never once have I fantasized being raped by Genghis Khan's hordes. Alone in the bedroom with Robert Redford, even in the missionary position, is a perfectly satisfactory turn-on for me. But, for heaven's sake, I must be peculiar. After reading *My Secret Garden,* a book about female fantasies, I felt more than deficient in that category. If all those other women had such interesting and bizarre fantasies, what was I repressing? And why did I continue to read that book if it made me feel so terribly inadequate? Because I had to finish my morbid measuring job. Oddly enough, Dick fantasizes more frequently than I do, and he often feels guilty when we compare. Which of us is normal? Which is abnormal? Such are the foolish and guilty questions we continue to ask ourselves, and such are the comparisons we continue to make.

There is another poignant sexual guilt for the happily married man or woman. It's the "what's wrong with me?" feeling one can get today for being faithful. If so many others are having affairs, why aren't we? Dick and I read the statistics, look around us, and find them basically accurate. Most of the married people we know, male and female, have had an affair. We have to wonder why a single sexual partner seems to satisfy us when one obviously is not enough to satisfy others. Is it that our sex drive is so low? Have we no spirit of adventure? Are we too timid? And what of that feeling of being odd man out? Dick has often been with a group of men who are playing on the road (and encouraging everyone else to play to alleviate their own guilt feelings), or with men discussing their latest affair or one-night stand. Silence contributes little to the conversation or the spirit of camaraderie. How sad to be made to feel out of step for being faithful.

Some of us feel there must be something intrinsically wrong with us because outsiders don't turn us on, or neither they nor we take the risks, make the moves, or follow through. A stunningly attractive friend recently confided that she had begun to wonder if she was totally devoid of sex appeal. She's been happily married for twenty years and very few men have made passes at her in that time. "I don't even know what I'd do if one did," she said, "but I can't help but wonder what's the matter with me. My other friends are either having affairs, or constantly fighting off drunken passes at backyard barbecues. I don't want either, but I'm getting a little concerned about my sex appeal. What kind of signals do I give off?" The signals of a sexually fulfilled person. She has no antennae waving, no leftover musk to be sniffed in the wind, and that has become a new worry and concern.

A couple can also be made to feel guilty today for being happily married and still sexually interested—in each other. Society applauds the obvious sexual interest of honeymooners, but assumes they will soon crawl into their sexual shells, never to be heard from again. To be blatantly sexually attracted to each other after five, ten—egad!—twenty years of marriage is an embarrassment, almost a perversion today. Some acquaintances who have been married for fifteen years recently built a mirrored canopy and headboard for their bed and turned the bedroom into a Hugh Hefner fantasy. But to whom can they admit it without feeling foolish—at their age? The few who have been told registered shock. And we all know shock is equivalent to disapproval. Dick and I had a queen-size waterbed for five years until it finally spewed its hundreds of gallons of water onto the bedroom floor last spring. Just owning one caused raised eyebrows. Waterbeds are for college kids who want to make out—not for a couple with four children.

And, ah, the children. Probably no other aspect of sexuality causes more guilt, confusion, and concern than our children's sexuality—and our own in relationship to theirs. Sex education is a fearsome guilt-producer, whether you approve of it or oppose it. Parents today who don't give a child an adequate sex education, regardless of those parents' own hangups, embarrassment, discomfort, or inability to do a good job, may feel guilty knowing their child is being sent out into a new sexual world unprepared. And for many people, the realization that they don't have adequate information or knowledge themselves is humbling, disturbing, and guilt-producing. The risk of appearing foolish or stupid to their own children slows other parents. "What if the kids already know more than I do?" The fear of the snicker wins, and they let the sex education slide.

Because of childhood fears and embarrassments we adults are still attempting to overcome, giving an adequate sex education is a difficult task for the most well-intentioned parents. As Dr. Wardell Pomeroy advises parents in *Girls and Sex*:

It may be necessary for them to review their own sex lives and ask themselves, "Has it been a life so perfect and satisfactory, so free of guilt and fear, that it has never given us any problems or affected the quality of our existence as individuals?" If the answer is no, the next question is unavoidable: "Don't you want something better for your daughter?"

Of course we do, but wishing does not make it an easy job. As Pomeroy states in *Boys and Sex:*

People are able to express their attitudes and give information to a child of any age in virtually every other area of life except sex. They can tell him what foods are good for him to eat, see that he is dressed warmly on a cold day, admonish him not to slam the screen door, and make an effort to see that he gets enough sleep, but a great void opens up between parents and child when it comes to sex.

Of course it does. Most of us were given little sex education, so we have no background to draw on. If we are breaking new ground ourselves, the question arises: How much is too much? Will the best information we can deliver really arm a youngster for the decisions she or he will later have to face alone? Or will it lead to promiscuity, venereal disease, and illegitimate birth? Or cancer in chickens? We don't know. Liberated parents are operating in the dark by new rules that seem logical and sensible, but have yet to be proven.

If you are among the liberated few who believe it is wrong to foist the fears and ignorance and guilt of your own past on another generation, you are also probably encountering daily uncertainties. If you have been teaching your children that sex is a normal, natural, joyous part of life, when do you advise them to begin enjoying that normal, natural, joyous part of life? Do you carry your concept through to its logical conclusion? As one father recently asked, "Do you leave a tray of cookies, milk, and rubbers on the coffee table when you go out for the evening, knowing your

teenager has invited his girlfriend over to watch TV?"
Aware that 95 percent of males and 85 percent of
females today will have premarital sex, do you provide birth control devices or the Pill for your adolescent children? Do you, as one forty-three-year-old
father did, fortify yourself with bourbon before sitting
down to talk about the Pill to an eighteen-year-old
daughter about to depart for college? He rationalized
that "prevention was better than pregnancy," but
claimed it was one of the most difficult things he had
ever done. "How do you begin a conversation with a
daughter about birth control," he asked, "when you
have no idea whether she is sexually active or not?
You are intruding on her privacy, assuming—and accusing—as soon as you begin the conversation."

The question of sex education is the one most frequently asked of us as parents. "How do you handle
it?" people want to know. How have our children reacted to openness? What repercussions, if any, have
there been? Even those parents most open, free, and
comfortable with their own sexuality stumble on this
issue and seek reassurance.

Having an open relationship with your children
poses problems. For one thing, if yours is the best-
educated child on the block or in the class, he or she
may share that sexual knowledge with others. Theoret-
ically, we would rather see correct information passed
around the school yard than the usual myths and mis-
information, but still we are concerned that other parents will be upset when Johnny comes home with a
tidbit from "the McDonald kid." Discussing sex openly
with your own youngster can be comfortable if the
family has been at it long enough. But many parents
have suddenly been embarrassed when other young
people—or adults—are around. We've experienced
this momentary flinch because our children are accustomed to asking questions whenever and wherever
they occur to them. When we begin to answer as we
normally would, and suddenly remember there are
three other teenagers, not our own, sitting at the kitchen table, the answers stick in our throats. How honest
should we be in front of them, knowing full well their

own parents may not be as open? And should we answer a sincere question from a neighborhood child, knowing his or her own parents would not give any answer?

The greatest stumbling block for parents is sexual freedom for the young person. There are many tricky sides to this issue. How many parents can be honest with their youngsters about adolescent sexuality—their own and their children's? If you admit that the first time is often disappointing because of fear, inexperience, early ejaculation, and a harried and secretive atmosphere, are you telling them that "practice makes perfect"? The discussion itself implies you had premarital sex, not an easy admission to your own children. Do you tell them you were pregnant before you got married? As Ben Wattenberg stated in *The Forming Families,* "Almost a third of American babies were conceived out of wedlock *before* the alleged onset of the Sexual Revolution!" The fifties and early sixties were hardly pristine; today sex has simply moved from the back seat of cars to the college dorm or apartment. Still, many parents feel guilty about their own sexual pasts and continue to fear an illegitimate pregnancy, even though today's adolescents have easy access to contraceptives and even abortion in most states. Despite the changed attitude of society—or at least the younger facet of society—parents act as if pregnancy may be as contagious as swine flu, or that their own guilty premarital pregnancy can be passed on genetically, like blue eyes and a turned-up nose. While a young woman today may barely flinch at the thought of having a child out of wedlock, her parents still do. "What will we tell the neighbors? What will we tell Gramma and Aunt Minnie?" they wonder.

Today's generation of parents is torn on the issue of living together. Many parents honestly admit that had they had the opportunity to live together first, some marital problems—and unhappy marriages— might have been avoided. But the guilt is difficult to handle for parents who are strongly opposed to premarital sex, who believe living together is a sinful disgrace. When their sons or daughters cohabit, they often blame themselves: "Where did *we* fail?" Others, less opposed or even approving, find it awkward and embarrassing to face the grandparents, the neighbors, and Aunt Minnie when their son or daughter moves in with a member of the opposite sex. A curious irony is that the unfairness of our Social Security laws has made it economically wiser for two senior citizens to live together rather than marry, and more and more of them are doing just that. One doesn't ask, "Where have we failed?" when one's own sixty-eight-year-old mother is living with a man, but it certainly causes embarrassment—and the added awkwardness for many people of facing the fact that sex doesn't disappear with old age.

Openness with youngsters is a delicate business at best. Do we explain to our teenagers that, old and crotchety as their parents may be, we still enjoy making love, and that it is becoming increasingly difficult and awkward for us to find a time and place to do so comfortably because they and their friends are draped all over the house until the wee hours? That degree of openness is still difficult for the most honest parents. Many prefer to sneak off and try to make love quietly and uncomfortably, hoping the young people won't hear, but fearing the snicker from the living room. Most of us do cringe when imagining a group of adolescents clustered around the TV set discussing *our* sex life.

When young people become accustomed to open discussions of sex at home, they innocently ask embarrassing questions: "Do you ever masturbate, Dad?" Dr. David Reuben has stated, "The only thing harmful about masturbating is the guilt drummed into children who admit masturbating, by parents who themselves masturbate, but don't admit it." Regardless of your current liberal attitudes, that is still one of the most difficult taboos to deal with honestly. The concept of privacy in sex battles with the desire to be honest.

It is never easy when children begin to ask personal questions. So much that we were once taught to be ashamed of comes back to haunt us. A friend was recently asked by her teenage daughter if she had been a virgin at marriage. She gulped and admitted that she hadn't, hoping the worst was over. It wasn't. "Well, who did you do it with?" "Your father, after we were engaged," she admitted. "Oh, just Daddy? How dull!" It's disconcerting to discover that your youngsters are more liberal than you are. You find yourself wondering, "Is this a healthy discussion? It doesn't feel right." That mother found the discussion enabled her to later bring up other points and attitudes with her daughter, but still, those few moments were awkward and unsettling. It had taken our friend twenty years to accept and live with the fact that she wasn't a virgin at marriage; her daughter shrugged it off in ten seconds.

Two years ago, Dick registered to take the YWCA course in sex education for mothers and daughters with our twelve-year-old daughter. Our reasoning was that by segregating the sexes, the educational programs themselves were promoting the attitude that males can only talk to other males comfortably about sex, and females only to other females. But someday our children are going to grow up and marry a member of the opposite sex, and we would like them to be able to talk to each other. We've tried to share the job of sex education in our home, and Dick's registration was simply a continuation of that concept. The officials of the program stumbled momentarily over the request, but then agreed that it was a sound idea for a father to register, since there are so many single-parent families today who are excluded by the mother/daughter, father/son programs. It was an interesting experience. The young girls in the program seemed to have no difficulty accepting the presence of a man in the room; many of their mothers initially felt awkward and uncomfortable. But when the program ended four weeks later, several women mentioned to Dick that they now planned to attend the next program with their sons.

It has become increasingly difficult for some parents to deal with a younger generation who seem to have no sexual hangups—or none that we recognize.

Some friends, on vacation with two of their teenagers and two teenage friends, were horrified at a Frank Zappa tape the young people played in the car. The open chatter between songs about groupies and homosexuality, and particularly the language, shocked this modern couple to the core. Yet the two fourteen-year-old girls and two sixteen-year-old boys listened to the same tape without a snicker or a flinch. Junior high and high school teachers often face the same clash of cultures, although they deal with adolescents daily. The language heard in classrooms and halls, the open and unashamed sexual conduct seen between classes, is often unsettling. The new freedoms and the newly free attitudes are too much of a departure from our own rigid and repressed pasts. They can't be right if we are so uncomfortable with them. Can they? Or are we secretly jealous?

And oh, the guilt that surfaces when our gawky adolescents suddenly develop into gorgeous young creatures. We feel jealous at times of the youthful bodies, and ashamed of the brief sexual thoughts: "He is getting sexy" . . . "She is developing quite a figure." . . . and hate ourselves for the thoughts that flit so quickly through our minds before we can banish them. These are the years of snapping at each other and of slamming doors because the kids are suddenly too big (or too sexually mature?) to hug. Oedipal? Me? You? Everyone! But whom does one discuss that with, unless one's best friend happens to be a psychiatrist? Fortunately, my best friend happens to be honest and open, and has the unique ability to laugh at herself and the rest of us as we struggle through adolescence—again— at forty. While she was writing a letter to me one day, a teenage house guest walked into the kitchen in his shorts looking for something to eat. She continued to write:

> *You should see this kid—a Greek god! I walked around all morning in short shorts humming "Oh ho ho ho, Mrs. Robinson." Adonis just walked into the kitchen in his underwear and I think I'm getting a hot flash. Did I take my estrogen this morning? That question did it. I'm all right again, but I think I'll fix him a ten-course breakfast anyway.*

This same friend was the first to admit to me that she was a crotch-watcher at football games. When the team huddled, out came her binoculars. How marvelous to be able to laugh and admit without guilt what so many other women hide—the fact that we are often just as interested in and curious about male sex organs as men are in ours. And to cure our own last vestiges of teenage guilt, she and I have laughingly talked about collaborating on a future book to be titled *How I Survived Adolescent Sexuality—at Forty*.

The ability to laugh at our foibles and our sexuality is a great gift, as is the ability to talk about them openly with a husband, wife, close friend, neighbor, or work associate. Laughter and openness may be the solution to the continuing dilemma of trying to live with a repressed background in a more liberal and often confusing new world. At least, Dick and I have found that talking to others who share our attitudes, guilts, and concerns helps immensely. Having each other's support and understanding helps immeasurably. Hangups cannot be vanquished while we still fear them. Fear cannot be eliminated unless we can talk to others who are fearless, or who share the same fears. Realizing we aren't alone in this tangled web that society, past and present, has knotted around us and our sexuality is the first baby step, and other baby steps then follow more easily. Once the first conversation with a husband or wife occurs, the next is not quite so terrifying. Once the first honest discussion with a friend is behind us, we can walk away secure in the knowledge we are not the only one who ever had this thought, this fantasy, this feeling, this wonderment, or this guilt. It's good to have a place to go back to, whether that place be your own bed with another sympathetic and understanding warm body filling the other side, a neighbor's kitchen table, the counter of a hamburger stand with a friend on his lunch break, or a classroom filled with supportive people who are also trying to free themselves and grow. We are attempting to understand ourselves, and often what we need most is one other person who will give us permission to begin the many baby steps this takes.

Since it was authority figures in the past who withheld the permission to enjoy our own sexuality, we now need new authority figures to give us that permission. They can be as close as a friend, a neighbor, or a spouse who will listen and merely nod without condemning. They can be as comforting as Professor Florence Schmitt, who repeats over and over to her students, "I give you permission."

With that beginning, we can continue on our own. We can give ourselves permission to be human, to try and fail occasionally, to be comfortably hung up about certain things, and to stop measuring. We can stop trying to conform and admit, without guilt, "I can't do it." Or, "I can't do it all, right now." So what? To whom do our sex lives matter except to ourselves? There are no Puritans today, nor are there perverts. There are only struggling people. As long as I know there is at least one other person who is comfortable with me sexually, that frees me to be me—whoever the new sexual me may be.

8.

Get Me off the Pedestal
(American Motherhood—
the Impossible Dream)

God could not be everywhere, and therefore he made mothers.

JEWISH PROVERB

All that I am my mother made me.

JOHN QUINCY ADAMS

HELP ME DOWN, for heaven's sake! Life on the pedestal is killing me! One more word, one more glorification of motherhood, one more pose that I am forced to assume, and I may self-destruct. My legs are cramped, my back is stiff, and how does anyone expect a 110-pound person with skinny arms to balance herself on an alabaster column while holding up so much guilt?

You don't believe American motherhood has been overglorified? You don't feel the burden has grown a mite heavy through the centuries? I challenge any woman to feel good about herself after snapping at her ten-year-old all the way to school because she had to drive him while still wearing her bathrobe. That may not seem like much provocation, but you haven't heard the rest of the story.

She had to drive because he was late; he was late because he remembered at 7:30 A.M. he had promised the teacher he would bring two dozen homemade cookies for the party. There was no flour in the house. The neighbors were sleeping. The grocery store had not yet opened. The trip to school involved many

117

angry words from the mommy, two tears trickling slowly down a ten-year-old face, and a screeching detour to the bakery two miles away. I repeat, I challenge any mother to feel good about herself after finally returning home, slumping over her coffee, and picking up the morning paper to read this letter to the editor:

> Whenever you see a man kneel to pray; whenever you see a man attempt some great object; whenever you see a virtuous woman, you know some good mother taught him and her. The good mother is literally a slave to love. No sacrifice is too great for her to make. She finds time to listen to stories of childish fun and frolic. She has limitless time to shape God's greatest gift—a human soul.

Honest to goodness, it happened just that way, and P. Richard Cuda, wherever you are, I don't love you for writing that letter.

Mothers haven't a prayer of navigating this life guilt-free. No group in history has been as consistently idealized, or given higher or more difficult expectations to live up to. It's easier to be a good Marine than a good mother. We are portrayed as superhuman, but I'll let you in on the world's best-kept secret: we are not. If, as psychologist Gordon Allport states, "Guilt is . . . a disgust at falling short of the ideal self-image," a lot of women are disgusted with themselves. For centuries, we have somehow managed to keep others from discovering we are imperfect, a mighty feat that's becoming harder and harder.

What are the expectations today? Well, for openers, in this era of wildly conflicting experts, we alone are expected to take full responsibility for raising Superkid. If your child grows up to be Marvin Marvel, take a bow. If he doesn't, it's all your fault. You probably overprotected or neglected him. And Dr. Spock isn't going to step forward to take the blame; neither is your husband, your pediatrician, your church, or the school system. The failure rests squarely on your shoulders, madam. Society has so decreed it. When technology advances enough to clone new human beings, you can bet each test-tube baby will be surrounded and hovered over by a full team of doctors, scientists, and child psychologists to ensure its perfection. In the meantime, that job is left up to us. But whoever taught us how to do any of it?

Mothers have become the mental throwaways of a slightly mad society that doesn't seem to care if we go crazy trying.

We are expected to glow when pregnant, go into ecstasy during natural childbirth, and cheerfully breastfeed a tiny person with two sharp teeth while the house painters swarm through every room. Let's stop and take a look at just that tiny portion of motherhood for a moment. I personally have never seen a woman glow during pregnancy. Balloon up, yes; glow, no. Perhaps the terms were confused in another century. As far as natural childbirth is concerned, I'm delighted it was not in vogue when we had our children. I am coward, I admit—but relieved I accidentally avoided that expectation and slept gracefully through all my deliveries. And breastfeeding? I nursed our children, like all good mothers in the sixties, and hid with our second child on the toilet seat of our rented duplex because the bathroom was the only room not being painted by the landlord and his thirty-seven relatives. And I felt ghastly and guilty because I just couldn't turn breastfeeding into a glorious experience during those endless weeks.

All three of those expectations of early motherhood were to be accomplished without turning a husband off sexually or provoking his jealousy toward the new baby. Surprise! It didn't always work that way. This letter written by a young mother to a Miami sex therapist is self-explanatory:

> *I have been nursing my baby, and my husband is not too happy about it. He says it turns him off. But, I've been told that breastfed babies are healthier, so I am afraid to stop until my baby is ready. He is now sixteen months old and shows no signs of giving up.*

Her husband added a postscript: "Please set my wife straight. Isn't she carrying this nursing bit too far?" He signed himself, "Neglected Husband."

No one ever explained that our obligatory roles of Good Mommy and Good Wife might conflict at times. Nor were new mothers ever warned that we might feel guilty while making love if the baby began to cry—guilty if we got up and guilty if we stayed in bed. And hard as we tried to be "normal," it was impossible to be spontaneous when our lives were being measured in two-hour segments.

Although colic in babies was said to be the result of nervous mothers, it was never mentioned that husbands might develop colic along with the babies; that they might pace the room and snap, "Can't you do something with that kid?" Many of us didn't know what to do with "that kid," but we certainly knew it was our responsibility. Oh, the guilt of living in a tiny apartment with a child who cried for three hours during dinner, law school finals, and "Kojak." Oh, the guilt of not producing the Gerber baby. A month into motherhood and we were failing already. And the poor baby had diaper rash, prickly heat, and yellow bowel movements. We were failing him, too. But never once during those first months of motherhood did a woman ever breathe aloud the secret thoughts: "This baby isn't all it was cracked up to be. I can't play with it; my husband seems to resent it at times; it doesn't *do* anything but drool, cry, and spit up on my shoulder. And it's hardly what you'd call a beautiful baby. Actually, she's really kind of homely—bald and toothless and wrinkled."

Most of us survived the guilty thoughts and conflicts of early infancy in silence and allowed the myths of motherhood to stand. We moved on to bigger and better expectations. Through subsequent years and stages, we endeavored to produce a small creature who measured up to minimal standards set forth by Grandmothers Anonymous and the Pablum commercials. But something wasn't quite right at our house. Our children didn't measure up. I was convinced it was my fault because never had I seen a child on television who threw a temper tantrum, needed a night light, spit strained spinach on his mother's white blouse, spilled three glasses of milk during one meal, picked his nose, wet his bed, had a reading problem, or urinated accidentally on the pediatrician. Our children did all those things—and more. Harriet Nelson's kids never did any of them. Lovable as the children were much of the time, there were moments when motherhood was grim. But no one spoke of it.

Never once did I see a television mother run shrieking from the room when her fourth child walked in with *his* first box of multiplication flash cards or *her* first reading book. "See . . . Spot . . . run." Television mothers didn't groan. They cuddled up on the couch, thrilled by the adventure of educating a young mind. Television mothers didn't threaten violence when their children showed signs of throwing up on the way to the airport to pick up Daddy's boss. They didn't speak through clenched teeth, dig fingernails into little arms, while continuing the hymn in church. All the mothers on television were continually smiling, serene, and content. All the mothers I know today are harried, harassed, and frantic much of the time. And all of us have had secret thoughts of taking the whining child and flushing him down the toilet, running away with the next traveling circus, or wishing, for a fleeting moment, we'd never had children at all. What a horrible thing to say! Those are the thoughts of a wicked stepmother, not a real mommy. I wonder. Columnist Ann Landers asked her readers in early 1976 to respond to the question: "If you had it all to do over again, would you have children?" Ten thousand readers responded, and 70 percent said "no." Ann Landers wouldn't lie to you, would she? But some of us, ten, fifteen years ago, didn't realize there were others wrestling with the enormous guilts and failures of motherhood. We never saw them, and thought we were alone. There were days when we couldn't cope; days when we, too, would have answered "no" to the question. A few women slashed their wrists when the guilt became overpowering; some were locked away in soothing places for a while to readjust their expectations or to rebuild their stamina; the rest of us managed to muddle through, classic examples of Normal Craziness.

How did this absurd guilt trip begin? Probably when the first caveman said to his woman, "Gee, Gleeka, I don't know how you do it. You manage to get little Tonga's swaddling clothes so white and fresh smelling. And his water buffalo skin doesn't cling to his loincloth anymore. You're wonderful." Millennia later, the guilt trip was still being expanded when a little Bronx girl sang the sidewalk rhyme with her friends, "Step on a crack, break your mother's back." A kindly grandfather stepped out from behind the porch swing and said, "Girls, for shame. Not your mother. Anyone but your mother. Your mother is a saint." We've been trying to live up to that expectation ever since the dawn of time. Well, mothers of America, gather round. We are going to shatter the myths of four million years, and the main myth is that we enjoy being perfect.

A good Mommy loves all babies and wants more constantly, right? I know a few who don't, and so do you. Most of us enjoy our children, want them, love them, but have a sensible stopping point in mind. It doesn't always work out that way. As a close friend confided, "When Susan was four months old, I got pregnant again. I secretly cried my eyes out, and lo and behold, I had a miscarriage. I felt an overwhelming sense of guilt . . . until I got pregnant again *the next month!*" She wasn't even Catholic, but another woman who is told us recently she had been asked to address the Christian Mothers Organization of a local church. She was sought out to speak because she had had thirteen children. "What do I have to say to them?" she asked. "I was dumb!" She wasn't dumb. She just didn't know the expectation was impossible. I don't believe there is a mother alive who, caught at the right moment (perhaps when she finds the Silly Putty plugging the toilet), hasn't asked herself, "How did I get into this?" Few mothers can admit that once in a while they feel a trace of envy for the childless couple, the childless wife. "How easy that would be," we sigh, and immediately hate ourselves for the thought. Few are honest enough to confess that perhaps they would have had fewer children if they had known what they now know. And when a poor honest soul does admit that the job entails more than she was prepared for, she is set upon by the myth-perpetrators: "Well, which one would you send back?" they hiss. That's not a fair question. We wouldn't send any back—or, at the right moment, we might send them all back—but that isn't the point. The point is we entered motherhood without realizing it would take all we have, and more, for most of a lifetime. We never knew the expectations were impossible until after we became mothers.

A Good Mommy never resents her children for an instant. It never crosses her mind that they will have freedoms and opportunities she will never have, and have them at the price of her time and commitment. One mother I know has felt guilty traces of resentment for years because her health began to deteriorate with the birth of her third child. That youngster is an extraordinary athlete today, and watching from the sidelines has been difficult. A San Diego mother admits, "I never realized my desires might change some day, that I suddenly might want to do something *else* with my life and resent the kids for holding me back." Isolated wicked mothers? No. Many mothers have had those same guilty thoughts. As Dr. Robert Gould, professor of psychiatry at New York Medical College, states, "Once you get into this [parenting], you can't get out of it . . . with children you are really stuck if it doesn't work. Some parents have to fake it." Many do. Much of the time, parenting is a joyous experience, and we wouldn't exchange it. But there are moments. . . . The Good Mommy has never been allowed to admit to those moments.

A Good Mommy never gets angry or violent. She talks like Haim Ginott and acts like Donna Reed. Did you ever try to talk like Haim Ginott? I dearly loved the man; I read his books and watched faithfully whenever he appeared on "The Today Show." I should have kept his image there instead of letting him creep into my kitchen. This wise pediatrician advised speaking sympathetically to your child, patiently drawing out his feelings of frustration and disappointment. "I know you must feel terrible being pushed into the mud puddles by Jimmy. You look sad. Tell me all about it." Sounds great, but as I quickly discovered, Ginott was addressing his advice to the mother with only one child. When four youngsters storm into the kitchen simultaneously after school, the patient drawing-out process sounds more like this: "I know you must feel terrible (For heaven's sake, give her the peanut butter, Eric, and stop teasing) being pushed into the (Kelly, don't leave! You have a dentist appointment) mud puddle by Jimmy (Will someone turn that radio down? I can't hear myself think) you look sad (Look out, Mike! You're putting your spelling book down in the jelly) tell me (Isn't anybody going to answer the phone? Well, tell them I'll call back) all about it." The child you were attempting to soothe has long since gone back to the mud puddle to play with Jimmy, and you are a nervous wreck.

We are so afraid of our natural anger because we have been brainwashed into believing that one screech, one crabby-day swat on the bottom, classifies us as child abusers. Nice Mommies don't hit or yell. Normal Mommies feel guilty when they do. We submerge our unpleasant or hostile emotions. Once in a while, though, they surface for an instant and frighten us half to death. "I'm going to kill that kid when he gets home," we say and laugh it off as we're saying it. But have you ever found gum stuck to the rug, a papier-mâché volcano constructed in the dining room without permission, or discovered your teenage daughter borrowed your best blouse without asking, stained it with ballpoint ink, and then tried to bleach it out? Have you ever gotten into the shower before going out for the evening and discovered, after lathering your head with shampoo, there is no hot water left because your teenage daughter spent the preceding hour shaving her legs? For ten seconds, we mutter, "I'm going to kill that kid," and mean it—and we're horrified by our own anger.

The Good Mommy has perfect children at every

stage of life, and she enjoys each stage immensely. She never dislikes her own child—not for an instant. She is never impatient with the growth process, even when the two-year-old hurls himself to the floor sobbing. Or when the five-year-old gets a stomachache before school each morning for six months, and has to be cajoled, pleaded with, and finally dragged off to the bus. Or when the six-, eight-, ten-, and twelve-year-old fight with each other, hate each other, tease each other, and bully each other every waking moment of every day. The Good Mommy adores her thirteen-year-old boys when they spend the year practicing long belches and loud farts; she thinks her girls are adorable when they spend a solid year on the telephone practicing their only two conversational tones—moans and shrieks. Even when both sexes find everything "gross," the Good Mommy does not consider adolescence a disease to be survived with the help of Erma Bombeck. She understands and is patient when her children turn from adoring little worshippers to miniadults who criticize. "Mom, your eye shadow is gross. And do you realize how *big* your pores are getting? Oh, sick! Why don't you ever cook anything decent like pizza?" Or as one fifteen-year-old daughter was heard to scream after her mother told her she had to be home at eleven o'clock, "You know what your trouble is? You're power hungry!" The Good Mommy is not rattled by adolescent rebellion; she merely watches lovingly while her hair turns gray.

Pizza? Not from the Good Mommy's oven! She is responsible for the children's health, their appearance, their weight (underweight is a sin with the pediatrician and Gramma; overweight is a sin with society), the amount of sleep they get, their cholesterol level, their vitamin intake, their shoe size, the shine of their hair, the white of their teeth, the number of cavities, the fit of their clothes, and their popularity. She checks to see if there is dirt between their toes, wax in their ears, if their homework is completed, and if they got a date for the prom. She pumps courage into them, picks them up when they are down, and assumes responsibility for the total happiness of the household.

No wonder our own mothers find it so difficult to let go of us when we reach adulthood. Look at the conditioning they have had. The burden of responsibility lasts for a lifetime. A thirty-two-year-old Whitewater, Wisconsin, woman wrote to her mother, who was living in Pakistan, to tell her that she was seeing a psychiatrist. The mother wrote back, "Oh, Baby, where did I fail you? What did I do wrong?" As this woman later said, "I couldn't even go crazy without my mother feeling she had to take the blame." Taking the blame is a difficult habit to break.

The expectations of motherhood have expanded through the years to include more than just child rearing. A recent survey estimated that the work of the average homemaker is worth $13,391.56 per year. That figure included only minimal requirements of the job, such as cooking, child care, cleaning, and chauffeuring. I think the survey barely skimmed the surface of the job requirements, and that no one to date has adequately listed what is expected of the Good Mommy. Let's try.

The $18,000-a-year version of the Good Mommy is organized and competent. The $13,000 model did it, but they didn't say how well she did it. This one is an efficient machine. She is a coupon clipper and a sale shopper. She totes restless children great distances to get ninety-nine cents off. She is able to remake hand-me-downs into stylish clothing that does not upset her children's psyches. She can magically transform old draperies into size seven Levis, complete with the little Levi tag. She is a good, creative, frugal cook, and does not discover Christmas pictures in her camera on the Fourth of July. In fact, the camera is always loaded with fresh film and flashbulbs ready to snap the "memorable moment." The photo album never has two years worth of unmounted pictures spilling out. She faithfully and accurately keeps up the baby books until her children are eighteen, and always knows the exact dates of their last tetanus boosters. She keeps mementos forever: tiny bean bags, plaster-of-paris hand prints, and hair from the very first haircut. (I actually have a jewelry box full of tiny teeth—try to top that one.) She carries at all times a purse filled with necessities: uncrumpled sticks of sugarless gum; a neat stack of "ouchless" Band-Aids held together with a rubber band; a separate compartment filled with unwrinkled, unused Kleenex to be used to wipe little noses *before* wiping little muddy shoes; wet towelettes for sticky fingers; a tiny sewing kit for mending on the run; and a limitless supply of pennies for the gumball machine. She is the family's keeper of knowledge; she knows where everything in the house is located and how it all works. "Mom, where are my track shoes? . . . Have you seen my science paper? . . . All right, I'll feed the dog, but I don't know where the dog food is . . . I can't get this channel tuned in . . . How do you turn on the oven? . . . The hide-a-bed won't open." She does not alienate her children by shrinking their clothes. She does not walk into the room and cheerfully announce, as I have done, "Look at the cute potholder I made out of your cashmere sweater."

The $21,000-a-year version of Mommy is not only organized and efficient, but creative as well. She is a jolly crafter who can make anything from practically nothing, and often does. She enjoys throwing themed birthday parties for drooling toddlers, and whipping up fondue on the spur of the moment for friends who drop by unexpectedly. (My cheese usually has mold on one edge.) During the holiday season, her house looks like Disney World. She does her Christmas shopping on December 26 for the following season in order to take advantage of the sales. I often bump into this mother at the post office, four days before Christmas, when I am mailing my out-of-town gifts; she is mailing her Valentine cards. In July, she hand-makes clever ornaments for her holiday tree, using old bottle caps, broken combs, and the lint from other people's coats for snow. Surprisingly, they look cute. And the tinsel on her tree always hangs straight.

The $25,000 Mommy is all those things and more. She is also Mrs. Clean. She doesn't find an occasional mouse in her spoon drawer, her vegetable bin, or her summer cottage. "Cleanliness is next to godliness," and no rodent would dare set food on her property. There are no ants in her kitchen, no silverfish in her bathroom, and her children do not have head lice. (Imagine the guilt a friend of mine experienced when her seven-year-old daughter had to be hospitalized for several weeks and came home mysteriously itching. When her face finally broke out in blotches, the doctor took a closer look. Head lice! How would you like to call the mothers of all your child's friends and warn them to expect lice? And imagine the guilt of masses of Good Mommies when Whitefish Bay was stricken with a plague of head lice last year. Whitefish Bay??? As one resident said, "They must have come in on a foreign exchange student.")

Then, of course, there is the Perfect Mommy, the epitome, the $30,000-a-year gem. She is most often seen on television. Besides doing everything well, she is cheerful at all times and serene in the face of disaster. She rises with the sun, makes a perfect cup of coffee, and takes it all in stride for the rest of the day. I moved up almost $2,000 a year last week while successfully emulating this woman—for once in my life. As our teenage son lay moaning with *at least* a separated shoulder in the back of my Volkswagen bus after a skiing accident, I remembered to put the dinner casserole in the oven before rushing him to the hospital. Is that cool in the face of disaster? I even remembered to turn on the oven. But the top-notch Mommy does other things I do not do cheerfully or well. In the interest of enriching her children's lives, she lovingly allows them to have any and all pets. She does not threaten to get rid of the bunny when its cage begins to reek from not being cleaned for a week. She does not threaten extinction of the kitten when it jumps onto the counter and eats the roast because no one remembered to feed it. She does not cry "Enough!" when the kitten eats the bunny, and even the mysterious disappearance of pet hamsters does not upset her. Nor is she the slightest bit resentful when the dog wakes *her* up each morning to be let out while five other people sleep nearby. Again, I once came close to matching this mommy. Once I cared for a two-foot-long garter snake my children had brought home from northern Wisconsin to show their various science classes. For six months, I force-fed that snake baby food and chopped liver twice each day with the end of a popsicle stick. But I didn't do it cheerfully, (though I was ecstatic to watch the snake slither into the woods in the spring—and so was the snake!). Try as I may, that eternal cheerfulness is what separates me from the Perfect Mommy. That and the fact that she daily creates glorious desserts for her family as a tangible and basic statement of her love. I only do it when I feel guilty or neglectful.

There is one other expectation of the top-notch Mommy—a genetic expectation. She, too, must have a Perfect Mommy—a red-hot Perfect Grandmommy who does not work, does not live in another city, does not lie about in Pakistan while her daughter is cracking up or her grandchildren are learning to tie their shoes. She is warm and fuzzy and wise and wonderful, and says soothing things like "Be strong and sensible for the sake of the baby" when her daughter threatens to commit hara-kiri. One of the more perfect mothers I know has lost numerous points having to apologize for her own mother through the years. "My mother was a wife," she told me. "Mother never came for the birth of any of our five children. I always felt guilty explaining to people why she wasn't there—and guilty for producing a bad grandmother."

Don't you think it's time we stopped all this? There are Good Mommies—to be sure. Many, many, many. But they are neither identical nor perfect. All of us do some of it well—and love it. Some of us do all of it well some of the time—and love it, but none of us does all of it well all of the time—because it isn't possible. The problem is we let the myths continue to grow; then we began to believe them. How can any woman maintain her own self-esteem when she believes she is the only one failing? For far too long, we've been afraid to share our guilty secrets. Perhaps it's best we start—for the sake of our families, our sanity, and ourselves. Go ahead, admit your imperfection. If nothing else, it will make me feel a lot better.

9.

Poor Dad

The mass of men lead lives of quiet desperation.
HENRY DAVID THOREAU

THE FOLLOWING PAGES represent a compilation of thoughts from many men, young and old, struggling and comfortable, all across America. We have taken the liberty of allowing them all to speak through the mouth of one man whom we will call Joe.

I guess you could call me a provider. "Head of the house" was what people once called a man, but that's not quite true anymore. Decision-maker, disciplinarian, moralist, protector—a lot of that has slowly been taken over by others: my wife, the cops, the schools. Today, my image (my masculinity, if you want to call it that) depends primarily on providing for my family —as well as the next guy at least, hopefully better. I'm supposed to keep the family ship afloat, but somebody put monsters in the water when I wasn't looking. When did the standards go so high? How did it become so hard to stay ahead?

My kids are superconsumers already. I don't know who to blame for that. Society, TV—probably myself. I suppose I let it happen, but I don't really understand

130

it. They want Barbie Dolls with genitals now, and an expensive trip somewhere every year. Where do they get the ideas? A regular bike is not good enough anymore; it's got to be a ten-speed or a minibike or a motorcycle. Everybody seems to want more. And everybody is constantly comparing—with the neighbors, with their friends, with other kids. One new dishwasher on the block and they might as well ship out a truckload. "Millie just got one," she says, and the pressure starts. At times, it builds up to the point where even normal conversations make me explode. Joyce mentions that Millie might be getting new carpeting. Maybe it's only conversation. Maybe she isn't putting the squeeze on me, but it's starting to feel as though it's on all the time. The other night I blew up when she mentioned that the kitchen needed painting again. I couldn't help it. "What do you think I'm made of— money?" I screamed. It probably wasn't fair. The kitchen does need painting. But we seem to need so many things lately. Every time I turn around, somebody is standing there with a hand out. If it isn't my wife or the kids, it's the United Fund, the church, the Democrats, or the suburb assessing me for new curbing. Do you ever feel you're just a paycheck to people? Or a packhorse?

Who the hell set the pace—the Joneses? I've never met them, but we've been trying to keep up with them for years. I'd like to get together with Mr. Jones someday and ask him if he wants to get off this merry-go-round, too. But there isn't any Mr. Jones. My wife, her friends, the neighbors, and their clubs somehow get together and set the standards for all of us. They decide what's necessary to keep up appearances; I pay. They dream up the advantages for the kids—music lessons, camp, college; I pay. Did you know a beginner's drum set costs $350? I just about finished paying for it when my kid told me he was tired of the drums. We own so much. We have a house full of things I don't have time to enjoy, and furniture I didn't pick out. It looks all right, but it's not comfortable; it's too fancy. It must be to impress her friends. It sure isn't for me. The only place I really feel at home is in the basement.

Maybe I'm oversensitive about the money thing, but it's getting so hard to keep up with what everyone wants. And if I don't, I feel like a failure. When we were first married, Joyce's parents used to send us things: toys for the kids, clothes for Joyce; they even bought her a fur coat once. I should have been happy for her, but it made me feel inadequate. I couldn't provide that for my own wife. Now when Joyce's mother comes, the first thing she does is take everybody shopping. I shouldn't care, but I do.

The kids use the house as a hotel and a bank. I often wonder if they respect me . . . love me. They hardly see me, but I get stuck with the heavy discipline. They're suddenly *my* kids whenever they get out of line, or whenever money is involved. "How are you planning to educate *your* kids?" The whole family takes me for granted. I'm a fixture, like the heating system; nobody thinks about it unless it stops working. Sometimes I wish they would notice me enough to take me for granted. Most of the time, they either ignore me or circumvent me. I know when I'm being cajoled or manipulated. I just don't know what to do about it. "Let's talk to your father about it," Joyce says. The pretense is that I make the decisions, but it's a farce; everything is usually all decided before I ever hear about it. Why fight it? I let it go by and concentrate on teaching the kids the things I'm supposed to teach them whenever I have time—sports, games, fishing, hunting—so they can grow up like me and kill themselves competing.

You know what hurts most of all? My wife accuses me of being a workaholic. How can I not be? Sure, I work long hours and I'm on the road a lot, but why? It isn't because I'm crazy about working nights or sleeping at Holiday Inns. The harder I work for my family, the less time I have to spend with them. Still, she's after me constantly. "What kind of a father are you?" What kind of a father am I capable of being? I'm supposed to participate in their lives, but how? They have so many activities of their own; all I can he is a spectator in their lives most of the time. Providing for them keeps me away from them, and it doesn't seem fair. I feel jealous sometimes because their mother can spend more time with them, be a more significant part of their lives. They talk to her. She knows everything that's going on. I know I shouldn't resent it, but it's hard to live a lifetime on second-hand news.

Even the school shuts me out. Maybe they don't want fathers around. If they do, they sure don't make it easy for us. Everything is scheduled during the day —the conferences, the meetings, even the grade school sports activities are held right after school. I can't leave my job at three in the afternoon or at ten in the morning to get to a baseball game or a conference with the reading teacher. How is a man supposed to participate? I often can't even remember my children's teachers from one year to the next. I get their names mixed up sometimes, and the whole family scowls at me. I'm supposed to know, but how can I remember a teacher's name when I've never laid eyes on her? Ah, that's not completely true. There are some things going on with the kids at night—Scout meetings and school plays. But sometimes I'm just not up to them.

I know what my own shortcomings as a father are. There are times I can't live up to the image. I come home from work and I'm beat; I don't want to be nice. I've been selling all day and have used up the niceness on strangers because I have to. Sometimes, at six o'clock, there's no patience left in me. But what's the image of the good father? The guy who drives in smiling, gives his wife a hug, and throws the ball around with Junior for a half-hour until dinner is ready; then he goes off to the concert at school. Once in a while, I can be that man, but not very often. Most of the time, I have a headache before I even get off the freeway. All I can think about is getting home and relaxing. I turn onto my street and there are all those damn bikes blocking the driveway again. When I clear them away, squeeze the car into the garage between the junk, and walk into the house, does my wife give me a hug? No. The first thing she does is tell me what a rough day she's had and that the dryer broke down again. So I blow my stack at the kids and the bikes and another repair bill. I know I shouldn't, but God, I'm only human. Before I even finish yelling, I feel rotten about myself, but how do you explain that to a ten-year-old? How do you tell him what your day has been like? And how do you apologize? I guess I never learned how to do it right. It's going to be another one of those nights, I can tell. Everybody's mad at me, and no one will say a word on the way to or from the school concert. Hell! I might as well have a drink.

Joyce says I've been drinking too much lately, and she's right. I don't like it, but I'm not sure I can stop. I'm so tense. Sometimes I feel shell-shocked at the end of the day, and it takes me hours to unwind—so I drink to relax, or I watch TV, or do both. How can I explain that it's a safety valve? It keeps me from taking the tension out on the kids or snapping at them. Once in a while, when I've really had a rough day, I stop off at a bar instead of going directly home. I'm not ready to cope with the family yet. On those days, I get a scary feeling when I walk into the house. I look around and think, "Who are all these people? What the hell am I doing here?" It's better to stop off and get a little high than to take off and run. And some days, I just don't feel like going home right away. I couldn't even tell you why. But I look around the bar at the other guys sitting there after work and wonder if they are there for the same reasons.

I'm tired all the time lately. I feel guilty because it seems like I'm letting Joyce down in so many ways. I'm not up to the kind of social life she enjoys. What do I want with Chinese cooking clubs and bridge parties? Those are her friends and her interests. And I'm not up to facing big issues at night. When we're not going out, she wants to talk; to settle everything. She says she hardly knows me anymore. The truth is she's right, but I don't know how to talk about the things she wants to talk about. I can't cope with them, especially after work. The truth is she scares the hell out of me sometimes. She starts on communication and where we're going together, and I lash out at her. I

know I hurt her, but I don't know how else to turn
the conversation in a different direction. She keeps
bringing up our sex life lately, too. I'm hardly King
Kong these days, I know, but she's been reading—more
foreplay is what she wants. More peace is what I
want. I don't satisfy her, she says. Well, nobody ever
taught me how, and I'd feel like a fool having *her*
teach *me* at this stage of the game. But I can't tell her
that.

Dear God, how did I get to be a burn-out so soon?
It seems I was an old man in my thirties—that's when
I stopped growing up and started growing old. We
went to a big party a few weeks ago. All the women
looked happy and relaxed and young. Most of the
men looked haggard and worn. Is it happening to all
of us? I sit around watching other people having fun
on television, watching them do interesting things. I
feel guilty because I'm not doing anything but watching. At what point did the football player turn into a
spectator? I don't remember when it happened.

Middle age really scares the hell out of me. What's
the point of my life? Where's my place? Who needs
me? The kids are busy, and Joyce is all wrapped up
with them and with her own activities. Nobody really
needs me except the Internal Revenue Service. And
what ever happened to my dreams? I used to believe I
was unique—one of a kind. This kid was going to
set the world on fire. The Golden Boy ended up being
just another poor slob plugging away at it, and I don't
even know what *it* is anymore. I'm not an old man,
but sometimes I feel as though this is the end of the
line, the death of something . . . maybe my dreams.
If it is, I want to cram in one last fling, one last
achievement, something . . . but what? I'd feel like a
fool even talking about my dreams to anyone now,
especially Joyce. I'm afraid she'd laugh at me. She
laughed when I bought that jeans outfit last year, and
I hated her for it. Gee, I'd love to get a little sports
car just for myself. I looked at a yellow Porsche the
other day. I couldn't afford it, though. Not without
depriving somebody else of something. I feel guilty

even wanting it so much—wanting anything for myself. Maybe I'll have an affair.

That's a scary thought, but it keeps coming back lately. I feel so trapped in this marriage. We were kids when we met. I never thought I would change; I never thought she would change. I never thought I'd get tired of her. It's different when you get out of the house every day. At least there are new ideas, things happening, different people to talk to. She doesn't care about anything but the kids and the neighbors. I'm ashamed to admit it, but she bores me lately. I feel guilty as hell even thinking about pulling out because she's so damned dependent on me. And it wouldn't be fair because she hasn't done anything wrong. Maybe I outgrew her; maybe we just grew apart. How do you figure out whose fault it is? She did everything expected, but the expectations were wrong—for both of us. Sometimes I tinker around all night in the basement, just so I don't have to be alone with her. What if the thoughts slipped out? What if she could read my mind? It would kill her. It kills me whenever she cries. But it's killing me slowly inside to live this way. I wonder if she's ever had the same thoughts. I wonder if she wants out, too. What would I do without her? But what have we really got together? Two people sitting side by side in a room watching Johnny Carson.

Maybe I just need to get away for a while, take a vacation. I wish we could go away without the kids just once, but we can't afford two vacations. It's funny. I wait all year for a couple of weeks that always disappoint me. Disillusioned might be a better word. You "do it for them," and they don't seem to appreciate it. It sure takes a lot to impress kids these days. We were at Disney World during the recession. We shouldn't even have taken a vacation that year because my commissions were down, but I didn't want to disappoint the family. We went in hock for the trip, did everything, saw everything, and the kids never showed any enthusiasm. We blew a hundred bucks in one day on rides and food at the park alone, and it was nothing. They didn't even say thanks.

A family vacation isn't a vacation for me, anyway.

I still have the responsibility for making everything go right. I still have to perform; check the reservations; check the car; tip the waitress; tip the bellhops; organize and round up everybody constantly; find our way there and back; pick a good restaurant; get a good table; and make sure everyone is having fun. If the rooms are too small, it's my fault. If we get lost, it's my fault. If it rains, it's my fault. At least it seems that way. I'd love to get off in the woods alone and not have to worry about anybody else, not have to be responsible for anything. That would be a vacation. But I can't. I'd feel like a worse father than I am taking the time off to go fishing or hunting without the family. I spend little enough time with them as it is. I probably couldn't do it, anyway; I feel guilty just taking a night out with the boys to play cards. Is there such a thing as enjoyment without guilt?

The pressure scares me. I read the statistics. I don't want to die; I don't want to have a heart attack or a stroke. But I've been building a life insurance program for twenty years for just that reason—so I can die without guilt! So I won't look like a crumb at my own funeral when people ask, "How did he leave her?" I wonder if other men ever resent the fact that women live eight years longer than we do. The biggest joke about this whole farce is that I have to fight Joyce for the insurance money. She'd rather buy new drapes because she can hang those up and look at them. She acts like I'm depriving her when I finally get her to agree to expand our insurance program. It's crazy! I'm not going to enjoy the money. I'll be dead, but I have to convince her every year. I ought to just skip it, but the family has to have insurance. It's my duty as a father.

I have to pile it up for retirement, too—so we can live with "dignity and security," as they say. Retirement—I'm afraid of it. I've seen what it does to other men. They break their backs for most of a lifetime so they can stop working someday. Then they don't know how. When all you've ever been to anybody is a provider, what are you when you stop? I wonder if it will happen to me. And I wonder if we'll be like other couples I've seen. A woman nags a man all his life because he isn't home enough. When he retires, she complains because he's underfoot all the time. A poor guy can't win. Somebody got it screwed up. You ought to be able to start your family after retirement; then you could spend time with them and everybody would be happy.

Do you ever get scared? Scared about the future, scared about your job, the economy, security? Scared that you've lost control over your own life? How did it happen? I've been working for twenty years and I'll work another twenty. Every day I get up at the same time, drag it out of bed, put it in the car, and go off to sell something I don't really care about. And I go to meetings and study reports and read the latest company manuals to learn how to sell it better. When it comes right down to it, I don't really care about what I do, just as long as it keeps bringing in the income. I don't even like my job, but I was supposed to know at twenty-two what I wanted to do for the rest of my life, and I thought I did. I got on a conveyor belt, and now it's too late to get off. I can't change my mind at this point without looking like a failure. And I don't have the right to take chances. There are too many commitments. I can't drop out like an eighteen-year-old. I can't go back to school or train for a new career like a lot of women are able to do today. Who would subsidize me? Who would keep the family afloat while I tried new things? There are no second chances for me. It's too late. I'm hooked like a fish by mortgage payments and car payments and insurance payments and educational expenses and school clothes. You want to hear something funny? My oldest son told me the other day he wants to drop out of college at the end of this semester and bum around the country for a year. "College is too much pressure," he says. I should know; I'm paying for it.

I feel guilty sometimes because I resent the freedom Joyce and the kids have. I'm jealous of them. They still own their lives, they still have opportunities. They can be anything they want, or nothing if they want. I'd like to be nothing for a while to see what it feels like. I'd like to have somebody else support my freedom just once. When you're locked into a regular job with regular hours, when you hustle to compete and have to conform because you know if you don't, they'll find someone else who will, the housewife's life sounds like a dream. Joyce can be her own boss; she can sleep late, and put the work off until tomorrow or next week if she wants. Who does she have to answer to now that the kids are all in school? Who's going to fire her if she doesn't get the ironing done on Wednesday? She can shop, go out for lunch, or play tennis whenever she wants. She has time to make friends; time to be a friend. That sure doesn't sound like a bad life to me. I'd like to try it sometime. Maybe the thing I'm most jealous of is a woman's freedom from failure. Nobody knows when a woman fails. How can you tell if they don't do everything right? Who measures them? They don't have any quotas to meet, any deadlines. There's nobody really looking over their shoulders week by week, month by month. Me? I'm transparent when I fail. If I don't get the promotion, if I get fired or laid off, if my commissions are down, the whole world sees me naked.

I wish I could make some sense out of it all. At twenty, I was asking myself what life was all about . . . who I was. At forty, I'm still asking the same questions. Shouldn't I know by now? And there's a new question that keeps creeping into my mind lately, no matter how much I try to shut it out. "How did I get here?" I feel trapped. There are so many hooks in me, but I never felt them going in. It all snuck up on me; the obligations just piled up. Sometimes I want to run away from my own life. I feel guilty because the good life doesn't seem to be enough. And tricked —it's not what I thought it was going to be.

Is that why so many guys drink hard and play hard? Is that why they spend all their free time tinkering or watching TV? Maybe they're trying to blot out the same thoughts. Maybe, like me, they're afraid to look too deep inside, afraid of what they'll find. Are we all sick, or is it only me? I wish I knew because that's what scares me the most. I wish I had one good friend I could trust and talk to—just one—to find out if I'm crazy.

10.

Make Me Proud of You
(Guilt and Parenting)

For you it will be hard,
You faultfinders and fighters.
We are not sorry this first world is passing.
People of the next world will not be long in coming.

It is for them my song is sung.
I watched the making of this world.
I shall see the coming of the next,
And I shall be proud.

TRADITIONAL AMERICAN INDIAN POEM

His own parents,
He that father'd him, and she that had conceiv'd him
in her womb, and birth'd him,
They gave this child more of themselves than that;
They gave him afterward every day—they became
part of him

WALT WHITMAN

"I HOPE you grow up and have children just like you," our mothers cried a generation ago when they were out of patience with us. The implication was that if we turned out rotten, it was none of their doing. It was possible then to have "bad" kids without being a bad parent. In fact, the world sympathized with parents when a kid went wrong or did wrong; nobody thought it was Mom's fault or Dad's fault. Today, everything our children do has become our responsibility. As Eda Le Shan stated in *The Wonderful Crisis of Middle Age:*

141

We are the first generation to blame ourselves for everything that ever went wrong with our children . . . we were victims of the nurture theory . . . we are the generation of parents who blamed ourselves for shyness, bedwetting, stuttering, nightmares, selfishness, rivalry, and every other normal problem of growing up.

It wasn't fair, it wasn't possible, it wasn't even realistic to expect we could totally control our children's lives from birth to death, and yet we tried. And in the fifties and sixties, when "getting involved with the children" became the new norm, we took on an incredible new smorgasbord of guilts. If childhood was to be treated as a separate culture, apart from the mainstream of society, then there had to be new rules —for children and for us. If we were going to give them every advantage, then there was no reason for them not to succeed. Our parents were reeling from the Depression and trying to manage in the midst of the Second World War while they raised us. The times made them conscious that their own self-preservation came first; it was necessary before the needs of the children could even be considered. When we became parents, the world was tranquil and prosperous. There was no national crisis to divert our attention, and therefore no reason for us not to dedicate our lives to our children—or so the propaganda of the times went. And if you spend your whole life tinkering with something, it had better turn out perfectly, because what excuse do you have if it doesn't?

So it was that we became the first generation to spend our lives worrying about our children. There was constant self-evaluation: "How do I measure up as a parent?" And constant comparisons: "How is my child doing against the others?" A horde of conflicting experts rushed in to help us compare. Books were written; the talk shows overflowed with child psychologists; and pediatricians were revered like priests. "Are we doing it right?" we constantly asked others. "What if we screw them up?" we continually asked ourselves. The certainty, self-confidence, and common sense of our parents were out. Guilt was in. To insure against failure, we kept getting more deeply involved, and the more facets of a child's life we involved ourselves in, the greater our responsibility for that child's success or failure. We could not simply allow our children to grow up. Once we took it upon ourselves to walk with them step by step through childhood, holding their hands each step of the way, it became our fault whenever they tripped and fell.

If we became involved in the schools, if we sewed the costumes, chaperoned the field trips, and faithfully attended every function, there was no excuse for the children not to become successful school citizens. If we helped with the homework, or did it for them, there was no excuse for them not to be good students. If we bribed them with money for grades, held the flashcards, reviewed the spelling words, how could they become poor readers? There were no more poor students, only poor parents. If they were lazy or slow, if they fell below the national norms, if they didn't like fractions, it was because we had somehow failed to motivate them. We took the blame squarely on our shoulders and involved ourselves even more deeply. There are mothers who have been room mothers for their children's classes every year since kindergarten. "In order to stay close to the classroom," they have told us. "In order to keep an eye on Billy and make sure everything is going well." Is that really the reason? Or perhaps it's insurance, and the ability to say someday, if necessary, "I did everything possible"?

The entanglement became total when we began to watch each other as parents, when involvement began to be measured. We signed up for the PTA, wrote our names on the blackboard at the open houses, and wore our little name tags at the orientations. Because we wanted to be there? Not always. By the time your third, fourth, or fifth child enters kindergarten, you know the routines by heart. If the teacher conducting the orientation meeting fainted dead away, many of us could have taken her place and given the speech verbatim. We came to be seen. If anything went wrong later in the year, or in life, at least people would know we had been there. Sometimes we had mixed feelings about the necessity for such a high degree of involvement, but we kept those to ourselves, even though our own very different childhood memories nagged. Dick's father was away in the South Pacific fighting a war for four years when Dick was in grade school, and yet he was considered a good father. Dick's mother had TB and was hospitalized for a year during the same period, and Dick somehow turned out all right. I don't remember my parents ever setting foot in a school except for graduation, and they certainly never helped me with homework. Somehow, incredibly, I became a good student—in spite of their lack of pushing. They were all good parents, and we were all good kids, primarily because no one was comparing notes.

When our turn as parents came, "Make me proud of you!" became the collective cry. And oh, there were so many ways they could raise our status or shame us: grades, activities, motivation, sports. Everybody wanted an outstanding child. And why shouldn't our children be outstanding? After all, we took them to puppet theaters, let them tour the cheese factory, and filled their rooms with educational toys before they could even sit up. "What! Quit the piano? Gramma gave you a year of lessons for your birthday. You can't quit." "Don't shame me," we seemed to be saying continually, "let me show you off," and we tinkered and tinkered. "Be a beautiful child. Have straight teeth for the dentist. Have a sweet personality and good manners for Gramma. Get a haircut for Grampa's sake. Be talented for my sake. Be a jock for your father. You know he only got to play second string himself. He wants to be proud of you. Be neat and clean for Aunt Minnie. Be angelic for the minister. Be popular for the neighbors. Have a boyfriend, have a girlfriend, have lots. Start early. Don't let anyone get ahead of you. Why don't you have more friends? Don't be shy. Use a mouthwash. Try a training bra. Have a nose job. Get a jock strap. Start a band. Have an interest. Buy a camera. Take up ceramics. Be an astronaut. Don't sit in your room and write poetry. Get out there and make me proud of you!"

The more cultural and material advantages we gave our youngsters, the more we became caught up in our own dreams for them, and our own sense of competition. Collectively, our generation strove to give them the best, hoping it would pay off someday. If the boy down the block didn't get an A in Spanish, it wasn't because his parents didn't provide the opportunity. They sent him to Mexico City with the Spanish Club on its annual field trip. There were summer exchange programs available for students who wished to visit Europe, and summer sessions for those who stayed at home, who got behind, or who wanted to get further ahead. The little ones had Scouts, Indian Guides, Indian Princesses, teams, teams, teams, and every other activity parents could dream up. We drove them everywhere to make it all possible. We gave them their own rooms so they wouldn't feel deprived. We gave them everything, and suddenly saying "no!" became a guilt trip in itself. What if other parents said "yes"?

It didn't take the children long to learn how to manipulate the new crop of parents. If parents already felt guilty, all the children had to do to get what they wanted was make us compare further. "Everybody else can go . . . Everybody else has one . . . Everybody else can stay out . . . You're ruining my life. Why won't you drive us? The Smiths always do . . . Why can't I go to camp? Take skiing lessons? Why don't we join a club? Everybody else belongs." Permissiveness was in, and we were easy marks because of our growing insecurity. Even the little ones caught on quickly. Our youngest son, Mike, is adopted, and in the midst of normal bouts of frustration at five and six years of age, he would frequently use the adoption as leverage to get what he wanted. "Boy, I wish I was back with my real family. They had six speedboats, ten motorcycles, five dogs, and I'll bet they'd let me stay up till nine o'clock." As tempting as it often was to give in, the nagging comparisons from the past still made us pause in confusion. Our own parents would have dismissed the demands without a word. Just a scowl would have done it. But the other parents around us weren't scowling. They were frequently giving in, or waiting quietly in their own confusion to see what we would do. Who was right? What was right? Paddle or hug? Were we being too lenient? Too demanding? Were we really pushovers? Would all of this really make them perfect children? Would it make them succeed? Would it make us proud of them? Was it really good for them? Even though there were doubts, the culture swept most of us along.

For some parents, the innocent involvement became vicarious living. The competition and the planning of each step of a child's life gave them an opportunity to relive their own lives. Two years ago at a party, a suburban mother of three was quite frank with us. "I want Rob to succeed," she said. "Maybe I'm pushing him too hard. Maybe I expect too much of him, but he's all I've got." What about her two daughters, we wondered? Her husband? And what about herself? So many parents seemed to be urging their children on, as this woman was, with a subtle new message: "You have a chance to fulfill the dreams and meet the expectations I could never meet myself. If I'm unhappy, I'll make it better for you. If it was wrong for me, I'll make it right for you. Don't fail me. This is my last chance." When parents' own self-esteem entered the picture, the competition grew stiffer. From swim club to the classroom, it was "Win one for the Gipper!" But the Gipper, in this case, was Mom or Dad or both.

A few years ago, Dick worked for a little over a year on a community committee to reevaluate the grading system of our four local grade schools. There were numerous meetings with various parents throughout the community to determine whether the grading system should be depressurized. Over and over, when discussing a less strict system, the same remarks were repeated: "We've got to have a tough grading procedure and competition. That's the way the real world is." The vast majority of parents had a personal motivation for wanting an exact grading structure, though: "How will I know how my kid stands? What his class rank is? How he's really doing? How he compares to others?"

That same intensity of parental involvement has been creeping into children's sports for the past twenty years. Win one for the Gipper in the stands, so he can brag about you at the office tomorrow. A close friend who was a Little League coach until a few years ago was virtually stymied at times by the interference of parents in their youngsters' games. For the sake of the team, he was finally forced to rule that any father or mother who swore at an umpire or disrupted the game with abusive language would be penalized by having his or her son benched. Another friend was horrified by the competitiveness of parents when her eleven-year-old daughter joined a local swim club. Mothers and fathers frequently stood at poolside with stop-watches and clipboards, screaming at their youngsters —during practice. "At a swim meet last summer, I actually saw a parent from another suburb slam his son's head against a chain-link fence when he didn't do as well as expected," she told us. "Make me proud of you or I'll murder you!" seemed to be the message of parents whose needs were not being filled.

We have all watched the competitiveness grow, or helped it along ourselves. What may have started out as an informal Saturday afternoon Pee-Wee soccer team (for the kids) suddenly turned into a full-fledged league complete with uniforms and refreshments (for the parents). It was difficult not to become overinvolved, and not to push once we were. Two friends with strong antiviolence feelings were astounded to find themselves in the stands with very mixed emotions during their son's first high school football game. The first half of the game was spent trying not to watch; the second half screaming for blood. And Dick and I have had the same mixed emotions concerning competition. Is it the atmosphere of sports? Or have we parents succumbed to the belief that winning is everything? What would the youngsters do without us around? Without adults pushing them to maintain "a winning tradition"? Bob Albrightson, head coach of Whitefish Bay High School's football team, took a most provocative stand for a coach in a recent article:

*Unfortunately, the purposes of athletics too
often are misunderstood or distorted by some coaches
who envision the game, meet, or contest as an end in
itself, with winning as the only goal; by some members
of the community who see a school's teams as home-
grown legions sent forth to battle the forces of enemy
towns to capture or protect community pride; or by
some parents who vicariously live through their student athletes' achievements. Winning is nice, losing
isn't disaster, and playing is enough.*

Playing is enough? Many parents today disagree.

This guidance, involvement, and push for success
through our children could not help but diminish parents as people. We all become vicarious livers to some
extent. Look at the letters most of us send and receive, the news we pass on to relatives, long distance.
Listen more closely to the normal conversations over
dinner tables, over cocktails, at lunch counters, bridge
tables, and in cars. "Rick is state tennis champ." "Eric
placed second in the ski tournament." "Em qualified
for the regionals." "Mike is playing first string." "Billie
was accepted at Stanford." "Our Tom married a terrific gal. She's from a fine family, and she'll be such
an asset to him." "Sharon is going on an archeological
dig this summer." "Jim scored the winning touch-
down." "Leslie is engaged to the most wonderful young
man. He's a lawyer." "Sammy is just fascinated with
electronics." "My David is getting to be such an outstanding photographer. And still in high school! Why
just the other day. . . ." How great a portion of our
social conversations is concentrated on our children's
successes? Three-quarters? Half? Where have our own
lives gone? Have we so little that is meaningful to talk
about without them? We're bragging—and we're not
even grandparents yet.

Somehow we allowed our children's successes to become an important measurement of our own success.
But none of us can afford to tell the whole truth about
our children. We know they are far from perfect, but
how can we admit that once we've been forced into
a game of "my kids are better than yours"? We worry

continually about preserving the illusion and disguising the reality. What will others think? Are their children really perfect, or do they, too, secretly wonder where they have failed because what they see at home never measures up to what they hear about from other parents? If parents use their children as a crutch, what happens when the crutch can no longer support the full burden?

A few parents actually do believe all the myths. Like ostriches, they refuse to take their heads out of the sand and look around. A year ago, I was sitting in the high school bleachers watching an afternoon track meet. Behind me, a local father was holding forth to a group of five women about a newspaper article on a recent drug crackdown in a small, rural Wisconsin community. "Thank God the drug problem is over, here in our suburb," he said. "It's moved from the inner city through the suburbs, and now it's out in the country." I was stunned. This intelligent, involved man, the father of four children, evidently hadn't looked around lately. Our suburb does have a drug problem. So do most others. So does most of America. Our suburb has had its quota of troubled and delinquent youngsters, of vandalism, shoplifting, thefts, burglaries, drinking, and premarital sex. White-fish Bay, like every other town in America, has high-spirited youngsters who are not bad kids, and a few who are. But it's difficult to admit that. Some local parents have tried unsuccessfully to convince the community it would be wise to hire a juvenile or youth counselor to help deal with the problems intelligently. "We don't have the need" is always the reply.

Some parents who are not ostriches find it easier to pretend they don't know what's going on than to be the first to take a stand. The unspoken message to children is: "Stay out of trouble with the law. Keep up your grades. Don't embarrass me, and I'll look the other way." There is an athletic code in our village that high school athletes and their parents must both sign before any youngster can participate in sports. It prohibits smoking, drinking, and the use of drugs. Many parents sign it, knowing that their sons and daughters smoke and that they drink beer as a matter of course on weekends, because if they refuse to sign, they and their children will be embarrassed. Many coaches look the other way when they see the football player three blocks from school with a cigarette in his mouth. If they enforce the ruling, they will lose a necessary team member, and they know the community wants a winning team. It is often easier for everyone to pretend, to avoid the confrontations, to say "I don't want to know." But there is guilt on all sides, and justifiable anguish. "Why should I be the only one to step forward and make an example out of my kid?" a parent naturally wonders. Why indeed? And yet, how many live with the uncomfortable knowledge that all is not quite perfect under the surface?

Because we have allowed ourselves to be manipulated into accepting full responsibility for our children's every action, we are forced to hide much that is normal. All young people have faults. Sisters and brothers do not act like Donny and Marie Osmond at home. Instead, they fight like samurai warriors while we wonder where we have failed. There are children who are selfish and lazy, and who mumble when asked to take out the garbage, who get F's in algebra, do a sloppy job on the lawn, and would rather read *Mad* magazine than *David Copperfield*. They are very much like we were when we were growing up. Only the placement of blame has changed. I can remember my father telling me with great glee about the pranks he and his friends played as adolescents. Greasing the streetcar tracks on a hill; howling as the streetcar went sailing past, unable to stop. Had he been caught, his father would, most likely, have beat him to a pulp and ranted about what a rotten kid he was. The neighbors and society would have agreed. But my father was not caught, and should his four grandsons be caught today pulling the same stunt, the reaction would be quite different. Everyone would cluck, not about the youngsters, but about their parents. My sister, brother, and I would dutifully hang our heads in shame, and the children would most likely be offered some guidance counseling. Though the world has changed, adolescents have remained basically the same. They are still out there greasing the streetcar tracks (or doing today's equivalent). Some never get caught. A few do. Others are caught only by their parents, who don't tell, and who don't know about the rest.

It becomes increasingly difficult for parents to hide their children's imperfections during their teen years, and increasingly difficult to cope with normal adolescent shortcomings because of the standards and the secrecy. But we are hardly the first generation of parents to tear our hair and wonder if we will survive. Remember Tom Sawyer? It is easy to laugh when you are not Aunt Polly. It is easy to be understanding and indulgent when you don't hold yourself to blame. As adolescents, some of us smoked, some of us drank, some of us experimented; we tried out all the language for size, screeched the tires, borrowed the car under false pretenses, grew sullen, criticized our parents, stayed in our rooms, talked on the phone, and confided only in our friends. Children today do the same, and we feel like failures. They make mistakes in their struggle to grow up instantly as we did ourselves during that same desperate struggle twenty years ago. The mistakes may be different (there are certainly new things for them to experiment with, and new dangers), but the process of testing one's wings is the same. The only major difference is that our parents put the blame on us. We were disgraced, not them.

Each generation rebels in its own way. When we gave our children everything, we left them with little except our values to rebel against: our lifestyles, our religious beliefs, our work ethic, our marriages. Why should it be easier for them to find themselves today than it was for us? Because we gave them so much, and involved ourselves so deeply? Then maybe *we* are what they have to rebel against. A friend recently commented on the anguish currently being experienced by some neighbors with a teenage daughter. She wrote,

Their eighteen-year-old daughter announced she was moving out, and in with her boy friend. She

*doesn't believe in marriage. They are sick about it . . .
feel she is making a mistake. They are very devout,
still go to church, and feel disgraced and let down.
They are about to celebrate their twentieth anniversary. And the girl's timing couldn't have been worse.
We thought we were pretty liberal, but it struck us
both in the gut. "There, but for the grace of God,
go I." It gets scarier as the kids get older. Starts you
wondering about your own equipment, your own
ability to handle the inevitable low blows of life.*

The *inevitable* low blows of life. She said it without
realizing it. We expect perfection *knowing* it can't be
had. And it does grow scarier as our children grow
older; the payoff is approaching, when all the thousands of small expectations and successes are supposed
to culminate in one final success: adulthood. A good
job, the right marriage to the right person, exquisite
grandchildren, and perfect replicas of ourselves. Why
do we feel they have to adopt our lifestyles, our beliefs, and become us? Because that is what is expected
in this culture—and because we will look bad to
others if our children don't fulfill that expectation.
Childhood ended, and we were expected to assume responsibility for our own lives—and our own problems
—far earlier. We, as parents, are still worrying about
our children at twenty-five.

When they come home from college and refuse to
allow us to solve their problems; when they sit around
moping and don't confide in us like the Walton children do; when they ask for the car keys before they
even unpack their suitcases so they can tell everything to their friends, we blame ourselves. We fear we
have failed again. We don't realize that almost every
other parent is experiencing the same anguish, and finding it equally difficult to let go.

We were so involved for so long that it makes us
feel guilty when they no longer need us as much;
when they try to grow up. Several months ago, one
of our teenagers asked to have a party. "We'll take
care of everything ourselves," she said. "All you have
to do is chaperone." Dick and I stayed home,

we turned down the volume occasionally and made sure that no more than ten girls crammed themselves into the bathroom at one time, but that's all we did. They supplied the food, planned the party, set it up, executed it, and cleaned up after themselves. And they didn't want our help. That isn't easy for parents who once picked out every little party favor and napkin; who baked every little cupcake, and stayed in the party room every moment. Nor are the other natural steps of letting go easy. Once a sleep-over meant Daddy was called upon to perform as the teller of ghost stories late in the night. Today, ghost stories would embarrass them; Dad isn't even allowed in the room. The summer bonfires were once a family affair with singing and monster stories. "Sing? Ah, c'mon, Dad. We've got the radio out here and there's a whole hour of Blood, Sweat, and Tears coming up."

The only familiar aspect of parenting left in the teen years is problem-solving, and that, too, diminishes. Others take our places: their friends, the counselor or understanding teacher at school, someone else's parent. It is the most natural evolvement in the world for teenagers to want to confide in someone other than their own parents, to look for other perspectives when forming their values (they already know ours). But it is difficult and guilt-producing for parents who have centered their lives around the fulfilling of needs, to discover they are no longer needed as much, that others are fulfilling the needs. It's healthy, but unsettling, and it feels like failure when it isn't.

A year ago, Dick was mourning a sudden change in his relationship with our oldest son: "Eric never talks to me anymore." And it was apparent that Dick blamed himself. Where had he failed? Fortunately, my perspective at the moment was a little clearer, and I pointed out that Eric had spent the past several months casually passing through the house (and the family) on his way to or from the bedroom with only an occasional detour to the refrigerator. The only words I had heard him speak were "We're almost out of peanut butter, Mom." I was able to maintain my own perspective only because he still needed *me* for food. I suggested Dick call him on the phone because it was the only stimulus that caused him to speak more than a single sentence at a time without prompting. Fortunately, that stage ended as quickly as it began. He now speaks again. He turns down the music and comes out from behind his closed bedroom door occasionally. We have little chats . . . then he asks for the car keys.

They are not perfect children, and we will never be perfect parents. But each parent suffers that guilty knowledge alone or we suffer quietly in pairs. We compare children within our own households, and expect the same from each, knowing we shouldn't.

Sometimes we favor one child over another temporarily because that one makes it easier for us to look good. And we know we're wrong. We're torn continually between common sense, understanding, and the impossible expectations. Was it really so terrible two years ago when one of our sons streaked around a garage after watching half the college kids in America streaking across the TV news each night? No. But it seemed disastrous for a moment. "What will the neighbors think of me?" I wondered. A successful parent does not raise streakers. I'll admit it took days for me to put it into perspective, weeks before I could really laugh about it. And that was only when another mother of three teenagers said, "I think it's hilarious . . . thank God it wasn't my kid."

Perspective is what we need so desperately. If the expectations are too much, if perfect parenting has become the requirement, we are all doomed to fail—and so are our children. When did we last pause to look at the illusion from their point of view? While we have been coaching, cajoling, demanding, and imploring, they have been forced to perform. And many of them cannot.

A six-year-old failure finds himself in the lowest reading group in first grade. Do we imagine for a moment that he doesn't know where he stands? He knows, and in his own little mind, he has used the systems we created to label himself a failure. A shy eight-year-old child doesn't want to be pushed into a constant stream of group activities, so she gets stomachaches. She knows full well she is letting her socially conscious parents down. The stomachaches are her way of coping with failure. Sixth-grade girls and seventh-grade boys who are not ready to date realize they have sinned against their parents by being short, quiet, undeveloped, or unpopular. Junior high school boys or girls may want to drop a certain activity because they have outgrown it or because they realize they have gone as far as their talent can take them. It is no longer fun. But they can't drop it without a hassle, without feeling as though they've disappointed Mom or Dad. A third-string basketball or football player sits miserably on the bench for four years knowing he will seldom get to play, but he can't quit because of Dad. And he knows he will never be as good as Dad once was—or claims he was. The son of the doctor, lawyer, accountant, or Indian chief isn't capable of carrying on the family tradition—and doesn't want to. He wants to go to trade school instead of college, and he should, but he can't—not without embarrassing his family, without implying failure. And millions of children do what we once did: swipe a candy bar or a lipstick from the local five-and-dime, cheat on an exam, get caught up with the gang and the spirit of the moment and paint the school steps yellow.. They are children and they make mistakes, the same mistakes that have been made for centuries growing up, but never before has the pressure been so great to be perfect. And never before have children been labeled failures at five, ten, and fifteen years of age because of the mistakes, or because they couldn't cut it. We, their parents, who claim to love them, have made inevitable failures of all but a very few because of our own insecurities.

Our children have developed their own insurance against failure. Why do you suppose they confide in, and spend so much time with, their own friends? They are building a support group of other imperfect people. We might take a lesson from them and begin to do the same ourselves—search out and build our own support group of other imperfect parents. All but a few of us are doomed to failure, by the current standards.

The pretense couldn't last forever, and it is with relief that some of us have begun to give it up. It is so reassuring to confide in others and discover they are also struggling. When a friend tells us that two of her teenagers recently chased each other through the house waving corkscrews in a fight over the car keys, it makes us feel better. Ours have only threatened so far; they have not yet actually drawn blood. When another father describes the past school year with his freshman daughter as "Gidget hangs out," we feel better. And when he sighs and says, "Maybe two out of three isn't a bad average," we all laugh. It is a nervous group chuckle, to be sure, but it is better than lonely guilt.

Think how comforting it would be if we could all be honest with each other again; if we stopped taking the blame and playing one-upmanship and began to console each other instead. As one friend sighed after a recent battle with his teenage son over school work and motivation, "It could be worse, I guess. There are always comparisons to be made both ways. Maybe we've been picking the wrong ones. 'What ever happened to little Johnny, Mrs. Dillinger?' Ha! I feel better already." We all did—because of his honesty.

There are no clubs, but honesty is a start. Our children learned the secret before we did—or we knew it once long ago but forgot. They are not too proud to admit there are problems, but they get by with a little help from their friends. We are just beginning to recognize the wisdom of their secret.

Even though our children will never be perfect, few of them are doomed to fail. They may turn out differently from what we expected, but that is not failure. "Make me proud of you?" We can be proud of them as they are if we stop worrying long enough to take a closer look at them. And if we stop comparing.

11.

Going It Alone
(Divorce and Single Parenting)

What God has joined together, let no man put asunder.

Till death do us part.

True love never dies.

Don't be a quitter.

I am often asked, 'What is the most common cause of marital breakups?' And, in all honesty I have to answer . . .

> 'Two people who should have never married in the first place, or at least—should never have married each other.'
>
> REV. MARTIN PABLE

If at first you don't succeed, try, try again.

FEAR, guilt, anger, resentment, a feeling of rejection, and an overwhelming sense of personal failure: these emotions wrack the recently divorced. And with good reason. Although there were more than a million American divorces in 1975—the highest number ever recorded in a single year—although our divorce rate is now approaching one divorce for every two marriages, we, as a culture, refuse to forgive those who fail. Although the "good" marriage has become a rarity, the broken marriage has hardly become acceptable. There is little sympathy, gentleness, or understanding for those who fracture the American family, our most cherished institution. Those who defy the rule, "What God has joined together, let no man put asunder," are punished by being labeled, isolated, and abandoned. "Irresponsible," we whisper. "Selfish . . . wanton . . . callous . . . inadequate." Divorce is a synonym for failure and divorcés are homewreckers—even if it is their own homes they wreck. The only sympathy we show is for the children—"those poor pitiful victims of their parents' sins." We bury the divorced in guilt. Their only consolation is that soon there may not be enough of the only-married-once segment of society left to continue the stigma.

Is divorce really so terrible? It is for those who experience it. A Washington University study shows it to be the second most stressful human experience, exceeded in pain and anxiety only by the death of a spouse or a close loved one. If there are any carefree, guilt-free divorcés, we have not seen them. No one seems to emerge unscathed. Those who take the first step out of the marriage experience the guilt of abandoning another. They are the quitters who broke the commitment, tore the structure apart, jeopardized the happiness of the children, and defied society. Those being discarded grapple with the devastating guilt of rejection. As one of our friends admitted, "The most terrible reality to face is 'He doesn't love me anymore.' Do you know how hard that is to admit? To try everything—to try your very best—and realize it wasn't good enough? It leaves you hollow as a person. If you gave it everything you had and failed, you're nothing. You're left with a self-image about an inch high."

Even couples for whom divorce is a joint decision do not escape lightly because society points the finger of guilt at them even if they do not point it at each other. Everyone feels free to dissect their shortcomings. Friends frequently pull away, employers often disapprove, neighbors and business associates gossip, and grandparents fret openly about the children. The man or woman who spent two years pondering a divorce may be forced to spend another two years defending that decision once it is made.

One of the more painful aftermaths of divorce is the loss of friends. In a very married suburban society, the divorcé is the ultimate fifth wheel. Moral judgments aside, married couples do not cope well with the suddenly single, and even the best of friendships can become strained when you take on the new role of "extra person." This is especially true for the woman with children who attempts to maintain the suburban lifestyle. Friends who were for you originally, who supported you before or through the divorce, may drift away afterward because you have become an awkward person in their lives. Nothing is said; the drift occurs silently. If there is suspicion or mistrust of you as a newly single threat, it is never mentioned. You are left to wake up one day wondering, "What did I do wrong?" It is a private failure and a private pain. One does not pull friends aside and ask, "Why don't you ever invite me over anymore?"

The very process of divorce is often ugly and demeaning. Dividing up the pie, especially when the pie includes children, rarely makes for a friendly parting. And having to fight for one's fair share, no matter how well deserved, is degrading. But fear causes one to fight: "What will happen to me without money?" "How will I live if she takes it all?" Changing lifestyles, giving up the house, tearing up roots—it all feels as if we ourselves are being torn. And what grounds? When the courts demand that blame be placed, all of the choices stick in the throat when spoken aloud; adultery, mental cruelty, incompatibility, all are an admission of failure for two people and testifying in open court against someone you once loved can be a shattering experience. If sex should be private, so should agony.

But no anguish is as great for those contemplating divorce as the question of the children. "What about them?" everyone asks, assuming they have not been uppermost in your thoughts. "What will it do to them?" you ask yourself over and over while defending your decision to others. "And how will I tell them? What can I say? I don't love your father anymore? He doesn't love me. But you children go right on loving him. Everything will be fine, you'll see. We'll still have a happy life. Happier than before." But no pat answers seem satisfactory when explaining to youngsters. Fear and concern for the children have probably held together more unhappy marriages than any other factor. It is one thing to take responsibility for your own well-being in a divorce. Most of us grow shaky when assuming that responsibility for a child. It has been predicted that within a few years, children of divorced parents may be in the majority in this country, but that doesn't comfort us when making the decision for our own child. Nor is it comforting to realize that fathers in middle class families live on the periphery of their children's lives anyway, spending three to eighteen minutes a day with them. The experts tell us that one loving parent can provide a healthier atmosphere for a child than two parents who are not happy together, and many children could testify to that truth. As a Fort Meyers, Florida, boy wrote,

> My parents threaten constantly to get divorced. We children, ages twelve, fourteen, and nineteen (me) wish they would get it over with. Our life is hell. We'd all be better off.

But his words are not much consolation either. Ten and a half million youngsters may be growing up in single-parent homes today and managing quite well. "But what about my children?" every parent asks, contemplating the effects of divorce on his or her own children. Gramma and Grampa, who come from a generation that seldom divorced, often pressure their erring child to stay in a miserable marriage for the sake of the children.

Little do most adults dream that while they struggle with the question of the children, youngsters are often suffering their own agonies of guilt. "It's all my fault," the child secretly believes when parents fight. "It's probably my fault," the same child tells himself when they finally divorce. During and after a divorce, every guilt feeling the married parent experiences concerning the well-being, success, and perfection of the children is faced by the single parent alone—and amplified. The normal confusions, worries, and uncertainties of child rearing are doubled when there is no one to talk the problems over with. The divorced mother or father blames everything that goes wrong on the divorce and assumes the guilt for all the children's problems, even when they are not real problems. Thumb-sucking, insolence, a slump in grades—it must be the divorce. The adolescent who shuts herself away in the bedroom for months is agonized over. Never mind that every other adolescent in America is also barricaded behind closed doors listening to music. This one is from a broken home. And if her mother has custody and is forced to work, or wants to work, the guilt is tripled: Mother has failed in her own personal life, she is not around when her troubled children need her, and she's made sure their father isn't around either.

Teachers, friends, and neighbors often contribute to the single parent's guilt by their callous attitudes. When a problem arises, the poisonous remarks are dropped casually: "Well, what can you expect? The poor kid comes from a broken home. And his mother works!" The implication is that if you failed once (with your marriage), it is likely you will fail again (with your children). There is no factual basis for that prejudice, but it exists. Jane Burgess Kohn, a sociologist at the University of Wisconsin–Waukesha Center, claims that recent studies made of single-parent families have shown that the single parent can function as adequately as two parents in the raising of children. Still, the divorced mother or father is more than prepared to accept her or his own guilt.

Every aspect of divorce is more formidable and more distressing when children are involved. First there is the question of custody. One out of ten fathers in America today has custody of his children. We suspect there would be more were it not for the fear most parents have of dragging their children through a custody battle, and the stigma placed on the mother who gives up her children. A few mothers have honestly admitted they were never meant to be parents, or that the father of their children is capable of providing them with a healthy home atmosphere or better care. It is often a profound act of love to give up one's child for the child's own good, but society is a long way from accepting that viewpoint. The mother who relinquishes custody is looked upon as some form of mutation; an abnormal freak, totally lacking in motherly instincts, totally engulfed in her own selfishness. As a Denver mother who did give up her two daughters told us, "I knew I was no good for them at the time. I was so shot emotionally, I had nothing left to give. Their father was more stable after the divorce. They had a better chance with him, and it's working out beautifully. But no one will ever let me forget that I gave the girls up. People curl their lips in disgust before I get the story half out. It's something I'll have to live with forever."

Nine out of ten mothers do have custody, however, and that presents its own problems and guilts. There is often a new feeling of resentment once the divorce is over and normal life resumes. Loneliness and the restrictions posed by any children cause the parent with custody to feel cheated and trapped at times ("I got stuck with the responsibility for these kids while he's out there free as a bird") and guilty for having those feelings. Discipline is more of a problem when one parent has custody and the other is still on the scene. How can you fairly evaluate your own attitudes when there are conflicts? Are you really too tough, too unreasonable? Is he really too lenient because he sees the children only once a week—and spoils them? Do you secretly undermine each other? And how could you possibly be objective about each other's methods of discipline—or lack of them? You're divorced. But the children still bind you together and force uncomfortable conflicts, confrontations, and disturbing thoughts. "Maybe I am overreacting. Is it because I'm upset with him and not with the kids?" There's no one else to answer that question.

Visitation privileges can be equally difficult for both

parents. They must face each other each week—or find some excuse not to, a plausible one that won't let the children guess that Mommy and Daddy are uncomfortable confronting each other, incapable of dealing with each other because the wounds are still unhealed. "I should be above that," each parent may tell himself, "for the sake of the children." But divorced parents are human and not beyond feeling pain. Being an involved father is virtually impossible when fatherhood is squeezed into three or four hours on a Sunday afternoon. Men realize that, feel the guilt, and know that each week they are slipping a little further away from the meaningful role they would like to play in their children's lives. But what can they do? They don't have enough time with their children to have an impact, barely enough time to be a playmate. Bring them a toy this week, a toy next week, a toy every week. Take them to the zoo, to the park, to the museum. Take them out to dinner, to a movie, to a ballgame. But soon it has all been done. Start over? Or take them to Daddy's bachelor apartment, where they will be bored and crabby, as Daddy often is himself. The whole business is unnatural, abnormal, and any parent with visitation rights knows that. But isn't that what they deserve for failing? Apparently society and our courts think so.

Eventually, the loneliness pierces everyone. But that is hardly the image we have of the gay divorcée—a *femme fatale*, unshackled, and now doing everything she ever wanted to do, with everyone else's husband. Or the swinging new bachelor who evokes the envy of every married man at the office. It is assumed he never sleeps alone, that he also takes to bed every woman he takes to dinner. Ah, and all that money now, no more restraints, no more obligations, no more meat loaf. He's got the world by the tail and it must be great. It's not—at least according to the divorced men and women we have talked with. Instead of swinging, most of them suffer an aching loneliness. Men paying child support and alimony seldom have enough money left to support the gay bachelor lifestyle. Women rarely have the courage or verve to reenter the singles scene triumphantly. The shell-shocked feeling that often follows divorce reduces one's ability to be bold. Besides, where are the eligible men? And where can they meet?

Old-fashioned as it may seem to some today, many women cannot bring themselves to walk into a bar alone because it seems a cheap and blatant advertisement of needs. There are over eight hundred chapters of Parents Without Partners, but joining such a support group may seem an admission of failure in itself. "Failures reaching out for failures," as the past president of one chapter described it. "One single parent looks at another and makes a judgment. You figure they have problems or hangups, too, or they wouldn't be there. Our social events have an old-fashioned high school dance atmosphere to them. 'Will she walk over here?' 'Will he ask me to dance?' It's like shooting fish in a barrel because we're all so insecure and pathetically vulnerable." A middle-aged man described the social scene for divorcés a different way. "Everyone I meet is gun shy. They are either withdrawn, bitter, or hurt. No one is willing to commit himself to a new relationship."

Sexual needs and loneliness are not easily denied or ignored, but many women and some men experience intense guilt when they fill those voids. Masturbation does not relieve loneliness, and brings its own stigma of guilt and shame to those from a strict religious background. "Promiscuous" is an uncomfortable label for those who have spent years in a monogamous marriage. And as one mother of three asked, "Where can I go anyway if I do meet someone? I don't want to set a bad example for the children by bringing men home. Yet I cannot go to motels because—well, I just can't. I don't want to end up as a prune, but I'm still a prude deep down inside." And when it comes to beginning a new relationship, sexual or otherwise, there is often the fear of being a retread: "If I couldn't succeed with one person, if I couldn't hold one, how will I hold another?"

Eventually, after the pain and fear subside, new relationships do begin, and they often pose new problems with the children. Mom brings home a boyfriend and the children see him as an outsider, an intruder, a threat. One adolescent girl described the man her mother was dating: "He's fat and I hate him." He might be a saint, but he's still an affront to the image of her absent father. A father often fares no better. The children may see his new girlfriend or wife as a symbol of his total abandonment of them. He seems to be moving on to a new life—without them. While many children resent their parents' beginning afresh, the parents equally resent their children's interference and hostility: "Why are they making it so hard? Why are they forcing me to choose?" And which will it be? Loneliness for yourself or unhappiness for your children? "I feel guilty constantly," said one young mother, "because I always seem to be caught in the middle between their needs and mine."

"Caught in the middle"—that phrase, perhaps more than any other, describes the plight of the single parent. Confusion, uncertainty, and guilt at every choice. "Am I doing it right?" they ask themselves over and over. But there are so many facets to *it*. We asked a close friend who has custody of a six-year-old son to describe the feelings, concerns, and frequent disorientation of the single parent. Here is the poignant reply:

> *I don't know anything anybody else doesn't know. A lot of people know more. Be honest. Let it all hang out. When it's chopped off by someone who doesn't understand, grow more, and let that hang out. When there is no more, rest. But be strong, always. And luck. Have luck. If you don't, resign yourself to misery. Do the impossible. Daily. Don't give in, or up. Organize. Be in love. Lots of sex. Laugh a lot. Be rich. Be Haim Ginott. Be. One day at a time, one minute at a time. But live forty-eight hours a day, at the minimum. Get involved. Spend a lot of time with your child. Travel a lot. Stay at home a lot. Too much moving around causes insecurity. Too much staying at home makes Steven a dull boy. Have a friend over. Don't interrupt your home with other people. Don't let dates stay over-*

night—it builds expectations in your kid. Live your own life. Let dates stay for the weekend. Make sure your kid sees his other parent a lot. Don't let an abusive parent near the kid. Tell your kid his other parent loves him even though the other parent neglects him and doesn't contact him. Don't tell your kid his other parent loves him if you know his other parent does not. Know whether they do or don't, then tell him the truth. Know other truths. Know all truths. If you find out later they were not true, tell your son. Don't confuse a kid with contradictory information. Reassess your values. What really counts? If you say love, that sounds good, but do you mean it? If you do mean it, do you have love? If you do not, why not? Go get some. If you are lonely, you are missing something in your life and letting yourself and your child down. Don't take advice. Be your own adviser. Get all the help you can. Have confidence. Know you are a worthwhile person. That's why your friends don't call anymore, and why, when you call, they are busy. Don't think so much. Don't be so rough on yourself. Don't worry about mistakes. Don't worry about anything. Be concerned, but don't worry. Relax. Hug him a lot. Don't be overprotective. Let him make his own mistakes. Tuck him in every night. Cut the apron strings. Be kind. Be strong. Kids are strong. Be a shelter for him. Let him know it's OK to cry. Cry yourself. Be strong. Let your kid know he doesn't have to keep up with the other kids. Be sure he keeps pace with his peers. Be completely open about sex. Be careful with kids his age—they're very curious. Let him dawdle—kids are like that. Do the dishes. Leave his. Make him eat from dirty dishes if he isn't finished in time. Teach him table manners. Let him stick his celery in the milk, what the hell. Feed him three square meals a day, freshly bought and prepared. Let him eat junk food if he wants, trust him. Have a pet. Have a couple. Stay home so the pet will be cared for. Be kind to animals. Don't let your kid near strange dogs, cats, etc. Make sure his bed is firm. Let him sleep in the hammock, what the hell.

Make him wash his hands. Kids' systems can handle germs better than we think. Don't be perfect. Remember everything. Read Dr. Spock. Again. Follow your instincts. Instincts lie. Relax. Catch him! He's falling! Let him fall so he knows what it's like. If he's a faller, get him to a doctor. No matter what it costs. Be rich. When you're sick, go to work because when your kid is sick you'll have to stay home. When you're tense, relax. Don't let it get to you. This has got to be the most important thing in your life. Who really counts? You? Your kid? Don't worry about it. Caring is the most important thing. Who cares about you? Just relax. You gotta relax! Take time. Get all the housework done, then play. Play first and let the housekeeping go. Keep a clean house. Kill germs. Keep your kid away from insect poison. Make sure he gets plenty of sleep. Oh hell, let him stay up late once in a while. Keep his sleep pattern consistent. Childhood is hell and there is nothing you can do about it. Take care of your child while he is small. He'll be large for the rest of his life. Be a kid yourself. Let the child in you play. Be responsible. Don't act childish. Be a pal. Don't try to be friends with your kid. Just be a parent. He needs another parent. Get a step-parent for him. Grow one out of your rib, like it says in the Bible. Read him the Bible. Read him Charlotte's Web *instead. Be his mother. Be his pal. Be his father, too. Help him over the rough spots. Get over your own alone. Buy him a bike. A skateboard. Swimming lessons. Be rich. Teach him to swim. Don't let him near the water—he's all you've got. Take him to the YMCA for swimming lessons. But they say the YMCA is full of gay weight lifters. Kids have to know about that, too. Kids are easily influenced by adult male models. Then teach him yourself, while you're doing the dishes and laundry and house cleaning and math and spelling and reading and bed making. Don't bitch so much. Other people are in worse shape than you. Don't compare yourself with other people. Share yourself. Be careful what you tell others about yourself. Trust other people. Trust them sometimes not to be trustworthy. Live your life. Don't worry about what the court or your ex would think. Be careful. The court and your ex still have the power to take your child away from you. Join a group of single parents. Sure, they complain. They've got* problems. *Be responsible. Pay your bills. Be rich. Stop trying to control everything. Be vulnerable. Keep your weaknesses to yourself. You're all he's got. Get roaring drunk. Don't drink, except with grownups, and then not too much because baby sitters don't like drunk employers. Plan. Plan today. You'll never know enough to make clear decisions. Don't make a move until you are sure. Explore. Sit tight. Give him all the love you can. Love is not enough. Be rich too. Until then, keep struggling. Look on the bright side. Find the bright side. Find any other side. Struggle to find it. Until then, struggle without it. The only thing that keeps things from being as miserable as they may sound is the numbness. And that goddamn hope. It springs eternal, like those trick candles that won't blow out. I feel like mine has burned down to the nub. Then it lights again. It isn't real. It's a trick. A mean one. There are times when I am overwhelmed by such feelings of love, when I am so grateful for knowing Steven. But I question my ability to love. I've done it so sadly so many times. If it isn't love, it's such a powerful feeling, it's good enough for now. Hi, I'm* hoooooooooom!!! *Wow! What a feeling! But* what a job! *I'm not handling it well at all. Barely surviving and becoming worn down by the struggle. What others perceive as courage is actually being trapped and responding only to necessity. I haven't figured anything out, as you can tell, and the risks if I fail are too high to take gambles. Be well. Love well.*

BOB

No, it wasn't a struggling, divorced mother speaking. It was an honest single-parent father, who spoke, we believe, for all single parents.

When a new commitment is finally made, when a new marriage blends a partial family with a new stepmother or stepfather, bewildering new problems often arise. What does a family do with three sets of grandparents? From which family will their traditions come? Who disciplines? How much? And how long should a stepfather remain a pal before stepping fully into the parenting role? What if the children's father undermines their stepfather? And what if the children are not lovable? (Some children are not.) Treating everyone fairly is a problem in the most stable of marriages. In a blended family, it is an additional guilt trip. There is the guilt of not measuring up to the ideal image of a good parent, of secretly liking one child more than another, and of being caught in the middle again. Where does allegiance lie?

Mothers with custody often feel torn between the desire to meet the children's needs and the desire to make the new marriage work. The two frequently conflict. There are drastic adjustments to be made for any man who marries and becomes an instant father to partially grown children who are not his own. Most women realize this and attempt to smooth the way, but it is seldom smooth. What if he finally implies "them or me"? She may be forced to choose a new pattern of mothering and live with the guilt of doing less for the children than she has done in the past. Some parents opt for the new marriage and send the children off to Grandmother's house, to boarding school, or to camp. All are difficult decisions. None is guilt-free.

In every family, there are child-rearing problems. In a blended family, the problems may be amplified because of split allegiances: some of the children do not belong to both parents. What about the child with a learning disability or an emotional problem who needs extra time, patience, attention, and, often, money? What about the difficult teenage son or daughter who is not your own? The child who gets into trouble with the school or with the law? The new parent often resents the continual effort needed to solve inherited problems, resents the time taken away from other things, resents the husband or wife who is meeting the children's needs more often than the partner's.

Then there are expenses. Raising a family is neither cheap nor simple today. What guilts does the new stepfather feel when making alimony or child support payments to his former family? Does that check, as many men have stated, really become harder and harder to write each month? But they are his children, too, even though he now has other children to feed and clothe. And a man may feel doubly guilty when his new wife must work so that the check can be sent.

Fifty-nine percent of all second marriages fail. All things considered, it is a wonder any succeed. (And, given the expectations placed on marriage and child rearing, it is a wonder any of us succeed the first time around.) Much of the guilt suffered by those who divorce is undeserved, and not all of it is self-inflicted. We—society—point the finger, but do not step forward to assume part of the blame. We should. All of us— churches, schools, homes—share in the guilt. If marriage is an institution we are deeply committed to preserving in this country, then why do we provide no preparation for it? Instead of an adequate education in sex, child rearing, and intimate living, we send couples to the altar as vulnerable and naïve as babes. We fill them with unrealistic expectations, with dreams of romance, and visions of old Doris Day movies. We throw rice and expect it to be enough. And then we blame them when the marriages fail. Why?

12.

I'm a Stranger Here Myself
(Guilt and the Emerging Woman)

*I am a canvas I paint new each day. How do you like
the me I've made today?*

JUDY KLOMAN

ONCE UPON A TIME, women knew where they stood
with each other. If we competed ferociously on occasion, at least the rules were universally understood. A
married woman could walk into any group of strangers,
whether they were new neighbors, the new bridge club,
or a gathering of her husband's work associates and
their wives, and confidently carry with her a mental
road map for success. Given the right clothes, the right
hairstyle, the right makeup, all a woman had to do to
win approval from the group was plop down on the
couch, talk a little chicken casserole, a little needlepoint, or a little thumb sucking, and she was in. We
threatened each other only in the areas of sex appeal
and the contest to become Hot Hors d'Oeuvres Queen
—but both of those rivalries were open and above-
board. Today, we threaten and intimidate each other
at every turn as we painfully emerge from our cocoons,
or with equal pain, struggle to keep from emerging.
The couch is no longer the safe haven it once was because we are never quite sure whom we will find sitting
there now.

171

The dedicated volunteer feels of little value beside the dedicated career woman. The happy homemaker intimidates the working mother, who secretly blames herself for her children's poor grades and cringes inside whenever she gets a call at the office saying her son has been suspended from school or hurt in an athletic accident. The full-time mother is equally uncomfortable with her own internal comparisons. She quietly asks herself why *she* isn't making a "meaningful contribution," why *she* is wasting her education, why *she* does "nothing." The woman who has returned to school is looked upon by some of her homemaking peers as frivolous and self-indulgent; others envy or resent her courage. The wife who works because she must is regarded as a martyr by many, while she who enjoys working is often considered selfish and irresponsible. The old road map pointing the way to easy acceptance and approval has blurred beyond recognition. At each gathering, we now find ourselves cautiously examining each other to see who's changing and in what direction, and where we are being left behind. As soon as one woman in any group alters, the rest of us are forced to reassess ourselves. The process is often painful and disturbing. Everyone is left on the defensive, everybody feels guilty, and even chicken casserole and thumb-sucking are no longer safe subjects.

"Where it's at" depends on the game being played at the moment, and which players currently surround us. Mere mention of some formerly innocent pastime can now cause the raised eyebrow of disapproval, the curled lip of contempt (or so we imagine). Baking bread, playing bridge or Mah-Johgg, belonging to the Junior League may be scorned by some of our friends today. And we know that. We also know we might evoke equal disapproval in another gathering by mentioning last week's psychology lecture, the business trip to Chicago, or the latest news on the Women's Movement. In some groups, it is no longer entirely safe to admit you are happily married, enjoy your children, or like to keep a tidy home. In others, it is unsafe to mention you dislike aspects of housework, cooking, and child care, are struggling toward an egalitarian marriage and can't play tennis next week because you are scheduled to work at the Rape Crisis Line. Nothing is totally safe today except silence, and more than a few women have retreated within their own minds to try to sort things out.

We've paralyzed ourselves and each other with insecurity and confusion as we attempt to walk an impossible tightrope—the one stretching between our past expectations of womanhood and the new expectations of a liberated future. Because the changes have been so rapid, because so many women are changing at different rates, no matter which role a woman chooses today, some other woman can make her feel guilty. If ever there was a case of "damned if we do, damned if we don't," American middle-class women are experiencing it now. Has it really been only ten years since that couch became such dangerous and alien territory?

What did you want to be growing up? To be married and a mommy probably. The expectations were not always easy to live with, but they certainly were easy to define. The conveyor belt began at the pink bassinet and ended at the altar. Getting a man and keeping him was the ultimate goal, and to accomplish it, we *willingly* became sex objects; we willingly climbed on that conveyor belt. We worried incessantly about our appearance, our sex appeal, our weight, and our bust size. We tortured our hips into submission, secretly bought falsies, fretted about the chewed cuticles or fingernails that made our hands unappealing, and tortured our hair into whatever style was currently in vogue. As a teenager, I faithfully sent away for every self-improvement product on the market: Mark Eden bust developers, hair thickeners ("Grow Longer, Thicker Hair in Two Weeks"), and acne creams for the ugly blackheads that never did develop during adolescence (but I was prepared nevertheless). As young women, we plucked or tweezed or dyed or bleached every hair on our bodies. And we did it all in the name of love. We did it because it was expected of us. How else could we compete with what author

Carol Wald calls "Myth America," the shining-faced girl who would quickly catch a man of her own?

We were encouraged to play dumb so as not to frighten the boys away, to appear dependent so they could feel more manly—and never, never to beat them at anything. It was a difficult deception for many of us: we were as smart, as fast, and as independent as the boys were, but we learned quickly enough to hide those traits and talents. We continued the cover-up after marriage because keeping a man was as vital as catching one, and we realized intuitively that cementing a marriage with children was not enough: it was also necessary to remain forever "cute." Never mind that the other two national images of "Myth America" were the mother with child and the kindly grandmother. We instinctively knew better. Sex appeal, cuteness, and dependency were the important feminine qualities, and they had to be maintained for a lifetime. How else could he refer to us as "the little lady"? And who wanted to be known as his "old lady" instead? Never mind that the expectations proved to be impossible. We tried. God knows, we willingly tried.

Aging became an unspoken terror, despite the kindly grandmother image. Once married, we worried about varicose veins, sags, bags, thigh bulge, and stretch marks. We applied wrinkle cream and prayed not to grow old too quickly, not to lose our sex appeal too fast. We believed it was all we had going for us. One could not be old and cute simultaneously, and growing old gracefully was something for other women to attempt. As one woman of fifty stated at a recent Milwaukee conference on women's issues, "I don't know how you feel, but I'm still terrified of growing old. A sex object without sex is an object." Not long ago, a close friend was honest enough to share her own feelings concerning an approaching fortieth birthday. "You asked about being forty," she wrote. "Little wonder that I hate the idea. 'Life begins at forty' is bullshit! I am still a little girl inside—a perpetual child-woman, giggle and all. My lack of self-confidence is gargantuan, and I am totally emotionally dependent on Bob. He used to say, 'You'll really be great when you grow up,' and that was a compliment. Well, chronologically I've arrived. Otherwise, I have practically made a career out of being 'cute.' What an achievement to look back upon when I'm eighty-five and still giggling. Do people constantly tell me I don't look my age because I don't *act* it? When will I be considered mature? And is it too late to start now?" A more disturbing question might be how will the people around her react to the sudden maturity of "Myth America"?

What will happen to those of us who suddenly decide to grow up at thirty, forty, or fifty? Or to those women who cease the frantic and fearful struggle to remain forever cute, sexy, and dependent? What will happen when we finally discover we have more—so much more—than that to offer? To whom will we offer it? Our husbands? Our parents? Our children? Our friends? Will it be accepted? And will it be enough to carry us? We don't know, and therein lies the terror of our rebirth.

Three separate magazine ads during a single recent month illustrate the confusion. All three featured a beautiful female model. The headline for the Literary Guild ad read, "Sure, sexy and gorgeous turns him on. But it takes more than that to keep him. Like turning on his mind, too." The advertisement for Emeraude perfume stated, "More of a woman. More honest. More open. Less helpless. I used to think being more of a woman meant acting hard to get. Today I think it means not acting at all." The third, for Elaine Powers Figure Salons, featured a model showing at least ten inches of bare midriff. The headline: "After a few visits to Elaine Powers, people stop talking about your personality." Which is the American woman today—the woman on the couch? Take your pick.

"What is it that people expect of me now?" women ask themselves, and everywhere we turn, the answers are different. "Fulfill yourself . . . be a person . . . reach out for your full potential . . . you can do it," proclaim the magazines and the leaders of the Women's Movement. Dear God! Which of us—homemaker, career women, volunteer—doesn't want that? But they make it sound so easy, and it's so hard. Everywhere we turn there are conflicts and guilts. Every baby step of change is immeasurably painful. There is the husband who encourages his wife to find a satisfying job, and then writes "dust me" on the furniture. There is the elderly mother who baby-sits so her daughter can pursue a budding career as an artist, and while baby-sitting, scours the bottom of her daughter's electric fry pan, scrubs her stove burners, and cleans the oven to boot. There is implied guilt and failure even in such an act of love, as there is when a little boy proudly tells his friends his mommy is studying to be a nurse, and then makes a Mother's Day collage consisting of pictures of other mommies baking cakes, stirring soups, and arranging flowers.

There are mixed signals everywhere. A husband claims to hate phoniness, professes to prefer the new natural, nonartificial woman of today (which his wife is), and then comments while watching an eye shadow commercial on television, "Wow! Would you look at that broad!" A modern "with it" boss backs the principle of equality, but is heard to say on the phone, "I'll have my girl call your girl for an appointment." Grandmothers express quiet concern for the well-being of their grandchildren while encouraging their daughters to "do something with your own life; don't let it dribble away as I did mine." Those who mouth the words of support but resist change when it affects them personally are best at muddling our minds and evoking guilt. The husband who packs his wife lovingly off for the first two-day convention she has ever attended alone, and upon her return says, "We couldn't find where you put the flash cards so Johnny failed his math test." Or the husband who says, "Don't worry, I'll handle dinner. You go on to the meeting," then leaves the dirty dishes for her to clean up at midnight. The children themselves can simultaneously be the most avid encouragers and the greatest guilt producers when the changes in Mommy affect them personally. There are the teenagers who criticize Mom for doing "nothing," but loudly resent the subsequent loss of their chauffeur and laundress when Mom goes back to school, to work, or gets involved in outside activities. There is my own fourteen-year-old who, after being told she was capable of making her own lunch while I was working, announced daily that nobody could make peanut butter and jelly sandwiches the way I could. Guilt? If we are alert, we can find it everywhere. And we are more than alert these days; our antennae never stop waving.

Some women attack the first tentative steps of change in other women because they feel threatened by it. Neighbors and friends may band together and gossip about the first Bad Mommy on the block to return to work or to school: "Those poor kids. She's *never* home!" Others criticize more liberated, freer, nonconforming, or just different methods of child rearing that produce imperfect (non-stereotyped) children by the old standards. "How will you feel," they ask the mother of the little eleven-year-old tomboy, "when your daughter has no boyfriends? After all," they state with authority, "the little boys are already passing notes this year. Next year, they'll be getting more serious, and then where will *your* daughter be?" In jeans, happily climbing a tree—we hope. But will she really be happy in an only partially liberated world? Or will she be ground up in the process of change? Who is in the majority today, we wonder? And who is right? Those neighborhood mothers? Or the grade school football coach who encourages the little tomboy to try out for the team because she's a fine athlete? We don't know. There is suddenly so much we don't know, and it terrifies us at times.

"What would you like to be when you grow up?" little girls were once asked—in jest. Is it too late to answer now? We were channeled into a world that has since rearranged itself. We recognize fragments of the past, but they exist now in an unfamiliar crazy-quilt pattern. Is the yellow square still attractive, we wonder? Necessary? Does the gingham patch still fit there? And will the blue corduroy one clash now that we have discovered shiny vinyl doesn't equate with happiness? Or that being part of someone else isn't the same as being a whole person? We have tiny but terrifying new questions and monstrously important ones to answer. Our very lives seem to hinge at times on sorting them out, but who has the answers?

What will happen if I take off my apron on Thanksgiving and sit down with the men? And why should so small an act seem so defiant, so symbolic? What will happen if my husband disapproves of the new me growing inside my head? And why should a question of such magnitude be left unasked? How will those around me react if I stop pretending to enjoy meaningless portions of my life? Will I simply trade one kind of loneliness for another if they abandon me? I want to be more than a sex object, but are my recently discovered inner qualities enough to carry me? Can I give up the standing appointment at the beauty shop? Will I feel insecure at the party if every other woman is trimmed and coifed and sprayed and smashing? Can I go without eye shadow? Nail polish? Why should I be so hung up on such little things? What if I stay at the table and finish my conversation at the next dinner party when all the other women pop up to clear the dishes? What will they think of me? Why am I so concerned by what others think? And why can't I turn my secret thoughts into actions? I'm afraid. I'm not strong enough to do it all alone. But I don't know who is for me and who is against me anymore. And I don't know where I'm safe. I don't even know what I really want. Where is this road *taking* me? That is the most terrifying question of all.

Women are experiencing an unprecedented rise in anxiety and confusion today because we have only unanswered questions, conflicting expectations, and the belief that others are somehow managing to juggle the guilts—or are not experiencing them at all. "I'm happy. I'm happy," married women cry. But, as sociologist Jessie Bernard states, "What else can they say? The alternatives are so grim—she could be roaming the streets—that she has to say she's happy. But, on all the objective criteria that you can apply, she's very badly off." As a bright, talented thirty-three-year-old woman told me several months ago, "I'm afraid to say it out loud. People would be shocked.

'You have everything!' they would declare. 'A fine marriage to a successful man . . . two beautiful, healthy children . . . a lovely home. How dare you be unhappy!' But that doesn't help *me!* It's like saying 'Clean your plate. There are starving children in Europe.' "

If the alternatives are grim, they are also obscure, and insecurity and indecision are the worst of a woman's current problems. Even our longings are vague. The problem might be described as a loss of equilibrium. Our lives have tilted out of balance. Listen to the voices as I have listened in the past years.

Barb: *I wanted so much to be what society wanted me to be. But that's not enough anymore, and I don't know what else is.*

Carla: *It must be wonderful to have a career and feel independent. I am no more than a household drudge, taken for granted by my husband and children. But what else can I do at this point in life?*

Mary Ann: *I wanted something meaningful in my life, but what?*

Kathy: *I'm dissatisfied with housework, but I can't admit that—and I can't live with a dirty house.*

Judy: *Why isn't everyone else going nuts? Am I the only one?*

Marcia: *I need to get in touch with myself and decide where I am, who I am, what I want.*

Bea: *I don't know where to start.*

Nancy: *I don't seem to belong anywhere with my new thoughts and my new doubts.*

Pam: *Maybe I married too young.*

Mary: Maybe I should never have married, never had children—but those possibilities didn't exist in the world in which I grew up.

Gail: Do I know what it is I want? No. I only know what I don't want.

Dorrie: It isn't that I want to go to China. It's just that I'm so trapped by tradition I can't even make it across the street alone.

Kate: I don't mean to resent my family, nor to reject it. But I know I do at times. I hope we can, all of us, gracefully grow through this somehow.

Linda: We were taught that motherhood and wifery are so fulfilling, and then we had to learn to live with the secret guilt when they weren't fulfilling.

Laurie: The growing pains almost kill you at times. I get so scared. And I wonder who I will be tomorrow.

Bitter women? Angry women? Neurotic and crazy women? Not one of them. I know these women well. They are married, and struggling, and I have listened and shared their pain as each has recently looked honestly into her own life—for the first time. It's been a privilege to listen, and learn that others are asking the same frightening questions.

Perhaps a short history of one very sane, very honest, and very dear friend, Judy Kloman, will bring the picture into sharper focus. This is a poignant letter she wrote last summer, less, perhaps, to explain her life to me than to explain it to herself.

When I was in high school, a social studies instructor said I had an inquiring mind and lots of potential. So this creative genius was encouraged to go to nursing school ($400 total fee for three years;

uniforms, meals, and valuable work and learning experiences included). Sound familiar? Like maybe the Marines? I hated nursing school from the very first minute. Question: What thirteen articles are found on the top shelf on the bedside table? Answer: I don't know—I'll look when I get there. Result: an F in Nursing Arts and the threat of deportation back home. Well, I didn't like home much more, so I decided to stick with nursing school, if only to rise above my environment (and prove my teachers wrong). Also, there were no other choices.

Fundamentally, a good nursing school in the 1950s was run efficiently by exploiting the sweet young things who had enrolled for idealistic reasons. During the first year, we had three suicide attempts, plus a 50 percent dropout rate. I came out of nursing school intellectually shattered and groping for an identity. What I found was a comfortable, congenial husband who encouraged me to give up any career dreams and/or nightmares. At that time, I wanted nothing more than to escape the deprivation and anxiety of nursing school. I wanted out. I escaped into marriage and motherhood.

For the next sixteen years, every day I would wind up this enormous ball of string that someone had tangled about the house, knotted around toys, furniture legs, lamps, doorknobs. From morning to night, I untangled and wound string. The next morning I would find the string was once again unwound, snarled, and looped everywhere. I would begin over —winding and winding and winding and crying and shrieking inside. "Enough!" I shrieked one day. "I want out!" Again?

Luckily, I have an ally this time. Tom is on my side. Maybe the reason I don't identify with my mother, my overweight ex-classmates, my PTA-oriented neighbors, my vacuous country club set— slick, tanned, hard, and wrinkled—maybe the rea-

son I don't even enjoy them is because I don't belong in any of their lives anymore. Okay. So where do I belong? My problem is to identify my problems. What do I want? What do I need? Where do I find a meaningful place for myself, unchained from the stove or the bed? Why have I tried so hard to belong in the wrong places? Why do I feel guilty being bored by people and subjects everyone else finds fascinating? How did I get to be so confused about my own identity? I only know what I don't want at this point. You have now encountered the result of sixteen years of string-winding.

I'm burning bridges behind me and trying to put some meaning into my personal identity. Maybe I could contribute more than homemade cookies and clean toilet bowls to the world. Maybe I do have something worth developing at thirty-nine. I'm just beginning. I know, at least, I am a person. And should I survive, I'm interested in learning and growing again. I think I just began my growth in the wrong places in the past. Conclusions? None. I'm a stranger here myself.

Like Judy, we were all similarly channeled. It was wrong to lead us to believe that the end of the conveyor belt—teaching, nursing, marriage, children, housework—would be enough to satisfy each and every one of us for a lifetime. But whom shall we now blame? Who was the villain? I can't point a finger. I *allowed* myself to be led. And those who pointed the way—our mothers, our teachers, our society—believed in the way themselves. Besides, what were our options? Independence then equaled spinsterhood—"old maiden Auntie Paula." The words today are not even frightening; once they were terrifying.

Even though I had personal role models to follow that others didn't—my mother and my grandmother both had careers—I was swept along like Judy, Nancy, Kathy, and the rest. I married in the late fifties when no other carrots were being dangled, when there were no other expectations of fulfillment but wifery and motherhood. And I did my damnedest to be only that, to survive on only that. It took years (with the best of marriages and four startlingly nice children whom I would not send back) to admit to the vague guilty gnawings inside. What was wrong with me? Why wasn't string-winding enough for me if it was for all the others? It took more years to admit, like Judy, "I'm a person, too. I need more." And as I was slowly gathering my courage to say that aloud, someone else shouted it from a mountaintop. The Women's Movement exploded across American newsstands and television screens; almost overnight, the consciousness of a nation was raised, tilted, and changed again. Whether we agreed, disagreed, or attempted to remain neutral, no one escaped the impact. Suddenly there was a thing called Sisterhood, and the secret questions we had never allowed ourselves to ask aloud were being screamed in the headlines.

Those of us who had buried the disquieting thoughts for so long breathed a monumental sigh of relief. At last we knew we were not crazy, or at least, we were not alone in our craziness. There were others, perhaps not close enough to touch or see, but we could read about them. "What's wrong with me?" quickly became widespread awareness of the years of conditioning. Awareness soon changed to militancy. "How do we right this mess?" And then the anger exploded. Questioning was quickly replaced by resentment for the lost years and lost opportunities. There were cries of rage when the full impact of injustice hit; centuries of role stereotyping, inequality, tokenism, job discrimination, and submission were examined overnight. We learned more about ourselves historically, culturally, and personally in a few short years than mankind had learned in entire lifetimes. We ferreted out each personal and universal injustice, and dragged it into the full light of day to examine and poke it apart with sticks of horror and revulsion. There was much to examine and the fury increased. Justifiably, some women howled and raged and invented phrases that won us battles, but almost lost us a new war. "Male chauvinist pig!" "Herstory." We pointed fingers and declared an enemy. We had found a villain at last—man. How absurd.

If men had done this to us, we had allowed it to be done. And if anybody did anything to us, it wasn't the men we lived with, worked with, or loved. It was their forefathers (and foremothers) and our own who had spun the webs and allowed them to settle over us. Our lovers, our husbands, our male friends had also been channeled by the culture of the times. Their conveyor belt was separate but equally unswerving. If we had all been conditioned together, how could it be their fault? But women needed a scapegoat, instant retribution for the hurts and the wrongs and the omissions. We expected change overnight, but history can't reverse itself that quickly. Our men were unable to undo their conditioning that fast, which shouldn't have surprised us because, after all, we couldn't undo our own.

Which brings us back to our awkward position on the couch—awkward for ourselves and awkward for other women. What do we do with it all now that we understand it a little better? Now that the fury has cooled for most, where do we go from here? There are many new guilts, internal and external, to resolve as we emerge, not as housewives or legal secretaries or executives or volunteers or students, but as people. We have stopped blaming for the most part, and have begun to realize we are responsible for our own lives, but we are still confused by mixed expectations, the loss of equilibrium, and the fear of the tightrope. How do we begin?

We have already begun. Knowledge of others and the comfort of numbers are the first pain-relievers in the struggle to reevaluate our lives. Knowing there are others who worry and wonder is reassuring. And from competition with other women, we are inching toward camaraderie. I can feel it, I can see it daily now, a new aura of spiritual support among women. We like each other better than ever before. There is genuine respect and admiration, and that is new to me. I am prouder of women—all kinds of women, known and unknown—than I have ever been. And I am more sympathetic to their pain and problems. One can almost grasp the feeling that author Sue Kaufman has accurately described: "Here among my own kind," she said, even though we may still be individually "stranded on the linoleum." If the poignant aloneness with her own thoughts is the special plight of the home-maker, at least she now knows there are millions of others. That is change.

And there are other changes. More than a million women returned to school in 1972. Four million did so in 1974. Fully half the mothers of America with school-age children now hold down a job. One of every three mothers with preschool children now works. Four out of five teens of working mothers now do the weekly grocery shopping. And, according to pollster Daniel Yankelovich, just over half the women in America believe women are overly concerned with household matters, such as cleaning and cooking! There is a growing awareness among both men and women of the stereotyping and manipulation of both sexes that occurred in the past. There is a new anger at advertisers who portray women only as functional drudges experiencing orgasms over the scents of their new fabric softeners. There have been changes in our federal and state laws, in our school policies, our athletic programs, and our textbooks to upgrade the images of girls and women. Progress is occurring; change is happening.

But, with change, there are always new conflicts. Housewifery and motherhood have been two of the most painful reassessments. Letting go is far from easy. I've read two conflicting studies during the past year concerning housework. One claimed that two-thirds of American women were dissatisfied with housework; the other claimed the opposite. Frankly, I don't care which is correct. The pain and guilt lie within each individual wife/mother/woman as she tries to change her own self-image, as she tries to let go of anything formerly considered a major part of her self-esteem. Whether a woman has gone back to work, to school, off to the garden club, or to the Help Line doesn't matter today. It doesn't even matter if she has gone nowhere but merely wishes to read a book in the afternoon or watch Merv Griffin. Having a messy linen closet, a greasy stove, a cluttered basement is guilt producing—traditionally. Not making lunch for your children, not baking for the school or the church, letting the mending or the ironing pile up, being too busy to chauffeur is guilt producing—traditionally. Not being totally child-centered is guilt producing—traditionally. But how old are some of those traditions? My grandmother never owned a car. I don't recall my own mother chauffeuring us around constantly, baking for the school, or making my lunch. And she certainly wasn't child-centered. Was yours? Many of the "traditions" we are abandoning we started ourselves when we swarmed into suburbia. But still, we feel guilty ceasing to do what *we* have always done.

The opposite side of that coin is the new guilt unfairly draped across the shoulders of today's full-time homemaker—the woman who enjoys that role, and happily still does it all. Other women who feel trapped by the role or who have recently rejected it have done irreparable damage to the homemaker's self-esteem in the last five years. They, we—not men—have made her feel guilty, useless, and degraded for finding joy in *her* work. But why shouldn't the homemaker enjoy her role? It's a helluva rewarding life for those who freely choose it. We were not all cut from the same mold; we were only taught we were; and the disparaging comparisons are like pitting engineers against accountants, and declaring a winner and a loser. I enjoy baking a cake; I enjoy rearranging a bookcase; I enjoy taking a dozen children for a hike through the woods—but not every day. I also enjoy writing, and not many people can survive the loneliness of the typewriter for eight hours a day. We are all naturally unique, and there is such a marvelous range of choices available to women today, we should be ecstatic. Why have we suddenly begun instead to make each other feel guilty for the very differences men have accepted in themselves for centuries? Is it to cope with our own guilt feelings and to justify our own changes that we now dump the guilt on other women who still do what we formerly did? Perhaps. And perhaps we will only be fully liberated when we can choose to do what we want without feeling defensive about those things we no longer want to do.

If the homemaker has been made to feel her role is invalid, insufficient, so has the volunteer. The lack of pay suddenly separates her in her own mind from the new working woman. But it is not a lack of talent, dedication, or energy that diminishes the volunteer. It is the abrupt loss of stature that volunteerism suffered when so many women began bringing home a paycheck. "How do I compare?" the volunteer began to ask herself as she looked around. "Could I cut it in the business world? Am I good enough? Am I as good as they are?" She will never know until she tries—but what if she does not want to try? Once happy volunteers are less happy today because of new expectations, new guilts, and new differences.

The "empty nest" syndrome, the luxury of the "last child in school" freedom, has recently turned to panic for many other women. "Now, I have no more excuses. I *have* to do something to justify my existence." Another new norm, another pressure, and another guilt. While many women long to emerge from their homes, others simply feel they must. Neither has an easy time. As one of my friends said recently, "A debut at forty—'a coming out'—is probably the most frightening step in the world. I desperately need a label to call myself. 'Retired Mother' doesn't cut it. I need a job that will give me an identity now that my old one is gone. And I need money because that's the way the real world values people. It is a tangible, visible, bankable sign of achievement! But what am I worth? And to whom? What can I do? I haven't had a job interview in twenty-two years." Another friend was equally intimidated: "I've started reading the Help Wanted columns. Try that once if you want to cure euphoria! No one seems to be looking for a fortyish lady whose last previous experience was eighteen years ago, who has little, if any, office skills, who can't even keep her house clean enough to satisfy her husband, and whose kids are even starting to complain about her cooking and laundering. I am probably qualified to be a cocktail waitress—Lord knows I've had enough experience at that!—a telephone canvasser, or a cleaning woman (if I really tried hard)." Just where does the bright, skilled, talented, creative homemaker take her talents? What does she put on her résumé? Little League driver? Room mother? Hot Hors d'Oeuvres Queen? Prom Queen, 1956?

Even with the most supportive of families, the most understanding and encouraging of husbands, an emerging woman experiences indecisiveness and fear. How does she find the right words to explain to a husband and children who have finally accepted her as a separate person with needs of her own that she has no idea what she wants to do? She was an almost-graduated political science major fifteen years ago before she quit school to put Dad through; she is no longer interested in political science; it isn't her fault the world has changed since then; she herself has changed and political science isn't her thing anymore, but she doesn't know what the hell *is* her thing. How could she know? She has no recent experience in knowing. But to satisfy her own new expectations and those she has recently created in her family, she must walk out of the house after fifteen years, find a fulfilling, meaningful career (not a job—a career) that doesn't take all her time and energy, that leaves her enough flexibility to remain a good and beautiful Mommy and wife. I know men who have been working for thirty years who haven't discovered their "thing" yet. So how does the emerging woman—who is battling so many guilts simultaneously—accomplish this on her first try with no training, no experience, and no help? "Everyone is being so good to me," she tells herself. "They are letting me out. I can't let them down."

Perhaps the reason so many women have gone back to college is that it is a semisafe limbo, an unpressured transition. One can get a C there and not be considered a failure. One can hardly expect even a grade of C from a family after fighting, pleading, and demanding to be considered a fully mature person at home, and then falling flat on one's face when one steps out the door. Sometimes the rigors of the business world are too different, too fast, too demanding for our experience, but one can hardly ask to be coddled by IBM because society channeled us in the wrong direction twenty years ago. Or demand time off to chauffeur the children to the orthodontist because we can't even conceive of asking a husband to take time off from *his* job.

Academia is less threatening than the cold, cruel, value-paid-for-value-received business world. Some of us can't cope with that much change the first time off the linoleum, and we're realistic enough to admit it to ourselves, but too proud to admit it out loud. School gives us a label, an identity, and the prestige we need to emerge gracefully, dignity intact. I don't think of it as a copout; I did it myself. I consider it a holding pattern, a temporary haven where women can test their wings, a step toward liberation without full commitment—and without the stigma of failure. Unfortunately, many emerging women never emerge from school. Limbo is too comfortable, so they become professional students.

The sharpest new guilt feelings are those experienced by the working mother. She has emerged physically, but emotionally, it is a different story. *"She should be home!"* said suburban society, and her guilt at not being home will never entirely fade until the last child marries and her husband joins the Marine Corps or the priesthood. People who point the dagger of guilt at working mothers needn't bother because we stab ourselves with it so much more frequently and deeply. Did we think when we went back to work (for whatever reason) that we would be able to do it all—work, make lemon meringue pies, run the pet rabbits to school for pet day, throw intimate dinner parties for eight with coordinated candles and centerpieces, keep our floors spotless and our Revere Ware gleaming? We fantasized that the transition would be painless; that the most loving of families would not squeak at the changes in their own lives; that husbands would not sigh and say "Hamburgers, again?"; that children would not continue to make their endless, innocent demands on our time and energy; that nothing would ever go wrong with their young lives (that the peanut butter would never run out)—and that we would not endlessly blame ourselves when it did.

I believed it! And when my standards around the house dropped, when I found myself cooking more simply and spending more money and less time at it, I felt guilty. When I looked into the corners of rooms on bright sunny days, I felt guilty. And when our youngest son wrote in a fourth-grade composition, "I wish my mother didn't have to work so hard," oh, how I felt guilty! And I have a husband who helps, understands, and encourages—and is fair; I have children who take on more than their share, and are as fair as children are capable of being. I pity the working or emerging woman who has less. How does she survive her guilt when I can barely cope with my own at times?

Success is another new problem for today's working woman. Rosie the Riveter was encouraged by society to enter the work force and told she was needed. We were never told that. The moves are our own, and we are still unwelcome in many working worlds, especially when we do well. We threaten many men and we know that. We threaten ourselves more. Women who were taught it was smart to act coy and dependent have difficulty just acting smart. And when we succeed despite our conditioning, when we are promoted or given more responsibility, we are expected to assume an aura of authority alien to our backgrounds. How does the woman conditioned to be ever-smiling and sweetly submissive get the late supplier to hustle; reprimand co-workers or subordinates when their work is not satisfactory; hire and fire; make decisions; make demands; and take charge? The very qualities necessary for success run against the grain of twenty, thirty, or forty years of typecasting for some of us. And through it all, we know we are being scrutinized—not always fairly. A recent Harvard study done by psychologist Matina Horner showed that men described a successful woman as "unattractive, unpopular, unfeminine, and overaggressive." Working women are already conscious of those attitudes; plus so much more: never mentioning menstrual cramps at work, never taking advantage of our sex, and certainly never crying on the job. We who were taught anything could be resolved by weeping are now expected to "act like a man" at work—and usually resented when we do.

Worst of all, we can't go home again. When it all gets to be too much, when we find ourselves in over our heads because of our lack of training and experience, or our conflicting expectations, we can't back out gracefully. We can't tell the family that helped us cross the street that we don't like the other side. Even less can we tell the family that fought us every step of the way. We wanted a fresh start and some of us made declarations of independence to get it. The woman who emerges and then has second thoughts is like the smoker who quits, piously informs the world, and then relapses. How can we face those around us (whether they helped or hindered) after creeping back to the nest? Some women would genuinely like to go back. Will we allow them that choice, knowing they will live with the guilt of not meeting their own new expectations? Isn't that punishment enough? Or must they, as a few women we know have, become pregnant again to gain a graceful escape hatch?

New conflicts and guilts accompany each of our growth spurts and changes. The latest is a sense of disloyalty or of torn and confused allegiances.

Many women feel a sense of loyalty to feminism, which created the new awareness in us all. But what if you can't buy the whole package? Or all its merchants? What if you genuinely love your husband; enjoy being with men as well as women; enjoy rearing your children? What if you would feel stupid demonstrating or burning your bra—or after thirty-five years of conditioning feel incredibly stupid, foolish, and naked not wearing one? What if abrasive feminists turn you off, as Rosie Casals did me on the night of the Billie Jean King/Bobby Riggs tennis match? I wanted to say, "Stop, Rosie. Enough! You are destroying a sweet victory with your venom." I knew why she was angry and hostile, I understood and sympathized, but I wanted her to be quiet—and felt a stab of disloyalty for that. Disloyalty to what? To "my own kind"? Guilt for what? Disagreeing with one of them? Or what if you are pro-abortion and "free choice" in principle, but could not have an abortion yourself? What if you aren't sure how you feel about some of the issues of the Movement, and believe some of the rhetoric ridiculous, alienating, and damaging? Is that disloyalty or maturity? Can we allow ourselves to differ without guilt in the process of growing up?

For the emerging woman, there are often poignant but acute feelings of disloyalty to a husband or any man close to her. We have stood by, often passively in the last few years, as good men have been tarred with the broad brush of chauvinism by bitter and angry women. When we do nothing because of our own confused feelings, we feel guilty. More poignant is the guilt experienced when we cannot immediately share all our new feelings with those men who have helped us, tried to understand, and waited patiently on the sidelines during our personal struggles to find ourselves. I feel it with Dick at times when a problem unique to women hurts or enrages me. As sympathetic as he is, he doesn't have the same frame of reference, he hasn't been hurt in the same ways. He isn't me; he isn't a woman. And at certain moments, I have neither the time nor the energy to help him understand. There are guilt feelings he can't always identify with, moments of despair he can't always track, at times rage he only partially comprehends. But I have women friends who have been similarly hurt, and they often identify instantly. At such moments, they are closer to me than he is. I need instant compassion, and the effort necessary to be fully understood is so great that sometimes it seems less exhausting to turn to a friend who has also been through it. Dick and I love each other deeply; he tries, I try, but we are imperfect as emerging people, and for that, I feel disloyal and guilty at times.

Emerging women also suffer an overflow of confusion and resentment when liberation doesn't happen quickly, easily, or guiltlessly. We are subsequently overwhelmed with despair for ourselves and for our children—despair at our own snail's pace, despair at the mixed signals and emotions within us. "We'll make it better for them," we claim, and wonder why we still secretly hope our daughters will be slim and pretty and popular, and our sons will be jocks and play football. There is a lack of consistency in our feelings and beliefs we don't like to acknowledge, and don't know how to cope with. "Dammit! I won't cry!" we say when everything goes wrong, and yet we lead our little sons to the television set to watch *Brian's Song,* hoping they will learn to cry, as their fathers never have. Sometimes we feel we are fighting an entire culture alone and losing, as we watch our children, boys and girls, becoming hooked as we once were on games, macho, coyness, and swagger. As the mother of two high school daughters wistfully asked, "What will the world be like for our daughters? Is it too late to change things for them? How do we discourage the double standard? And why do we still prepare our daughters for a career in homemaking, teach them little housewifely skills, take them shopping with us? Is it because that's all we *can* do—the limit of our usefulness as parents? How do we turn them into human beings—make them self-reliant, the opposite of us, when they have us for models?" Her questions were not really questions, but a quiet, naked moment of despair. There is despair for ourselves when we try and fail, or suddenly realize there are areas where we can never succeed—when the legal secretary realizes she can never be promoted to lawyer; the medical technician cannot move up to doctor. Those are opportunities forever lost. There is equal despair when we take a step forward and are knocked back two by our own guilts. "I have the feeling I had my one chance and blew it," said a friend who is currently struggling with the demands of a busy family and her own college courses. "Back there in the late fifties when I should have, could have made my move. Now it is too late." But she is still trying. We are all trying.

Although the heat and the anger have cooled as we inch forward, many raw nerves still run close to the surface. I no longer bare fangs when the gruff but well-meaning seventy-year-old real estate broker calls me "girlie" and asks to speak to my husband because he has something *important* to discuss. I can't change him, and it no longer seems necessary for me to ferret out chauvinism from under every rock and destroy it with bombs of hatred, or etch my mark on him in acid. There are bigger, more important battles for me to fight, and most of them are internal. But the rage against blatant injustice or unfairness still surfaces at times, as it did when I read a recent article in *The Milwaukee Journal* about author Wallace Reyburn. He stated that even married men can be lonely. "By being married, they are condemned to talking only to ugly women." That evoked rage.

There is another common rage women are experiencing today. It stems from not being taken seriously, and it is very difficult for men to understand. They have always been taken seriously, so they can barely comprehend what it is like to have your fragile self-esteem routinely choked off time and again. It occurs when a woman tries desperately to express her needs and a well-meaning husband tells her to get a sitter and go out for lunch. A few hours away from the children will solve any woman's problems, right? For me, the problem occurs over and over on the interview and lecture circuit. Dick and I write, work, and travel together, share every television show, and every microphone. We have done so for years. And yet, approximately every third male interviewer begins his interview this way: "Dick, I understand you run an advertising agency. And Paula, you're just a house-wife, right?" "Then why am I here?" I want to ask. The alternative opening is this: "Dick, you run an advertising agency, and Paula, you're an artist. Do you sell your work?" At times, when I have heard it often enough in one week, I want to scream, "Why don't you ask Dick if he gives his ads away—or runs his agency as a cute harmless little hobby to keep him out of mischief?" Trying to explain that type of rage to men is like trying to explain life in a foxhole under fire to someone who has never been in the army.

Though we can certainly look back and pride ourselves on the progress we have all made—men and women—it is discouraging to contemplate how far the road ahead still stretches. We are impatient with ourselves and the world, and there is still so much to become comfortable with. Despite our new camaraderie, women are still intimidated by each other, by our leaps and baby steps of different sizes, by what we have been and what we could be. I am simultaneously intimidated by Ginny's Eggs Benedict and Pat's Ph.D., by Ann's bread hook and Flo's ease in the lecture hall. Margie and I are both writers and dear friends. We have literally grown up together in the last five years—dragged each other kicking and screaming into maturity. And yet . . . I intimidate her because I can dive into her pool and get my hair wet. She intimidates me because her hair looks beautiful when we go out to dinner that night and I look like a drowned rat. Judy caught me last summer making a patchwork quilt and was surprised. I caught her in a moment of sheer delight over a miniature Indian doll. I was surprised. Karen asked who had done all the needlepoint wall hangings in our summer home, and was astonished to find they were mine. "I can't picture you doing that," she said. Why? The psychology student does not collect dolls? The writer does not sew? The career woman does not bake? Ever? None of us can measure up to the compartmentalized new images we have boxed ourselves into—at least not consistently.

What is the liberated woman really like? Who knows, but surely she isn't the same all the time. I can visualize Gloria Steinem in the executive offices of *Ms.* magazine, confident, assertive, and surrounded by a stalwart feminist support group. But what is she like out of her element? When she goes home to visit her mother in Peoria, or wherever? When she visits her sister, the housewife in Schenectady? Or when her old neighbors flock around to see how "little Gloria" is doing? Is she as consistent and self-assured as we imagine her? Or is she, too, a little ill at ease at times because she doesn't always know who else will be sitting on the couch? If there is comfort in numbers, there is also comfort in that thought.

"What do you do?" was not a question asked of women twenty years ago. Today it is, and we should each be able to answer with pride. But first, we will have to make peace with ourselves again, and with each other. There is the need for a great many baby steps alone as we overcome our separate guilts, our self-criticisms, and our fears. And a need for many more steps to be taken hand in hand with other women; still more to be taken with men. Most will not be easy. In a surge of confidence, a fifty-year-old woman recently exclaimed, "I will run as fast now and jump as high as I damn well please." Terrific! But does she know how much she will hurt the following day? It's true: the growing pains almost kill you at times. But, as my friend Judy has said, "I have hopes for my own survival." So do I.

If we need vast amounts of patience with ourselves, a woman today also needs all the supporters she can muster, whatever she chooses to be. We have to find those who care, who will share with us their own pain, who don't threaten us, who won't attack us, and who understand the insecurities and agonies of change themselves. They are legion and they are near. "Our own kind" may be as close as a loving husband, a supportive friend, a daughter or son who encourages us to be what we are best. But to enjoy their support, we have to give them a chance. We also have to give ourselves a chance. We, who for years were told we were dependent and who are now being told we are independent, must admit we are only human. Are we so different from each other in our guilts and fears? No. We are all among our own kind, but in a vastly changed world, and except for guilt, we're neither trapped nor "stranded on the linoleum." But God knows, you and I need each other's help to believe that today.

It is going to take time. In the meantime, I would be proud to sit beside you on the couch. I'm a stranger here myself.

13.

Men Don't Cry, They Bleed
(Guilt and the Emerging Man)

They also serve who only stand and wait.
JOHN MILTON

A man gets tied up to the ground,
He gives the world its saddest sound.

PAUL SIMON

IF THE SITUATION on the couch is intimidating, think what it must be like in the men's huddle over near the fireplace. If women are threatening each other these days, imagine how they are threatening men. Ten years ago, the man who strolled into the kitchen to refill his drink found only other men clustered around the set-up bar. Today, he might also find a female neighbor—not washing glasses, but holding forth on urban renewal, while the men around her listen intently. On his way back to the fireplace, he pauses to light the cigarette of a woman obviously struggling to juggle drink, purse, and paper plate. "No thanks," she tells him. "I can manage perfectly well by myself." And as he approaches the huddle at the fireplace, he discovers a petite little thing in pants has taken his place. He admires the view from the rear, but as he gets closer, he realizes she is discussing Bart Starr's coaching ability with the same knowledge and conviction as the men around her. Leaving the party later, his wife snaps at him because he forgot to hold the car door open for her. What is expected of the poor man today? God only knows; he certainly doesn't.

Like women, men were rigidly conditioned twenty, thirty, and forty years ago. Their expectations were as clearly defined and as narrowly limited. If women were destined to be sex objects, men were programmed to grow up and become success objects, objects of prey, "good catches." What made a man a good catch? The ability to protect and provide. A real man was expected to be stable, virile, emotionless, know all the answers, solve problems, set the moral tone for the family, remain clear-headed at all times, and run a steady ship. In other words, he was to be tough, strong, and masculine. A good man could be leaned on and relied upon. He was conditioned for respect, pride, and efficiency. The family name was to be carried on by him, and when he assumed his rightful place in society as "head of the house," he was expected to assume responsibility for each member of that household.

As a little boy, he was taught to "bite his lip," be John Wayne, be Humphrey Bogart, be a little man. "Big boys don't cry," little boys were told, "they bleed!" If toughness and the ability to cope were highly respected male qualities, sentimentality decidedly was not. Size and muscles meant strength, emotion meant weakness. Strength gave a boy the ability to compete, and competition enhanced his self-esteem. Tenderness did not. The football field, the basketball court, the baseball diamond were the proving grounds where the only safe emotional demonstrations were the backslap of victory and the helmet hurled down in anger. After a defeat, the team bus returning home was silent. He who could run the fastest, jump the highest, climb farthest up the tree, do the most daring or dangerous stunt, was the acknowledged leader of the pack; those who could not follow were sissies. Charles Atlas ads were read and memorized: "Add two inches to your biceps in only two weeks." Little boys sighed, checked the mirror daily, and waited. Big boys flexed and rippled. Big girls giggled and blushed. The penis was a special muscle, and it was compared as carefully as the rest—more carefully—with infinite and endless

care, as a matter of fact. The future status and performance of each potential sexual stud, each future
sexual tour guide, depended on the length and thick-
ness of that vitally important little muscle. If ever
penis envy existed, it existed in the boys' locker room,
not in the girls' dorm.

Boys shoveled snow, dug gardens, cut lawns, and
did the heavy work around the home, preparing for
their future roles. They built model cars, and dreamed
of racing real cars, squealing real tires. They pushed
toy trucks across the floor and longed to grow up and
shift the gears of giant trucks. When asked what they
wanted to be some day, they answered, "Cowboy, fire-
man, policeman, spaceman . . . doctor, lawyer, Indian
chief." Their parents smiled happily. They never answered, "Daddy," and no one noticed the omission. Being a daddy wasn't being something special.

Little boys played soldiers, played war, played with
guns, and dreamed of bravery; dreamed of going off
to real wars, carrying real guns, flying daring missions,
blasting the enemy out of the sky. "Uncle Sam wants
you!" the ads commanded, and it was assumed he
wanted you to kill, not to vacuum the barracks. War,
whether played with tin soldiers or flesh-and-blood
bodies, was an acceptable pastime for our future lifelong protectors. The defense of a corner of the playground was as much a matter of honor as the defense
of the nation—only the size of the territories differed.
Honor demanded a boy beat the bully, right injustice,
and save all damsels in distress. Girls existed to be
fought over, won, and evermore defended. Protection,
as with the playground territory, implied ownership,
but it was honorable ownership, all parties agreed.

When the little boys grew up, they made the ownership legal. They became daddies after all, and tried to
live up to the expectations of being a good catch. They
worked hard applying their childhood training—shoveling snow, digging gardens, and doing the heavy work
around the house. They provided a good home for their
families, educated their children, built up estates and
inheritances, and established themselves in the community. They put their toughness, their competitive skills,

their manly virtues to work for the family. Men did everything they were expected to do, and generally, they did it well. They followed the rules explicitly, as they had been taught years before on the playing field. Some men were almost reaching a point in life where they could ease back and relax a little, when suddenly it all blew up in their faces. Women changed! The rules changed! The game changed! Overnight, men ceased to be protectors and became oppressors without doing anything differently. Along came Betty, Gloria, and Maude, Bella, Billie Jean, and even Mrs. Jones, followed by—my God!—the man's own wife, daughter, or secretary. Macho met Ms. It was a teeth-jarring collision, not a casual handshake on the corner.

As author Gene Marine describes the impact, "A man can't live to be forty-five with any sort of social history, and then attempt to deal honestly with the ideas of Women's Liberation without suffering recurrent shocks." Dick compares it more to being in the midst of a surprise air raid. Without warning, bombs were suddenly dropping everywhere, careening crazily out of nowhere, and shaking the foundations of all that men had been taught to believe. What had always been right was very suddenly all wrong. Everywhere, women seemed to be questioning, scrutinizing, and then attacking. Cries of "Pig!" were heard across the land. In bewilderment, men asked, "What have we done wrong?" and women told them . . . and told them . . . and told them. The man conditioned to be respected found himself on the defensive. A mass movement was afoot that was critical of men in general. Each individual man was accused, labeled guilty, and forced to defend four million years of masculine oppression. It was guilt by association, and women piled it on at home, in the office, in the plant, socially, and on the street. Automatic courtesies so carefully ingrained over a lifetime became potentially dangerous or embarrassing acts. Open a restaurant door for a strange woman and she might just bite your head off, make a devastating crack, or slam it in your face. Was this someone's "little lady"? Wow!

No wonder a backlash occurred. Without warning,

a power struggle was on, a war was suddenly being waged, and men had not begun it. There was a new enemy—women! Could it be possible? And they had attacked first. As after the sneak attack on Pearl Harbor, the first reaction of many men was shock, disbelief, and confusion, quickly followed by anger and retaliation. Across bars, lunch counters, and desks all over America, hackles began to rise. "We shoulda kept 'em barefoot and pregnant! If they want to fight, we'll give them a fight! Let's see who runs when it starts to get rough." The competition, the pride of not walking away from a fight, the need for honor, all resurfaced from playground days. Only no longer were little boys fighting the neighborhood bully; grown men were fighting Myth America. Incredible! If the early outrage of the Women's Movement brought out the worst in some women, some women brought out the worst in men.

It took a few years, but when we stopped accusing each other long enough to listen, the anger cooled for most. And as in any sweeping new movement, the strident voices were eventually replaced by more moderate and thoughtful voices. Both are necessary. Awareness cannot be achieved without the shriek of pain; progress cannot be made without reasonable calm. For some men and for some women, it all fell into place. There were still hostile camps and pockets of militancy on both sides, but the honest cries were being heard and understood by many. "Yes . . . equality." "You're right . . . injustice." "I never realized . . . job discrimination." "Of course . . . equal pay for equal work." While Congress, the legislatures, industries, and unions began the business of legally righting the wrongs, we at home began to deal with a much more far-reaching consequence of the Women's Movement: the permanent change in the status of men.

Men have been more affected by the liberation of women than have women themselves. It is more noble to be the martyr than the persecutor—and infinitely easier in the long run. Yes, women have experienced pain, uncertainty, a swift change in values, indecision, awkwardness, explosions—and yes, we have been crippled (a few of us permanently) by our conditioning. But men have had the very foundation kicked out from under them by the emergence of women. We have emerged at their expense, for equality for women has meant diminishment for men—even if only in men's own minds. (And when we speak of men in this chapter, we are speaking of thoughtful, well-intentioned men who are attempting to cope with the changes, or those men caught temporarily in the middle but trying to understand. We have no frame of reference to speak of, or deal with, the Archie Bunkers of liberation.)

The man who has listened carefully to the voices of women around him is confused at times—as are the women themselves. And he is often very threatened because so much of a woman's growth affects his life directly. While he may respond to, sympathize with, and encourage the women in his life, he is also burdened with his own secret fears. His status as lover, provider, protector, economic power, and friend are all on the line. He faces a direct loss of power, stature, ego, and self-esteem when he utters the first word of encouragement. What a woman gains, he has to give up. And if she no longer needs him in the ways he was led to believe were the purpose of his life, then what is his purpose now?

The man who was traditionally supposed to have all the answers has few today, and is often filled with genuine bewilderment. "I did it all because I loved you and was told it was right. But if it's all wrong now, why am I the villain?" A good question. As Dick has pointed out, men his age were raised during World War II primarily by women. Twelve million men were away at war and it was women who taught the norms and values to those boys: mothers, teachers, nuns, and neighbors. The stereotypes, the images, the proper paths to manhood were implanted in these boys by adult women. "So why," Dick asked in the early heat of the Movement, "are women attacking men? Why aren't they attacking their mothers instead —who were also our mothers?" Sisterhood, I suppose.

Besides, it is impossible to be a true heroine without having a villain.

The secret fears take many forms for men, pose many disturbing questions. The emotional growth rate of the emerging woman has far outstripped that of the emerging man, and he realizes that. He has been forced to react or to watch or to wait while she changes. Of course, there is the natural fear of abandonment for the waiter. "If she continues to grow, she may outgrow me. If she becomes free, where and how will I fit into her new life? If she moves on, to work, to school, I may lose her. She may find another man who is more attractive to her, who keeps pace with her better." Aren't those the very same fears that have distressed women for decades as we worried about sex appeal, cuteness, and aging? And if we agonize over giving up what we were traditionally taught were our virtues, what makes us imagine men don't do the same?

There is another new fear for men: inadequacy. "She has needs suddenly that I can't meet." That is a devastating admission of guilt for the lifelong protector and problem-solver, for the saver of damsels in distress. He's falling down on the job, he believes, and more disturbing, realizes that he has no support group. A very real and difficult problem for the man taught *he* was the one to be relied upon, leaned on. While women are discovering camaraderie across the bridge table, the lunch table, over mimeograph machines, and at consciousness-raising sessions, men are feeling guilty about being excess baggage, and in the huddle at the fireplace they still pretend the problems do not exist for them personally.

Whom can a man talk to about feeling threatened and insecure and unsure? Traditionally, men have talked to each other about things—sports, politics, and sex—but not about themselves. The "be tough, be manly" conditioning prevents them from showing weakness to each other. It's hard for the problem-solver to admit he has problems; he has no license to let the mask down, man to man, friend to friend. Most men certainly can't do it at the office or plant.

If a man confides his insecurities and fears to those either above or below him, it is an admission of weakness that may jeopardize his present or future position. Bitch, yes. Complain, yes. Join the chorus of "Isn't it awful?" But confide, no. One does not show weakness to a competitor, and men were taught that every man is a potential competitor. As Bob Draper, then president of the John Oster Manufacturing Company, explained to Dick years ago, "If I ever even told my vice president I was scared at times, it would rock this company right down to the loading docks."

The man who was taught that feelings are suspect and emotions unmanly knows better than to risk confiding in other men. The man who was taught to cope silently and to be self-sufficient, the man who can't even ask for directions when he is lost, can rarely bring himself to ask for help from other men in coping with the changes in his personal life. Besides, he has no idea other men are wrestling with the same frightening questions. Where can he go with his new thoughts and self-doubts? Home? His wife was once an emotional safety valve for him, but now she may be part of the problem, perhaps *the problem itself*. She has her own needs to attend to at the moment, her own self-esteem to build. Ironically, her needs have doubled his. And how can *he* become a burden to her now? Besides, men are used to talking things over with other men and explaining things to women. How can he explain this? And what if she no longer wants to be explained to? He is left once again to find his own answers. But suddenly, introspection is more painful than usual. He would like to avoid it, but can't; the problem permeates almost every aspect of his life.

Women's recent sexual awareness and increased sexual interest are two more bewildering new threats. Modern man lost his status as the sexual tour guide when the tourists began to run ahead, or demanded that the tour move more rapidly, or take exotic new paths. The suddenly sexual female often causes impotence in the traditional man. A middle-aged Florida man speaks for many men when he states, "My wife is a Women's Libber. I am not against her activities, but now she's dictating my actions in the bedroom. When she comes on strong, I go limp." A younger man from Raleigh, married only six years, confides the same problem: "When I married my wife, she was as cold as an iceberg. I did everything that a man could do to make her normal sexually. I must have had a good technique because lately I can't handle her. She is now too aggressive and demanding for my mind, health, and body. She comes on so strong, she would scare a bull to death, and I lose my desire." Logically, a sexually active, sexually interested woman should make any man feel vastly complimented; instead, she often scares the hell out of him. But there has never been much logic connected with sex.

Many men feel threatened by such changes in their sexual routine as foreplay or the woman-astride position, by initiative on a woman's part, and even by the discovery of the clitoral orgasm. "If it doesn't happen in the vagina, then what does she need me for?" he wonders. "A finger, a vibrator can do as well. All that measuring in the locker room all those years for nothing!" It is another loss of power, he believes, and a devastating one to cope with. It is the same fear that makes so many men view vasectomy as a loss of power, even when they have finished siring children. "She doesn't need me for sexual satisfaction anymore, and when they invent test-tube babies, she won't need me at all." Those are a man's thoughts, not a woman's. For most women, sex is an act of love, not a locker-room competition. And as Gene Marine has stated, "If the idea of a free woman makes us feel unmanned, it is the fear, not the woman, that unmans us." If only women could make men believe it.

The traditional problem-solver suffers a guilty overflow of frustration as he quietly attempts to wrestle with his own new problems while valiantly trying to understand and ease those of his wife. Sudden, inexplicable eruptions occur from even the most encouraging and supportive husband when the burdens of liberation (his and hers) pile up: when he genuinely wants to help a woman emerge, and she keeps changing direction; when she claims to want change, but is unable to take the steps necessary to change herself; when their mutually thought-out and agreed-upon game plans and timetables for her step-by-step liberation are later discarded by her without adequate explanation; when his conditioning in logic and reason can't penetrate the cloud of emotion that surrounds her; when their lives remain in a holding pattern of indecision and unhappiness for months, sometimes years; when changes are made, demands are met, and new changes are suddenly demanded; when too much is expected of him too quickly; and especially when he asks, "What do you want from me?" and she doesn't know, but continues to want it anyway.

We've seen genuine frustration derail so many struggling couples, and Lord knows, Dick and I didn't escape unscarred during our first difficult year of changes. The problem is that neither side really understands what is happening under the surface. Things seem to be progressing well, but one day an innocent and unexplained straw too many causes an explosion, a boomerang that catches women by surprise. "I love you, but this time I've been pushed too far," seems to be the momentary message. It happened to some good friends not long ago, and this letter will bring the conflict back vividly to any couple who have experienced it. It was written by the woman a few days after returning from her first three-day trip alone to visit friends:

> *Jesus! Trouble at home. All of a sudden I have a surly, ill-tempered, argumentative monster where there used to be a nice, supportive, agreeable husband. What happened? He's been picking apart everything I try to communicate before I get out two sentences. He's finding a negative for every positive. He's arguing and angling off on irrelevant points and frustrating me to tears of hopelessness. I get very confused in my thinking when I cry. (And besides, I look vile.) Since I got home, it's been like, "This time, wife, you've gone too far! I've put up with these foolish notions about self-improvement, but honey, the ball game's over! Get back to where you belong. Where my opin-*

ions are your opinions, my choices are your choices"
... *etc.*

Do you suppose I threaten him? Why me? Why now? He's been with me all through this evolution; why should I suddenly come off as a radical, prejudiced feminist? I feel we've regressed twenty years, and only wish I knew whom or what I'm fighting—and why. It's kind of sad, but my initial impression after going over these past three days is that I've gone too far in searching out my own identity. That maybe he was more comfortable with repressed, bored, and largely silent me. That I've estranged myself from him, without intending to, without wanting to, by expanding my own little life. Whatever it is, it hurts. A lot. I feel so vulnerable. What has happened here? Isn't it odd, just when our relationship seemed to be really getting in gear, to have trivial differences blow it all to bits?

Perhaps not so odd. Trivial differences piled up make for enormous adjustments that suddenly seem overwhelming—incredibly too much for any man, even the best of men. And the best of men are those who feel the most helpless, the most frustrated at being unable to make it better for the women they love, at being unable always to understand completely or to comfort, at being asked to watch so much of the struggle from the sidelines—and dismissed to struggle alone themselves. There is a growing feeling in many men that women are so immersed in their own problems they have lost their perceptiveness: they recognize no pain but their own; they no longer realize how much they are asking of men. Think about it. The solver of problems, the captain of the steady ship, the righter of injustices, the savior of damsels in distress, the protector of others in pain—he can't handle it all. And flex-ripple does no good. The protector does not handle powerlessness well, so he sometimes lashes out instead. Contrary to tradition, men are human, too. They do feel—as much and as deeply as women. And the best of men feel the new pains most acutely. How does our man conditioned to lip-biting handle the pain today? Sometimes in ways women find strange and upsetting. John Wayne would have gone out and busted up a bar. Today's man may explode and retreat in silence to sort it out and find his bearings again.

There was no manual written for the liberation of either sex, and the man who struggles to free himself of his conditioning often finds himself an alien among both sexes. If he begins to let his feelings show to other men, he is quickly suspect because the man who is sensitive, open, tender, understanding—the man who can express emotions—is a threat to other men who cannot. And the specter of homosexuality still looms. But there are men who are beginning to beat that specter down; who realize the ability to be human is freeing. And who realize that without support and understanding, without reaching out, they are as lonely at the fireplace as women are on the linoleum.

The man who is supportive of his emerging wife or of other women faces another specter—the label of Henpecked Harry. He sometimes faces the contempt of other men, their criticisms, their snide remarks. "I'd never let any woman run all over me!" he hears. He is unable to explain adequately to other men that running side by side is exhilarating and not at all the same as being overrun. But some neighbors, work associates, and friends see his growth only as a loss of stature. Dick asked just recently if I realized what a threat our relationship poses to many men, and what he often faces because of it. I hadn't realized because the nuances often slip by me, as they did when we gave a recent speech together. The master of ceremonies spent several minutes of the introduction commenting on how unusual it was that my name appeared before Dick's on our last book. I missed the significance at the time, but Dick states this type of comment occurs frequently when he is alone with other men. "How can you let Paula . . . ?" they ask. Whatever the end of the line may be, it is assumed Dick does not want to let me be, grow, change, write, or speak for myself. And that each of my changes or successes is a personal assault on his manhood.

There are other lonely battles for the emerging man

to fight. Comfort and conformity of appearance depend on the group a man finds himself in, and there are so many varied groups today. In a short decade, men have evolved from the Prussian military look to the accepted gray flannel suit to sport coats to leisure suits—to really anything. Or have they? Individuality of dress, the ability to wear jewelry, beards, longer hair, and interesting clothes is hardly universal. The recreation director of a Midwestern college was recently telling us he enjoys the freedom of wearing neck pieces, jewelry, and jeans on campus, but when he returns to his small Ohio hometown to visit his parents and three brothers who are engineers, he encounters raised eyebrows and jeering comments: "Are you supposed to be 'with it,' or are you trying to get yourself picked up by some fag?" Dick has frequently faced the same raised eyebrows in the business world because he hates ties and avoids them at all cost, is more comfortable in Western boots, and started wearing Indian jewelry ten years before it became popular. We may scoff at conformity verbally today, but no matter how self-assured we are, it is difficult to be alone, ahead, behind, or different in any group.

In the eyes of some feminists, the well-intentioned emerging man is categorized and branded for the sins of a few men. In the eyes of some men, he is a traitor for being supportive to women. Thus he may be trampled on at any given moment by either sex. No wonder he feels paranoid at times. What is now right and what is still wrong? And with whom? Whom does he address as Ms., for example? As Mrs.? Miss? Any one of the three titles can be insulting today if innocently misused. Does he open that door, hold that chair, light that cigarette, suggest that dish on the menu, and allow that woman to go first or not? Which women still expect the courtesies; which will glare at him? And who now pays for the business lunch? Does he let her reach for the check? Whoever pays, it may be an awkward moment. Does he tell an off-color joke in front of her at the lunch table or in the office? Does he laugh or choke if she tells one instead? How does he handle himself now that the "little lady" has become one of the boys? And sometimes she wants it both ways: she wants to use the same language he does and enjoy the same privileges and freedoms, but still wants help with her coat. How does he handle that?

When the many women in any man's life are on different rungs of the liberation ladder the mixed signals are more confusing. He may live with a contented homemaker and find himself surrounded by emerging women at the office or plant, at the school board meeting, in the car pool, or in a community drive. His own daughter and wife may be of totally different philosophies. Which one can he support and still live peacefully under the same roof? While the women he works with may now want to be treated as equals, his own wife may enjoy her dependency. How does he remember to change mental hats on the way to and from the office each day? Women are doing "men's work" all around him, except perhaps in his own home. Would he enjoy dropping some of his burdens at home, or changing them? How can he ask if she doesn't bring it up? Women want equal pay, and that seems fair to him, and to his wife, until they are threatened the bread will be taken from their own table—by a successful woman. The "go-fer" at the office suddenly won't go anymore, and he agrees in principle, but he doesn't know how to start the office coffeepot because he's never had to do it before. Can he ask for help? Will the retired "go-fer" give him help? And what will his associates think if he is the only man in the office fetching his own coffee? Then there is the astonishing new concept that women and men can be friends—just that, with no sexual overtones. He likes that idea; it makes sense. Why eliminate half the human race as potential friends? But there is the snickering of other men to contend with, and frequently the jealousy and misunderstanding of his own wife.

Perhaps the most difficult problems to cope with for the emerging man at work are the frequent changes of direction in the emerging women around him. He listens, attempts to understand and support, and is baffled when women no longer seem to want what they wanted yesterday. Even though he realizes that assuming a position of authority and responsibility is difficult for everyone, the transition period is often more tension-filled and troublesome for women. "I want advancement," say the women around him. "I want more responsibility," some insist, and then balk at the accountability, the pressure, and the extra time and effort accompanying that responsibility. "I didn't think it would be like this," they claim, and they genuinely didn't. They don't have the years of practice in deeply ingrained toughness, assertiveness, and competitiveness men have. And he understands that; he wants to give them a chance to grow into it gradually . . . but still, he has his own division to answer for, his own boss to report to, his own quotas to meet. How long a transition period can he safely allow? How supportive can he be without jeopardizing his own position? How long can he afford to wait for results?

If there are women who continue to find chauvinism under every rock, there are also those who continue to find discrimination under every desk. In 1971, two women working for Dick's firm mobilized the other women and presented management with a list of twenty-seven items of inequality. Management endorsed their meetings, allowed them to take place during company time, and readily agreed to twenty-four of the twenty-seven points. A lounging room for women was established, tables and chairs were purchased for it, and extra space was rented for a women's dining room. The new furniture and facilities were used four times. A year later, the furniture was sold and the extra space was sublet. The men asked, genuinely, "What are we to believe is important to you?" And wondered quietly, "Were they making a stand just for the sake of making a stand?"

There are men who want it to work. They are often stymied at home and on the job when it doesn't, and when the women who also claim they want it to work offer little assistance in solving their joint problems. The emerging man does not have an easy time with himself, with the women who surround him, with his friends, associates, fishing buddies, and with the world in general. But surprisingly, despite all the problems, insecurities, doubts, and agonies of liberation, a recent survey of men showed they were sympathetic to the Women's Liberation Movement by 42 to 39 percent. Men are more for women than women believe. Men are more for the freeing of women, and, in turn for their own liberation, than men themselves believe. It is only the continuing silences, the solitary and lonely introspections, that keep us all from realizing that.

If women feel they have been isolated on the linoleum, perhaps the emerging man has been equally isolated in his car—his symbolic twentieth-century horse, the only thing society has ever allowed him to stroke, polish, and caress. Riding alone, he can only wonder, when buffeted from all sides, what he has done wrong. Why the guilt and obligations to right the wrongs have been thrust upon him, and why he, too, is suddenly damned if he does and damned if he doesn't. What will he do? Take care of what he can and wait in his traditional, stoic silence to see what the outcome will be? In the meantime, who will take care of him?

If women were shackled in the past, so were men. What is worse, they were taught it was noble to bear their shackles in silence. That silence is the final barrier to be broken down between the sexes—between men and women, between men and men. "Enough!" someone has to cry out. "There are guilts being borne by both sides."

That we are all struggling, anyone with an ounce of compassion can see. Let the war between the sexes, if it ever really existed, be carried on by maniacs. The rest of us need each other too desperately to war. It is possible to emerge one by one, but it is an agonizingly slow and lonely business. It is still painful to emerge two by two, but it is infinitely more comforting. For God's sake, let us do it that way, instead. Let us do it together.

14.

Side by Side
(The Emerging Family—
New Lifestyles, New Guilts)

Let wives be subject to their husbands as to the Lord;
because a husband is head of the wife . . .

ST. PAUL (EPHESIANS 5:22-23)

Don't know what's comin' tomorrow.
Maybe it's trouble and sorrow,
But we'll travel the road, sharin' our load
Side by side.

HARRY WOODS

THE AMERICAN FAMILY TODAY often resembles a cat-
erpillar with its head and tail moving in different directions, and at different speeds. No wonder there is an
"ouch" from the middle at times. No wonder we trip
over each other's legs. Push Mom, pull Pop, drag the
kids along. Everywhere there is diversity: mobile families, liberated parents, traditional patterns, new lifestyles, old routines, working wives, role changes. There
is much to adjust to, and none of it is easy.

Who are the Joneses today? And what is their lifestyle? They are spread across the entire spectrum of
change, trying to cope with current trends and new
ideas in their own way. Some shifts in direction have
been rapid and startling. We have already stated that
more men favor equality for women than do not. A
1973 *Redbook* survey of 120,000 women (84 percent
of them married) showed that two out of three favor
the Women's Liberation Movement. Eight of ten single women feel the same. Four of ten married women

213

also desire a more egalitarian marriage today, and less than 2 percent feel most women could best develop their potential by being only good wives and mothers. Half viewed motherhood as a temporary occupation and intended to return to work. And that has already happened! In 1976, Labor Department statistics showed that in sixty-six out of one hundred marriages, wives also held an outside job. That single change alone has knocked the Jones family on its collective ear. What does it mean? Shared housework problems, "my money/your money" conflicts, child-rearing changes, multiple losses and gains for the modern family as a whole, and new guilts for everyone.

Money, not liberation, is the primary motivation that sends the American wife back to work. In 1974, the median family income was $16,928 for families with working wives and $12,082 for those with non-working wives. According to Eugene Jennings, a professor of management at Michigan State University, the disadvantages of a single income become painfully clear to the woman who remains at home as her children grow older and more expensive. "The irony of this is that while society and our corporations speak of the home as the cradle of civilization, every incentive is offered to get women out of the home."

A working wife is both a relief and a threat to Mr. Jones. There is less pressure on him as provider, and most men genuinely welcome that. At the same time, he experiences a loss of control, and therein lies the conflict. A woman's sudden economic independence is discomforting to many men. Two incomes are nice to have; two people instead of one deciding how the money will be spent is not always so nice. If a woman is earning income, of course she should have her fair say in the family's economic affairs, but often she has more than a fair say. Her husband's income may still provide the necessities while hers is used for luxuries the family couldn't afford before. The woman who expects total control over her earnings can also expect eventual trouble. If she now decides where the family vacation will be spent, which color television set will be purchased, and when a new family car can be afforded, that is not always a happy change for Mr. Jones. If she is working to pay for college educations or a daughter's wedding, naturally she will want to mastermind the plans and determine the economic limits. He, in turn, has been faithfully paying off the mortgage for years, but may not have the same deciding power over what goes into the house. If she has sole control of *her* money, and he does not have equal freedom with *his*, there is bound to be friction. "You don't realize what it symbolizes for me," she cries—and he doesn't. On the other hand, she may not realize how unjust her "what's yours is half mine, but what's mine is all mine" attitude is.

While men quietly resent their loss of status and power as the solitary provider, they feel a corresponding need to be grateful to their wives for the added income. It is a natural conflict, and there are natural new guilts when Mr. Jones finds himself torn between feeling genuinely appreciated at times and secretly resentful at others. Even though his life and standard of living have changed for the better, he still mourns the losses. It is another tricky tightrope to walk, and Mrs. Jones occasionally gives the tightrope a little extra twang just to remind him she is there—a new power to be reckoned with.

The scales of justice seesaw back and forth for the emerging couple, however, and the quiet new guilts are hardly one-sided. For the woman who earns less than her husband, as most still do, there is the guilt of not pulling her fair share. "How can I justify a fifty-fifty split on the housework," so many women ask, "when he earns more than fifty percent of the income?" A good question, and not easily answered. Even with the most willing of husbands, it is difficult for many women to ask for help on the home front. In the back of our minds, there is the nagging belief we are falling down on a part of our original bargain. When most women married, they willingly signed on for the housework, believing it to be a lifelong commitment. Changing that commitment at a later date, no matter how sensible or fair or necessary that may be, seems like a betrayal of the vows. Many working wives we know willingly take on the double burden of outside work and housework because they find exhaustion easier to handle than the guilt of asking others for help. There are women who vacuum at midnight, spend weekends scrubbing, mending, and cooking, and do the laundry at 6:00 A.M. because they can't ask—and never will be able to.

The problem of fair shares is even more painfully felt by women in the transition stage of emergence. "I can't get out of the house to retrain or to look for a job (or go back to school in order to get a better job) without help around here first. But how can I ask the family to take over my jobs when I'm not earning anything yet?" Many women delay asking for help because of those guilt feelings, and hope once they have a job, the family will notice their double burden and step forward gratefully to relieve it. It is often an endless wait. Families don't notice when one person is carrying an impossible load if their own lives have not been directly affected by the changes. It isn't deliberate selfishness; it's acute myopia. And if, because of her own guilt feelings, a woman can't ask for help, all the resentment building up inside her won't bring the family rushing to her aid. Husbands and children don't read minds. They don't even notice full garbage pails.

There is another problem women face when they earn less: their jobs are taken less seriously. The working wife usually finds herself working around sick children, family emergencies, and the sudden plumbing leak at 8:00 A.M. She stays home when trouble strikes, often resentfully, because her job is considered expendable—by both of them. There is the unspoken but implied message: "You can always quit; I can't." And it is true in most cases. Even though neither partner wants her to quit, the implication hangs there between them whenever the question of fair share arises; whenever she complains of double duties; whenever she suggests *he* stay home with the case of chicken pox for once; whenever she needs the car for work. The demands make a wife feel guilty because she knows she can stop working—and inconveniencing him. A husband feels just as guilty using the implication as clout. He does want her to keep working, and he does enjoy the new freedoms it brings him, but he doesn't like the restrictions and the curtailment of his old freedoms. Often he feels secretly guilty knowing he is not pulling his fair share around the house, but doggone it—he resents spending Saturday mornings cleaning the bathroom instead of playing softball. Now that he's discovered scrubbing floors is a rotten job and folding laundry is a bore, he may attempt to find excuses not to help around the house—sometimes he even pulls rank. But when he does, he feels guilty because though he may be lazy or genuinely chauvinistic, he is seldom conscienceless.

The problem of shared housework is one of the more troublesome for emerging families to resolve. Even with the most willing of children and the most cooperative of husbands, the guilts a woman faces are enormous. Asking for help is only the first step. Once help has been offered or given, her guilt doesn't necessarily disappear. Each job a woman relinquishes, no matter how gratefully, will forever remain an accusing finger of guilt stabbing just under the breastbone, as she watches others continue *her* work. The guilt is not present at every moment; just often enough to make it feel like a chronic case of heartburn. There will be lapses in enthusiasm and natural complaints: "Oh, c'mon, it can't be my turn for laundry again!" . . . "Why do I have to wash windows? Everybody else gets the easy jobs." . . . "I hate cleaning this stupid oven!" Mutter, mutter, mutter. Bitch, bitch, bitch.

Instead of hearing those complaints for what they really are—ordinary gripes about tedious jobs—a woman feels steadily reminded that she has turned *her* work over to others. She doesn't handle that well. Traditions are sunk bone deep, and she forgets that the reason she turned the jobs over to others was so she could do something else—for those same others.

Even the most innocent remarks can double us over with guilt. A year ago, our youngest son, aged eleven, decided to move his bedroom to a heated room in the basement because it was larger, and he thought it would be adventurous to live down there alone. He was trying to convince Dick and me to let him move, and used one final argument that withered me with guilt. "Besides," he said, "I'll be closer to the laundry." Ouch!

Neither are men immune to the stabs of guilt. Dick took over the grocery-shopping chores at our house three years ago, and most of the time, he enjoys the weekly trip to the supermarket. You might expect after three years we would have that routine worked out perfectly, but it still causes peculiar guilty problems for both of us. Dick has to shop in the evening, of course, and while he is out doing *my* job once a week, I find it impossible to sit down, read the paper, watch television, or relax. I have to do something equally productive during that time to justify sending a poor, overworked husband out into the cold dark night to gather food, even though I worked all day too, made dinner, and did my own share of the household chores. And when he comes home with the wrong cut of meat, three quarts of strawberries out of season, or two pounds of kidney bean salad that everyone hates, I have to gulp twice before telling him the truth. I feel guilty correcting anyone so willing to help—to help me, that is. Why can't I just relax and say, "OK, provider—go provide. Bring home the bacon—but make sure it's Oscar Mayer this time." It's absurd to feel guilty, and it is doubly absurd that Dick now feels equally guilty when he has to travel and isn't home to do the weekly shopping, when I push that grocery cart in his place. Now, I'm doing *his* job, he believes. He's falling down on *his* part of the bargain. A typical exchange of the Normal Crazies. We've discussed it, laughed about it, searched endlessly for alternative routines, told each other to relax. But I can't shake the "my old job guilts," and he now wrestles with his new ones. On-the-job training at forty for lifestyle changes is not easy for either sex.

Shared housework will never work fairly or perfectly. When one person has traditionally done it all, there is too much to teach, too much to change, too many tiny details to divide the work equally and satisfactorily. Each small transference of chores takes time and endless patience from all parties, and sometimes it does seem easier for a woman to continue doing most of it herself. Teaching a youngster to mop a floor takes time. Supervising the job to see that it is done properly takes time. And asking that it be done over because it wasn't done right the first time turns Mom the new Home Manager into Mom the Monster —at least in her own mind. And asking a husband to rescrub a poorly washed floor is virtually impossible for most women—or at least as impossible as telling him he bought the wrong meat.

The nagging reminders necessary to keep a shared household running smoothly make a woman seem both demanding and bitchy, often to the family, always to herself. The jobs have to be done, the family has agreed to do them, but everyone is human, and people forget; the burden is on Mom to nag further or do the job quietly herself.

"Make a list," Dick has asked over and over. "Tell us what you want done and we'll do it." But there is so much he isn't aware of, so many tiny daily facets of running an active household that even I'm not aware of until I find myself automatically doing them. Sure, the children agreed to feed the dog, but who remembers two hours later the dog dish is still unwashed? And because a particular chore wasn't prearranged, it seems unfair to ask for more help later—or again. Dick might be already settled comfortably in his chair for the evening when I remember there are still three loads of laundry to fold, and that the dishwasher must be emptied before breakfast. I hate to pry him out of that chair when he genuinely believes he's finished for the day, but I have only two choices, neither pleasant: I can ask for help and feel guilty, or I can do it myself and resent it. I thought I was finished for the day, too.

Choosing resentment instead of guilt is not uncommon. Until recently, I never realized that was the reason some mornings start off badly. Dick and I get up the same time, but on those mornings when we are leaving the house at the same time, Dick has an opportunity to read the morning paper and I don't. That half-hour of my time is taken up letting the dog out, wiping the table, picking up wet towels from the bathroom floor, and checking with the kids to make sure they are organized for school—while I drink my coffee on the run. All of those jobs have been routinely done at the same time each morning for years. I never thought to mention any of them when we divided up the chores. And before I began working, I read the paper after Dick left for the office. I never realized how much I missed that paper or resented the small change in routine until I exploded one morning in the car. Dick, in turn, never noticed there was a change in routine because there *wasn't* for him. He had watched me doing those same small chores while he read the paper for years. There is a legitimate lack of awareness in husbands and children. Because their conditioning isn't the same, they don't notice when the dog is wandering around with his legs crossed, when the stove is greasy, when the dining room windows are streaked, when we have run out of vanilla. The help women ask for originally is never enough, but it makes us feel guilty and inadequate to go back continually and ask for more.

While there are willing husbands and families, and men like Dick who say, "Help me learn," two other problems keep the shared-housework operation from running smoothly. Men often resist asking how to do a job they have assumed. Dick, for example, decided to make chocolate chip cookies for the first time last winter—a marvelous idea since everybody else in the family was busy at the time and he was the only one who wanted them. But he didn't ask how. It's difficult to step in and offer advice to someone who hasn't asked for it, especially when you feel they are doing your job. On the other hand, it's difficult to stand in the kitchen doorway and watch the wooden spoon splinter its way through the blades of the electric mixer. When Dick began to swear and mix the cookie dough with his hands after breaking the beaters, I disappeared, feeling very guilty. But he had put me in an impossible bind. Advice at that point would have been ludicrous. Stepping in to take over the job halfway would have demeaned him. Besides, I was too angry. Why did *I* have to feel guilty because *he* demolished the mixer? Why didn't he ask? I would have asked for directions if I had volunteered to run a complicated business machine at his office with no prior training.

The second problem is one of standards. Even when the family pitches in cheerfully to help, the average woman insists the chores be done her way, by her standards. Understandably, the family often resents that. But most women, myself included, find it difficult to lower their standards around the house after starting back to work. Even though we tell ourselves dustballs aren't a disgrace, that a corner cobweb or a blob of jelly won't bring the Board of Health running, that one messy hall closet won't destroy our precious self-esteem, we can't let go. What husbands and children don't realize is that we often have good reason for concern. It is still *our* self-esteem at stake, not theirs, *our* responsibility in the eyes of most of society. Women know that the friend, the neighbor, the father-in-law who drops in unexpectedly won't think to themselves, "Dick certainly keeps a messy house."

Then there are those husbands who won't help, those whose pride and fragile sense of masculinity seem to be automatically forfeited the moment they pick up a dish towel or a broom. For their emerging or working wives, there is nothing but frustration and overwork. While the problems of shared housework are frustrating, funny, or awkward at times in willing families, they are not impossible. In uncooperative families they are. There is no solution without a loser. A wife automatically loses if there is no change in the situation; her husband loses if there is. And even when circumstances force a change, there is guilt and a demeaning sense of loss for both. Any work is demeaning when you are forced to do it. One uncooperative husband who lost his job during the recession eventually did pull his share at home. He finally did vacuum since he was home all day anyway. He did make the bed. He did feed the dog and start dinner.

But there was no sweetness in that victory for his working wife. During the months he was out of work, he would call her office and ask if she preferred green or red peppers cut up in the salad. She got what she had been pleading for for years—a helpful mate. And a beaten one. There is no sense of victory to that when you love someone. There is only monumental guilt.

Lastly, the liberated family suffers the guilt of living in an only partially liberated world. Dick still runs into constant questions at the supermarket, people asking if I am sick or out of town, and raised eyebrows when they find out I am neither. I run into the same problem when dealing with mechanical problems around the house. That has always been my forte, but plumbers, repairmen, electricians, and carpenters refuse to believe that. They want permission from my husband before proceeding with a costly repair job. Or at least, they'd feel more comfortable discussing it with the man of the house first. How does a woman explain that the man of the house doesn't know a hammer from a hatchet and that's all right with both of us? She doesn't. She just quietly fibs that she is an aeronautical engineer. That ends most discussions, and is infinitely simpler than explaining life histories to the furnace man.

One of the more liberated couples we know has managed a relatively smooth two-year role reversal. She works at a highly prestigious job; he quit his highly prestigious job to keep house and raise their two young daughters while finishing a doctorate degree at home. And it's working well. But even they admitted recently that during the first six months of his home tenure, while wearing an apron and dusting with Pledge, he often found himself swearing colorfully in front of his daughters. It seemed to be the only way he could maintain "a real masculine image."

The emerging family deals constantly with a society strung out across the ladder of liberation. What is comfortable for the Joneses is not comfortable for the Smiths, so there are bound to be awkwardnesses. We recently had a male house guest whose wife waits on him hand and foot at home. I knew that, and also knew I didn't have the time to do the same, so his stay might be no easier for him than for us. But I realized I would be the one to suffer the most guilt by comparison. We explained, upon his arrival, that our family worked together to get things done. He smiled and agreed that was wonderful, but it didn't stick. After each meal, as the rest of us automatically picked up our own dishes and took them to the kitchen, he sat waiting for someone to take his. Me, of course. I foolishly kept waiting for him to notice; he kept waiting for his accustomed woman to appear. We had also mentioned that breakfast was "help yourself" in our house, and showed him where everything was. For three days, he didn't eat breakfast—wouldn't even pour himself a cup of coffee. I felt grimly guilty watching him slowly starve. Finally I offered to make him some eggs and English muffins on the fourth morning because I couldn't stand it any longer. Not his starvation; my own guilt at not measuring up to his image of a wife. And over the English muffins and eggs, we had a little talk. He was genuinely dismayed. He hadn't meant to make me feel guilty; he hadn't realized. Of course he hadn't. I knew that the entire four days. I just didn't know how to cope with my own mixed emotions: resentment for the guilt I felt he was causing, and frustration at myself for being cowardly so long. It is not easy for an old-fashioned Good Mommy, now liberated, to let a man starve in her own kitchen.

Dick and I, and other couples who are struggling with the myriad problems of change, sometimes look with envy at younger couples. "They, at least, don't suffer our guilts," we think, but they do. Younger men and women have a head start on us since they can begin their marriages on a more equal basis. But much of their conditioning has been the same as ours, and while they may not have to undo the patterns of years together, they still have to contend with society: their parents, their friends, their neighbors. One twenty-three-year-old university student was recently telling us of the guilt feelings she and her husband suffer because they have chosen to attend different universities, in different cities. It is a temporary arrangement necessary if each of them is to get the required training for a future career. They know what they are doing, and have chosen to pay the price of a year of separation. Their friends on campus understand, but Mom, Dad, Aunt Minnie, and friends back home do not. Sexual infidelity, swinging, and swapping are automatically assumed. And each trip home is an agony of explanations. "Is the marriage really all right?" "It's not normal for a young couple to live apart." "Is this what you call an open marriage?"

Young couples pursuing far less drastic lifestyle changes are subject to the implied accusations of a more traditional society. Why aren't they having children right away? Why do they work different shifts? How come they hardly ever see each other? How come they have different friends? When are they going to settle down? Stop traveling so much? Buy a house in the suburbs? It isn't natural. But by whose standards? Certainly not those of the young couples themselves.

Children, too, frequently suffer the raised eyebrows of the less liberated. Fortunately, they hardly ever notice, but their parents always do. There are no boys' jobs or girls' jobs in our house. Our four children split the chores right down the middle, and each takes a turn at lawn cutting, dishes, dusting, and snow shoveling. The boys are as handy with a bottle of Clorox as the girls are with an electric saw. They will all make great catches for some lucky men and women someday—should they choose to marry. And there hasn't been a comment, a raised eyebrow, a question about their lifestyle from any of their friends. But while most of our friends applaud, some are still bewildered, uncomfortable, and even embarrassed by our children. They don't know how to handle the teenage boy who whips out the ironing board to press his own shirt; the girl who does her best without worrying about whether she is too bright, too quick, or too independent. I feel sorry for those adults. And I feel sorry for Dick and me, too, because occasionally, just occasionally, those other adults can still get to us. They can make us feel a little defensive, and a little guilty, for being different.

There is a sad side to liberation. Some parents become so caught up in the intensity of their own differentness that they cannot allow themselves or their children any flexibility. It's a new sin for them to be the same as anyone else or to take any part in the traditional aspects of our culture. There are women who say, "No girl of mine will ever be a cheerleader, wear eye shadow, flirt." Fathers who vow, "No son of mine will beat himself to death on the playing field, act tough, show off." That is denying a child his or her own individuality, and the very freedom we so loudly claim to want for ourselves. It is narrowing a youngster's existence and experiences, and denying him or her the right to choose as we have chosen. Why can't the girl who pushes the lawnmower also be a cheerleader if she wants to? Why can't the boy who enjoys poetry also play football if he can handle both with his own friends? This kind of rigidity is reverse stereotyping, no matter what else people would like to call it. Recently, we had a weekend house guest who had just been through a bitter divorce, and an even more bitter awakening to her lifelong conditioning. She walked around all weekend stating, apropos of nothing, "I don't cook . . . I don't cook," as though cooking were some kind of vice. Well, cooking is not a crime—for either sex—any more than crying is, and I wanted to say, "I hope someday you'll be able to cook again. It's fun sometimes." But, from my own experience, I know she will never joyfully cook again until she realizes she has always been more than *just* a cook.

Liberating yourself from parts of the past is hard. It's hard for those of us struggling with new moves, new ideas, new lifestyles, and for those being dragged along, even willingly. It is equally hard for those who are not changing. They, like we, are surrounded by comparisons. The media barrage alone must overwhelm them at times. But each family must make its own comparisons, each individual must decide how he or she measures up to past and future expectations and together decide what they can comfortably live with. And each of us within the isolated Jones family must help the others because that's the only way it can work. Dick and I have learned that lack of forward motion is frustrating and deadly to a marriage. It satisfies neither the needs of women nor those of men who have tasted new freedoms and enjoyed them. Giant leaps are just as disastrous; they confuse and disorient men and children, and are distressing to women. We are left again with only baby steps and with the realization that it is going to be neither quick, painless, nor guiltless. "Change is inevitable . . . change is constant," said Disraeli, but he didn't say it was easy. We simply have to learn to cope, one by one, two by two, or in our family, six by six.

As a couple, Dick and I have learned to stop and reassess when we recognize the growing pains. We've had to make constant readjustments, reevaluations, and frequent changes in direction in the past five years, and through it all, we've discovered we complement each other's strengths and weaknesses. Life does not have to become a daily competition to get "one's fair share," to measure exactly. Someone always has to give a little more than the others, but in time and with goodwill, it evens out. We've learned it will never work perfectly, and that in itself is comforting because it saves us from having to be perfect people to each other all the time. We've learned it is freeing for a man to be released from many of his burdens of support and the constant burden of "manliness." It's awfully nice to let someone else help carry the suitcases once in a while, check the reservations, take the hassles, stand in the lines, and say, "I've got some money." It's nice to sit down and read a magazine at the airport or the train station, let someone else pack the car for a trip and let someone else deal with the responsibilities. And I find it awfully nice to know I can sit here writing this while someone else plans dinner tonight. I don't even know who's cooking, but I'm sure it will be delicious. And even if it isn't, so what?

We would be less than truthful if we painted a picture of the changes in a marriage and a family all in soft pastel colors. There have been raised voices and the clashes of reds against purples. There have been exhilarating days and days when it all seemed flat and pointless and too difficult to continue. There are still moments, and days, of anger, misunderstanding, resentment, guilt . . . and yes, even tears. I still cry, but so does everybody else. But we're laughing a lot more easily these days too—at ourselves. And we keep inching slowly forward. For us, there is the realization that women can never go back—and neither can men. There is also the belief we can work it out together, and that's what keeps each of us going. And when we look back, when we see how far we have come, we are in awe. Even though there is a long road ahead, the road behind stretches so much further back.

The greatest fallacy of liberation, for men and for women, was the expectation it would be easy. It never is. But the hardest step is over once we have begun.

15.

Making It—The American Dream
(Guilt, Money, Success, and Status)

Success against the odds is the American ideal.
EDWIN ROGERS EMBREE

At the end of the rainbow is a pot of gold.

You can be the happiest person in the world, but if you are not wealthy, you are not successful.
JERRY APPELL

"HEY, BIG SPENDER!" Anyone who shouted that out in a group of typical middle-class Americans would get an immediate response. Every head would turn, to see who the lucky devil being addressed was. Big spender? That's the American dream in a nutshell. The number-one American goal is success, and success is measured by money. The good life is galloping consumerism. As a nation, we have it all, but nobody has enough. What's next on the spending agenda? A mink for Mom? A sailboat for Dad? A camper for the family? A second TV for the bedroom? Almost all the families we know are living over their heads—perpetually reaching. Ambitions rise with income; money dribbles away. Middle class isn't enough anymore. At every level, Americans would like just a little bit more, to be truly comfortable. Twenty-five percent more, as a matter of fact. Why? Because those ahead of us look a little bit more successful, and perhaps a little bit happier. But everytime we struggle up another rung in the ladder, we look around and see others climbing higher. There's no stopping place in the American Dream. It's like Gertrude Stein's description of Burbank, California: "When you get there, there's no there there."

What do Americans think about, dream about, fight about more than anything else? Money and sex. Both are elusive; both carry impossible and confused expectations. We were taught not to speak of sex by a generation of adults who spoke of it in hushed, embarrassed whispers, if at all. We were cautioned it was impolite to talk about money by a generation of parents who talked about it constantly, worried about it continually, and struggled ferociously to accumulate it. Television taught us to crave everything we saw. A booming postwar economy encouraged us to buy now, buy more, buy on time. Spending was patriotic until the recent recession, and we lived by phrases our parents never heard of: debt counseling, consolidation loan, Master Charge. Eighty-two million people are living off credit cards today. We're spending like there's no tomorrow. Depression era parents sometimes look at us with bewilderment. "You don't know how good you have it," they say. And we don't. But times change, folks, and we're just following the herd, though sometimes guiltily.

First, our own parents often make us feel guilty about money, success, and status. We, in turn, make them feel just as guilty. Thrift to our parents meant, "Save it, fix it, mend it, make it do, make it last." To our children, it means, "Throw it away, get a better one, save yourself a mending job, it's cheaper in the long run." Somewhere between these two different cultures we find ourselves, listening to the voices of the past, listening to the voices of the present, and looking around to see how we measure up.

The competitive, get-ahead spirit was drummed into us by the very same parents and the very same culture that also taught us spiritual values were the most important. But their actions frequently contradicted their words, and we were started on the road to acquisition by the examples we saw. "My mother always said it is easier for a camel to pass through the eye of a needle than for a rich man to enter the kingdom of heaven," a forty-two-year old friend told us. "It was her favorite quote. But she and my father broke their backs all their lives trying to get richer." "I was told not to be materialistic by materialistic parents," said another friend. A middle-aged Kansas woman was reminded continually by her father of every possession acquired as a child. "Girl," he would say, "you don't know how lucky you are. I had to work five hours for those shoes you have on your feet." Then she would later hear him bragging to a neighbor about the shoes and about their price.

Our parents had a deeper pride concerning money than we have, and different fears. Being self-sufficient was an indelible badge of self-esteem to the survivor of immigration, the Depression, or the World War. Self-denial and self-sacrifice were the important paving stones on the road to success for them—with good reason. Their survival had entailed a struggle, and saving was important; security was vital. If a catastrophe like the Great Depression could strike once, it might strike again. Yes, buy . . . but only after you have saved. But we, their free-wheeling, free-spending, debt-happy children, living in a later, more prosperous era, said, "Save? Why?" Because they had struggled and survived, most of us never had to struggle. "Why save when we now have life insurance, Social Security, pension funds, health insurance, disability insurance, and a good retirement plan at work? We even have profit-sharing trusts. Stop talking about the Depression, Pop. That was forty years ago."

But our parents had watched too many around them go down in ruin ever to forget completely. Their pride and their fears will keep disaster from happening to them again, but they worry about us. As one sixty-eight-year-old father recently lamented, "I don't understand it. My son seems to have gone crazy. He's barely thirty, and he's already making more than I made when I retired. And he spends every nickel! What is he doing with it? How can anybody spend that much money and still have the bill collectors beating on his door? His debts are unbelievable and he's not even worried. If things get too bad, he says he'll declare bankruptcy. Bankruptcy! What did I do wrong?" Nothing, Pop. He's never known a struggle, he wasn't even born when the Depression hit, and you were the one who handed him his first credit card. It's the proverbial clash of grasshopper and ant. The grasshopper, never having lived through deprivation, is not afraid of it. The ant can never forget the days when there were no crumbs.

Welfare, bankruptcy, and debt were all shameful stigmas to the working men and women who survived the Depression. Fathers lament and feel personally disgraced today when their sons go bankrupt. Their sons frequently see bankruptcy as a fast and feasible way out of overindebtedness. Three hundred thousand Americans declared personal bankruptcy in 1975, and they were not our senior citizens! But perhaps the difference between the two generations is best illustrated by a story Jerry Appell, a Phoenix friend, often tells: "There are no Jews on welfare today. Ask any Jewish parents and they will tell you that. But look down the welfare lines, and lo and behold, there's the Jewish daughter in Levi's and a Gucci belt. She's the one holding the hand of the little girl in the Saks Fifth Avenue dress. The daughter's pride is intact; she believes it's her civil right to be on welfare. But go find her mother in the Bronx apartment building, and it's a different story. Momma is at home trying to convince all her girlfriends and the neighbors that the situation doesn't exist." Jerry is right, but the generational difference is hardly unique to the Jews. Several years before we met, Dick was on welfare in Dallas for six weeks. A new business venture he started at twenty-three folded at twenty-three. His father generously bailed him out—as fathers do—but never acknowledged the time on welfare. His dad lent him the money to pay off his debts, and we, in turn, spent the first few years of our marriage repaying him. The difference was we talked about it; he never did. For Grampa, it was a disgrace; for Dick, a twenty-three-year-old from a then comfortable middle-class home, it was only a temporary setback. How many other fathers scurry around, continually bailing out the boats of their grown children? We, as a generation, take it for granted that they will help if they are able. We feel a little guilty knowing they are concerned, but we borrow anyway. Meanwhile, they worry, wonder where they have failed in our training, and feel guilty about that.

Because of their own struggles to attain a comfortable existence, our parents desperately wanted us to succeed. And the message, "Success is money," came through loud and clear in many families whether it was intended to or not. Comparisons were made constantly. We were compared with the neighbors, the neighbors' kids, their friends' kids, our own friends, and most of all, with each other. "Money speaks" the old saying goes, and it spoke, and spoke, and spoke, in so many homes—around the dinner table, when relatives visited, and on the way home from church. I doubt that our parents ever meant to make us feel guilty by the comparisons, but they did. One friend's mother came to see her still empty apartment shortly after marriage and toured it, talking all the while about another friend's daughter and the beautiful furniture her new husband had just provided. Dick was so poor when we were married he had to borrow my savings to make the trip to Pittsburgh for the wedding. My older sister and her husband had started marriage a few years earlier on a more economically sound basis. We were compared to them. Dick and I eventually paid off our debts, became respectable middle-class citizens ourselves, and then became the comparison models for my younger brother and Dick's younger sister. His sister Pat recently told us that her years of struggling were harder to endure because of the constant comparisons to us. "After a while, I couldn't stand hearing Mom and Dad tell one more Paula and Dick success story." Everybody felt guilty, including us. No one intended it that way. Parents across America were just doing their best to urge us on, to protect us from disaster, perhaps. Naturally, they applauded those who succeeded. In many families, what was owned and what was in the bank became the criteria for success. A friend who was told years ago by his stepmother that he was a bum when he couldn't find a job—who was compared constantly to his two stepbrothers—has now become a success and sends money to his family every month—partly because he wants to, and partly because he enjoys being the successful comparison at last.

We all feel guilty when we can't measure up to our parents' hopes and dreams for us, or to the obvious successes of others we see around us. Not marrying as well as your parents would have liked, not becoming as successful as they eventually became, causes guilt that surfaces only after years of marriage. It may take ten years before it becomes apparent that the new husband and wife are never going to "make it" financially. The son or son-in-law who is a salesman may suffer from status and title guilt because he does not measure up well against another son who is a sales manager. The guilt may be very subtly induced. One friend described the way her mother introduced three daughters at a recent party. "This is my daughter Joan. She's married to Jack, the banker. This is Suzie. She's married to Bob—he's a successful lawyer. And this is Annette. She's married to Bill." Bill is a grade school teacher, and obviously his profession is not worth noting.

There is also the guilt of making too many mistakes: buying the stock that goes down instead of up; the investment that goes sour; the real estate deal that ends up costing an arm and a leg. There is enormous guilt when one has to be helped again and again at different stages of life by parents, the guilt of going back to the folks for more and dragging our pride behind. Yes, somewhere along the line, we grasshoppers developed pride, too—along with the competitive spirit. How could we not? We were taught to look around and compare, and it has become a habit.

Nowhere are the guilts of money and success felt more deeply than at home—among husband, wife, and children. Each of us compares and knows internally when we are not measuring up to the Joneses or to our own ideals. Most working parents love their families; most husbands love their wives and would genuinely like to give them the best. It is not always possible. We returned from our honeymoon sixteen years ago, a honeymoon we could not even afford to take, three weeks before Christmas. We entered our first holiday season together flat broke. Hardly enough money for a two-foot-tall tree, and none for presents. Dick felt guilty for years believing he had failed to give me a memorable first Christmas, one that measured up to those I had known in the past. Another young husband today, still struggling after eight years of marriage, told us not long ago he sometimes drives alone down Milwaukee's lake shore looking at the Lake Michigan mansions, with tears streaming down his face. "I want to give her that. She deserves that. But I can't even pay the department store bills." There are bill-paying guilts in so many families. Several years ago, the father of six children wryly told us the story of their early years of marriage, and of dealing with the constant pressure from angry creditors. His wife was always the one to receive the upsetting phone calls during the day. They made her frantic with worry, and caused continual fighting and tension between the two of them. Jim finally ended the calls from one harassing creditor by saying, "I'll give you a choice. Since we are not able to pay off all our creditors at once, I'll tell you my current method of selection each month. I put our bills into a hat, shake them around, and pull them out, one at a time without looking at them. I pay until the money runs out. If you call here and upset my wife one more time, I simply won't put your bill in the hat anymore." That story, however, was not told for years. It didn't become humorous until they were out of debt.

There are numerous smaller money guilts that plague families. To the working wife today, time is money. She can no longer afford to be frugal. Chops are faster than casseroles, but more expensive. Frozen foods are faster than fresh, but more expensive. She feels guilty being unable to save money on the grocery budget as she once did, but what can she do about it? We had a silly triple guilt trip on this one tiny aspect of modern living the last time Dick's father was here to visit. He, coming from a generation that often enjoyed "playing poor," mentioned, as we sat down to dinner one night, that he hadn't had lamb chops for years. "Couldn't afford them in retirement" was the assumption. "It must be nice . . . sigh" was the implication. I gulped and felt guilty as I set the platter of chops on the table. Dick felt guilty because the remark implied he was now more successful than his own father, and could afford to throw money around. Each of us read something entirely different into the remark —our own particular guilt feelings. But good lamb is rarely available in Tucson, a subject Dick's mother and I have frequently discussed. If she had been there, she too, would have felt guilty hearing the remark, and might just have dumped the platter of chops over Grampa's head.

We all wish to give our families the best, and can't help but glance around to see how well others are doing with their families. The comparisons are not always happy ones. Through the years, some friends inevitably become more successful than others, and are able to do and give more. Is it envy or guilt that makes people withdraw from their more successful friends? Does it eventually become too frustrating to try to keep up with them, or is it simply too hard to face lopsided comparisons time and again? Most people don't enjoy hearing about exotic vacations they will never be able to afford themselves. Most of us find it difficult to sit in the house so much more elegant than our own, drinking expensive liquor and eating expensive food we never serve. And most of us aren't comfortable with the self-inflicted indignity of having to return hospitality on a lesser level. "How can we invite them back and serve spaghetti when they served us steaks?" It is usually not the successful friend who breaks off the friendship, but the other, who can't bear the comparisons. As one woman told us last year, "The number of old acquaintances we normally saw dropped in half after we moved into our new house. We invited everybody, as we had always done. Half never invited us back." Frequently bitterness mixes with guilt as we watch others succeed. We snip and chip away at their achievements out of envy, belittling the new promotion, the raise, the fancy vacation, the fancy title, the big bonus, the inheritance that someone else got instead of us. Very few people are genuinely pleased when others succeed because we are then forced to take a close look at ourselves and ask why we are failing by comparison. "Why them, not me?" Luck, we claim, and find every opportunity to make the success look smaller. Snip, snip, snip. As a successful surgeon put it, "I must be doing well. The other doctors at my hospital have started to snip at my ankles. When they go for the throat, I'll know I've made it."

Status must be maintained with friends and others around us. Whatever income level we are at, the need to impress others is usually what makes us spend beyond our means. We feel guilty knowing we are overspending for the sake of appearances, but we do it just the same. We go into debt to look good because it's too hard to admit we can't afford what others seem to be able to afford with ease. We borrow for the trip to the out-of-town wedding, borrow for the dress to be a bridesmaid. We charge more when the old bills have not yet been paid in order to have new outfits for the coming holiday season. ("But I wore that dress to their party last year!") We go deeper into debt to throw a party because we have been to the parties of others. We even borrow, as one acquaintance did several years ago, to make an impressive charitable contribution. Borrow for charity? Everyone else in his "position" was expected to make a sizable donation to a particular cause that year; no one knew he happened to be short of cash. He borrowed the money because he couldn't bear for them to learn the truth.

If we received mixed signals years ago from our parents concerning money and success, we, in turn, confuse our own children with a different set of mixed signals. Our youngsters can't help but notice the importance of money in our lives, but they don't understand our secret guilts. They see the status climbing, the scrambling, observe the spending, and wonder why we sometimes explode when *they* ask for more. As our own parents did with us, we whetted our children's appetites long ago; we gave in, bought for them, and did for them because they were part of our appearances. But when their expectations outstrip our own, it suddenly becomes a little frightening. It doesn't seem quite natural that a generation of youngsters could want *so much*. We feel guilty, realizing we probably created the problem—and the problem looks suspiciously like greed—but we don't know how to stop it. Every parent hears the comparisons and the longingly expressed desires from every child around. A ten-year-old sits on our pier and says wistfully, in front of her own parents, "I wish we had a sailboat like the Mc-Donalds." Our own children come home the next day and say, "I wish we had a Honda 250 like the Smiths do." And everyone feels guilty because none of us can do it all.

Occasionally, the guilty fear of creating monsters makes a parent explode. We try to reverse the trends in our children because we're afraid of where they are taking us. The explosions sometimes turn into a Ping-Pong game of guilt. Unfortunately, teenagers can play that game as well as their parents. "Fifty dollars for a grade school graduation dress that you're going to wear once! That's insane! If you had to work for the money for a change, you'd learn not to ask for the moon." "Oh, yeah? Well, I've seen you blow that much in one night taking people out to dinner! And I've been with you when you spent more than that during one trip to the liquor store!" A Ping-Pong game of guilt and parents give in because the youngsters are right, the money *was* spent as they said. But parents can't avoid the disturbing question that follows: "What kind of children have we created? What kind of future will it be?"

Children are different today; there is no doubt about that. But we wonder if different is right or wrong. At times, Dick and I look at our four youngsters, and the words of our parents come back to haunt us—words we often ignored ourselves. We try to inject in them a little of the past, a few of the Depression talks, as insurance. "I had a paper route at nine," says Dick, "and I didn't blow my money on junk," when our fifteen-year-old seems to be spending too much of her baby-sitting money on record albums. "I worked road construction in high school to help pay for my own college education," he reminds our sixteen-year-old, who seems quite happy working only part time to meet his needs. "Listen, I had to put half of everything I earned in the bank, and I was glad later that my father made me do it," he tells them all when they complain occasionally about doing the same. Parents try to inject a little motivation or a little thrift with pep talks from another era—forgetting that it's probably too late, forgetting that we are fighting an entire culture, forgetting that their needs are being met. For them, there is no more reality to stories of a nine-year-old paper boy than there was for us years ago in stories of the Depression.

It may seem wrong for a teenager to spend ten dollars on a single ticket to a rock concert. But a sixteen-year-old has the money today—he earned it and that's the way he chooses to spend it. What further motivation is there for him? Mom and Dad are doing well, the culture has told him it is unnecessary to save, and there are student loans and aids for just about everything. Still, we parents are concerned because young people have more than we had at the same age, want more than we did, and never seem to worry about the future at all. The struggle is less; the pep talks grow less effective with each generation. Isn't a reckoning likely at some point, we wonder? We haven't prepared them for one, and as the expectations keep spiraling ever upward away from the Depression, we're beginning to grow as nervous as our own parents once were.

But how to turn it around and do we want to turn it around? How much of this perpetual consumption is really healthy for any of us? We all have secret fears and secret doubts as we flash backward and forward in time. A comfortable middle-class suburban friend looked around her home not long ago and was suddenly appalled to realize how many things she owned that she didn't need: the Persian rugs; the collection of pewter plates; the antique rocker no one could sit in. She had just finished watching a news story showing earthquake survivors carrying their few possessions on their backs and had to ask herself, "How much of this could I live without?" "Most of it" was the honest answer.

Only a few weeks ago, I was reading one night with my feet up on our off-white couch. As I tried to keep my feet dangling uncomfortably over the edge, I suddenly wondered why we own a couch I can't put my bare feet on when I am usually barefooted? Who is it for? A young friend who recently declared bankruptcy expressed the same thoughts, a little too late: "So much of what once seemed important, so much of what we went into debt for, now seems absurd. I paid a heavy price to learn it didn't matter as much as I thought." Would my grandmother be stunned if she knew what our current debt level is compared to her cash-and-carry tradition? Would she be appalled at the cost of the couch, and the cost of so many other things we grasshoppers routinely spend money on, things that didn't exist thirty years ago?

Are those the disturbing thoughts in a father's mind as he tries to stem the tide a little with sermons to his children on the value of money? The realization that the average teenager *spends* twenty-two dollars a week is frightening to most parents—as is the fact that Schwinn's most popular bike sells for $135. Is that why parents occasionally bounce the guilt back to their children, hoping to make them appreciate what they have—just a little? "Why do you think we live in such a nice house? . . . a good neighborhood? . . . a fine school system? It's all for you. Appreciate it, dammit!" But is it really all for them? A lot of it today is for us—just as a lot of it was once for our own parents. But, we don't always like looking that closely at ourselves. Deep down, we don't always like the games we play, the comparisons we make, the words we speak, the things we need to be, or seem, successful. We don't want to fail, and yet . . .

Meanwhile, attainment of the goal, the American Dream, the stopping place, the final rung of the ladder, keeps creeping just out of reach—pushed upward by all of us and our guilts.

16.

All in a Day's Work
(Guilt on the Job)

We tend to judge others by their behavior and ourselves by our intentions.

ALBERT F. SCHLIEDER, MANAGER OF
MANPOWER PLANNING, BOWLING DIVISION,
BRUNSWICK CORPORATION

EVEN THE BOSS FEELS GUILTY at times. What? That can't be! He's the one who makes the rest of us feel guilty. Not always. Since 40 to 60 percent of our waking lives is spent on the job, there are myriad opportunities for guilt. Few of them are caused directly by Big Daddy the Boss, or Big Brother the Company; more are caused by the fellow sitting at the next desk, or the man or woman sitting at our own. There is the guilt of compromising one's own principles or values in order to succeed, to be accepted, or to get ahead. There is the guilt of "going along" in order to remain part of the team, one of the group, or one of the gang. There is the guilt of opening one's mouth when, ethically, it should be closed; of closing one's mouth when, ethically, it should be opened—and doing neither at the right time. Most of our guilts at work are self-imposed: We don't always like what we see ourselves doing for the sake of self-preservation. As with most other guilts, working guilts can be summed up in two questions: What do others think of me? What do I think of myself?

240

But let's get Big Daddy out of the way first. Bosses come in three varieties, and each produces a separate form of guilt in employees.

The warm, nonauthoritarian employer who brings out the best in people can also evoke tremendous loyalty guilts. Employees often find it difficult actually to do what they would genuinely like to do for him: perform at maximum capacity all the time. One can never do quite enough for the good boss; one is never quite satisfied with one's own efforts, even though the boss may be, and the positive work atmosphere frequently causes negative guilt feelings: "He deserves more; I'm letting him down; I'm taking advantage of him."

Far more common, however, is the human boss with faults of his own: traces of pettiness, areas of incompetence, moments of unfairness, and blind spots just like the rest of us. But—he *is* the boss, and most employees find it difficult to point out errors to their superiors, speak up honestly when their opinions differ from that of management, suggest changes, or offer unsolicited suggestions on doing things a better way. Because of our own insecurities, we let things slide when we know they could be improved. Better safe than sorry, we believe, while feeling slightly guilty for our lack of courage. "But what the hell," we think. "The company's gotten along for years this way. Why should I be the one to stick my neck out and tell the boss he's wrong?"

Then there is the boss who is never wrong. The domineering employer, who uses power and fear to drive his employees, is the greatest guilt producer. Everyone under him feels guilty constantly because he is impossible to please. Whether pushing a broom or pushing a pencil, an employee's self-esteem is quickly destroyed when the job is never done right. Reverend Dave Koch, a Lutheran minister who frequently counsels women, blue-collar, and clerical workers, describes this employer as dehumanizing. When people are treated like machines, objects, or sex objects, and have to endure that treatment in order to keep their jobs, a feeling of personal guilt begins to grow: "It must be me. I must be doing something wrong or I wouldn't be treated this way. I must be incompetent if I can never please those above me." Blue-collar women in particular feel this guilt, Reverend Koch claims. They are often forced to compromise their dignity in order to gain even the smallest shred of acceptance on the job, not only from their employers, but also from the men around them. That's the way the power structure often works, and it is difficult not to feel guilty when compromising your self-respect in order to keep a job. "I'm a human being, too," one would like to say, but can't when Uncle Scrooge is signing the paycheck.

More often, though, it is the small compromises we make with ourselves in order to get along that cause guilt at work—the "going along" because it is easier. There are women who feel strongly about equal treatment and their dignity in the office or the plant, who no longer wish to be "go-fers," but who do not speak up, do not snap back when the fanny-slapping salesman passes by. They know the eight hours a day they spend on the job will flow by more smoothly if they hide their feelings or beliefs and don't risk alienating the men around them. So, too, the union worker often compromises his own ethics to get along with fellow workers. He may believe in an honest day's work for an honest day's pay, but slows down anyway when pressure is applied. "Don't work so hard," his co-workers tell him. "You're making the rest of us look bad."

The desire to give an honest day's work for an honest day's pay poses other conflicts: most common is the problem of saying no to others who want to play when you have to work. Every conscientious worker is pestered at times by people who impose upon company time, who are bored or have nothing to do themselves, or who literally do not understand the working environment. One young woman we know of is frequently interrupted at her new job by calls from her mother. Momma has never worked a day in her life, and simply cannot understand why her daughter "can't take a few minutes out to chat each day." When the daughter explained that the calls embarrassed her and made her feel guilty in front of her co-workers, her mother dramatically announced, "You don't love me anymore!" The calls continue, and this young woman now feels trapped by her inability to take a firm stand and turn them off.

Even without such dramatic manipulation, most of us find it hard to turn off the time-wasters who want to waste *our* time. It's difficult to be blunt, honest, or downright callous with either co-workers, relatives, or friends. We have one friend whose father calls him frequently at the office and expects a long, leisurely telephone visit each time. While our friend is a commissioned salesman, and is not answerable to a superior for his time, he still can't make his father understand that the long calls keep him from doing his job—and earning money.

Working at home, as I usually do, poses its own problems—particularly with friends. I have one friend who drops in frequently while I'm working and interrupts me. She does not work, and finds it impossible to believe I can't take "just a short break for one cup of coffee." I usually can, but often don't want to if I'm in the middle of something, and from experience, I know that a "short break" when she is bored means several hours over multiple cups of coffee. I've tried to explain my work schedule to her, but she has no frame of reference, and unless I resort to brutal honesty ("You are screwing up my life!"), I know I won't get through to her. I'm not capable of tossing her callously out, but feel guilty for being timid and letting her waste my time. But no more guilty, I suppose, than the conscientious office worker who is annoyed by co-workers who are momentarily bored, or who are not busy themselves. When someone drops by your desk to talk, and then talks and talks and talks, how do you get rid of him without brutal honesty? Or when someone urges you to take a few extra minutes for lunch or a coffee break because she doesn't have to get back, how do you explain that you don't want to? Most of us are torn between our desire to do a conscientious job and our desire to be liked. We usually let the pests waste our time, and then feel guilty about it.

Getting along sometimes entails keeping silent about those around us who steal from the company, pad expense accounts, slough off, cheat whenever they can, are inept, or, as one junior executive put it, "have retired on the job at the age of forty." Does the secretary turn in her boss to his boss when she knows he's cheating the company? Do you report the fellow worker who pretends he's calling on clients when he's really getting a haircut or seeing the dentist or having an affair? Probably not. While most employees know exactly what is going on around them, few speak up. It's easier to pretend tunnel vision than to be known as the company spy. "Don't get involved."

The same lack of courage applies when we see others around us mistreated. We may console the coworker who was unfairly chewed out, or the secretary who is continually abused by her boss, but we rarely stick up for them if it means sticking our own necks out. "Boy, Bellweather is a real bastard," we snort indignantly. "I'd tell him off if I were you." I'll hold your coat is what we are really saying, but don't get me into it.

We also feel guilty and cowardly when we can't express our own non-work-related beliefs because they might be unpopular with those around us. The Republican union worker may not put a bumper strip on his car because it will stick out like a beacon in the overwhelmingly Democratic parking lot. He knows it will force explanations at least, arguments at worst, and mark him as different from his fellow workers. There is the guilt of agreeing with the boss when you don't agree with the boss; compromising your beliefs on politics, religion, and sex to stay in favor; biting your tongue or twisting your words just a little to get along.

Occasionally, there is the guilt of doing something personally distasteful or unethical because you are ordered to: padding a customer's bill, padding the travel expenses a client pays for, creaming a little off the top for the company because the boss tells you to. More often, employees face a personal conflict when choosing between doing the right thing for the customer and doing the right thing for the company. Allegiance lies where the paycheck originates, and ethics must sometimes be uncomfortably swallowed. For the good of the company, you ought to close the sale no matter what; for the good of the customer you ought to tell him the product isn't sound, isn't safe, or isn't right for him. But the truth may lose the sale: "That dress isn't right for you, madam," from the clerk; "This house isn't right for your family," from the real estate agent; "I wouldn't buy anything right now; the market doesn't look good," from the stockbroker; "We've had problems with these boots; the workmanship isn't good," from the shoe salesman. We know those are the right words, but they are hard to say when they mean less money for the company, which, in turn, may mean less commission or take-home pay for us.

Even insignificant conflicts between the good of the customer and the good of the employer can and do cause conflict. A former waitress told us she was frequently torn by her own ethics over nickels and dimes. If she advised one of her customers that the hamburger plate, which included french fries, cost less than the hamburger and side order of fries he had just ordered, she was saving him money, and that often meant a larger tip for her. Each time she did it, she felt guilty, knowing the restaurant and her employer made less profit. Each time she didn't do it, she felt she was cheating a customer by her silence.

At times, we do stand up for our principles, values, or beliefs on the job and then feel guilty when they backfire on us. Many employers or supervisors today genuinely want to give minority group members a chance. They hire the black, the woman, the reformed alcoholic, the handicapped worker, and sincerely hope they will succeed. When they don't there is the double guilt of not wanting to fire them, or worse, to correct or criticize their work. The supervisor may decide to "carry" the minority worker, though performance usually wins over principle in business, especially when a supervisor's own performance is being judged by those above him. Either solution produces guilt.

Standing up for your beliefs when they run counter

to those of the crowd can cause guilt feelings—especially when your way doesn't seem to be working. Our local Whitefish Bay football coach, Bob Albrightson, believes in playing for the sake of the game rather than playing exclusively to win. He sees football as part—he hopes an enjoyable part—of a youngster's education, and for this reason, Bob refuses to drive his teams hard. There is no hype on the bus while on the way to the games, and instead of sitting in tense silence preparing for the grim assault, the boys are allowed to play rock music and enjoy themselves. There's no psyching out of players on opposing teams, no sharpening of the killer instinct in his boys. And in midseason, once they have learned the drills, he gives them a day off from practice occasionally, as do pro coaches. "They know it all at this point," Bob explains. "Pushing them would be overkill." All of this seems sensible and humane . . . until the boys lose a game. Then a classic and almost universal reaction from the working world applies: A lone believer can guiltlessly buck the crowd only as long as things go well. When the criticism begins, when the principle fails (or appears to be temporarily failing), there is the guilt of being out of step, and the guilt of being blamed. "If he had pushed them harder, if they had practiced more, they would have won," Bob often hears.

Sometimes when we try to uphold our principles we are misunderstood. Several years ago, two sensitive and perceptive high school teachers spotted a boy with behavior problems. His parents were divorcing and he had a hellish home life. Both men worked with him for a year, attempting to father him through a difficult period and add some stability to his life, but all the while, he grew more troublesome. The boy's mother eventually turned on the teachers, claiming they were entirely responsible for her son's problems. She attacked them everywhere "for what they had done" to her boy. The men felt terrible, of course, and more than a little guilty. They had tried their best, but in the eyes of the community, their best had failed. Several years later, the young man returned to Whitefish Bay specifically to look them up and thank them. He had finally straightened himself out, and attributed it to their patience and their efforts during that hard year.

There is a particularly difficult guilt for the white-collar worker who has to sacrifice a portion of his family life in order to get ahead. Perhaps the boss wants him to stop off regularly for that drink after work, or join him in taking clients to dinner. These are command performances, and while they may advance the man's opportunities with the company, they don't help his homelife. The extra requirements necessary to get ahead—the business done on a bar stool, the night work or weekend work, the seminars, workshops, or out-of-town meetings—usually conflict with the best interests of the family. Men realize this, but they are torn between two "gottas." "I've gotta be here, and I've gotta be home." And the conflict of values is more difficult when a man can't adequately explain to his wife or family the pressures, or his own insecurities that make him give in to them. He feels guilty being criticized at home, while knowing he has little choice.

The blue-collar worker experiences the same conflicts and the same pressures, but they come from a different source. He is often kept from his family by the need to be "one of the boys." When payday rolls around and everyone else is cashing that check to begin the Friday binge, it's difficult not to go along. He might genuinely want to be home with his children instead of shaking for drinks at the corner tavern; he may not like spending that amount of money on booze; he might honestly wish to be a better father. But he needs acceptance on the job in order to get along, and the crowd at work, with their norms and their values, occupy a major part of his waking life.

All working men and women pay a stiff price when choosing their personal values over the "gottas" of their co-workers. Being different is never easy, as a friend of ours discovered when he stopped drinking entirely last year. He was slowly excluded from his group of associates when they realized he was serious about quitting. In phase one, his co-workers would declare over lunch: "Aw, come on! How long do you think you can last?" In phase two, a month later, the comment over the now occasional lunch invitation was: "When you finally fall off the wagon, it's going to be a mighty crash! I can't wait to see it." In phase three, several months later, curiosity dominated. Over the desk, rather than across the lunch table, his colleagues would ask, "How long are you going to stick with this program? Do you miss it? Is it tough to quit?" In phase four, six months after quitting, no one talked about drinking any longer, their own or his. No one kidded or mumbled about their hangovers in front of him because he had established himself as different. There were few invitations to lunch; none to go out after work. It frequently takes more courage than most of us have to stop being one of the boys, whether the boys are men or women. Instead, we allow ourselves to be sucked into personally distasteful actions or patterns because we do not think we can afford not to "go along."

There is a strange new conflict of sexual ethics on the job today, primarily for the white-collar worker. It is widely assumed that fellow workers will not expose the extramarital affairs of their associates. And while tacit approval—or at least acquiescence—is given to affairs, the situation is rarely handled as nonchalantly when two single people live together. Why? Because living together is a public embarrassment, awkward for the company and many of those in it. Affairs can be kept under wraps; living together cannot One junior executive working for a New York publishing house finally married the man she had been living with for four years—not because they felt the need to get married, but because she was ordered to by the powers on high. Her lifestyle was a constant source of embarrassment to other company executives and their wives at parties and business functions: company wives disapproved; no one knew how to introduce the couple without awkwardness. Because an extramarital affair is kept out of the limelight, only the parties involved need feel guilty about it; an open sexual relationship makes everyone uncomfortable.

Even innocent relationships between the sexes at work can cause guilt—at home. Men and women work side by side today in offices, factories, and ivory towers. It is impossible to ignore the existence of the opposite sex, and difficult not to form friendships when men and women spend a third of their lives together. While those friendships are almost invariably innocent, they seldom seem that way to the wife at home who has little or no experience in the working world. Working women are frequently seen as a threat by housebound wives, and the jealousies and suspicions are not easily disguised. Guilt by innocent association is unfair but real. Some men find themselves forced to exclude all references to the women at work in normal conversations with their wives. Silence may be safer, but most men feel guilty for the unnecessary deception.

Probably most on-the-job guilt is caused by our concern over what fellow workers think of us. We frequently keep our mouths shut even when we know an associate is wrong. We don't want to be the ones to point out his or her mistakes; we don't want to rock the boat or hurt someone's feelings, so we let the mistake or error in judgment go by. "What the hell? Why alienate a friend or associate or get them in trouble? Let the company suffer instead." While this may mean only the loss of a little money or productivity in business, it is far more frightening in medicine, where covering up for each other's shortcomings has been a dangerously widespread practice. Many doctors routinely look the other way if they discover another doctor is incompetent, alcoholic, or unstable. "I wouldn't let him operate on my wife," they might think to themselves, but they continue to allow him to operate on or treat others. The brotherhood closes ranks because no one wants to be involved in an embarrassing license revocation procedure, or cause a fellow doctor's practice to be diminished. Nurses maintain the same silence, and frequently don't report mistakes because they fear it will jeopardize their own jobs or alienate other doctors. Medicine is hardly the only profession that pretends to wear blinders. Architects do not report other incompetent architects; realtors complain to each other but seldom turn in the shady or unethical agent; lawyers close ranks behind their own; teachers criticize but rarely take action against the unjust or incompetent teachers. Nobody wants to squeal, and whatever our profession, there are times when we prefer not to see.

"What will the others think of me?" We try not to rise too far above the crowd or sink below it in any way. "We fear our best as well as our worst," said psychologist Abraham Maslow, and while failure has its own guilts, so has success. One can hardly remain "one of the guys" after a promotion puts one in the position of supervisor who gives orders to the others. Being silently excluded after getting the promotion, the raise, the praise that others did not get is part of the price of success, although an unexpected price. "What did I do wrong?" we wonder as we find ourselves just a little more lonely.

"What will they think of me?" we also wonder when we have to ask others for advice on the job. Will they think we are incompetent? That we can't handle our own assignments, tasks, or decisions? Or what if we do seek help from associates and get poor advice or unusable ideas in return? For some, there is guilt in the asking and a different guilt in ignoring what others have genuinely offered. On the other hand, if we never ask, never confer with others, we may seem aloof, arrogant, or autocratic. And, of course, there is the problem of bullheadedness. At times, our own ideas do seem best, and we block those of others only to discover later they were right. Often we can neither apologize nor admit errors to those around us. While we may feel guilty for that, we rationalize that our positions are too shaky for us to admit mistakes.

Many people find it difficult to give advice to those around them even when the company and the person would both benefit. Last year, a local business executive was asked to train another executive on the same level. The new man soon felt he was beyond the training stage, and capable of proceeding with his own ideas and methods. Our friend, having had more experience with the company, could see potential mistakes before they happened, but no longer felt comfortable interfering. His unsolicited advice would have seemed belittling, so, instead of intruding, he sat back, feeling guilty and wondering what else he could do while the man made his own mistakes.

Orders are far more difficult to give than advice, so we often play little games to get people to do what is necessary instead of telling them honestly or directly. We feel guilty about the deception, but know it is easier to live with than the fear of appearing overbearing. Even when we legitimately need others to get a job done, or done right, we frequently feel we are imposing when we tell them what to do, or order them to help. Who enjoys asking a secretary to stay late, or ordering anyone to do a job over because it wasn't done correctly the first time? "What will they think of me?" we wonder as usual, and frequently find it difficult to be tough even when it's necessary. We would like to be liked by everyone, including the office cleaning lady, but jolly good fellowship and productivity seldom go hand in hand.

Unintended misunderstandings crop up between coworkers just as often as they do between family members and friends. A man may not realize he is using the women at the office as "go-fers." A senior executive may not realize he rarely thanks his subordinates or that he treats them shabbily at times. The boss may not realize he uses those around him as mechanics, and neither delegates authority nor seems to take their suggestions seriously. An executive may be genuinely unaware that he takes his secretary as much for granted as he does his wife. But rarely do any of those being inadvertently abused speak up directly. They suffer in silence or gripe to others, who then might inform the offender. When this happens, the guilty party usually feels double guilt: first because he unwittingly mistreated people, and second because he obviously created a climate that made it impossible for them to talk to him openly. How can anyone help but feel guilty knowing someone else has suffered in silence for months or even years?

Perhaps the greatest peer group guilts arise from the constant measuring done in work situations, and the feeling of being out of step in performance. As in every other aspect of life, different usually seems wrong. A good example of this, as explained to us by a high school faculty member, are the many teachers who compare their performances to those of other teachers by comparing the grades they have given. One member of the English department asks another at the end of a semester, "How many A's did you give? How many F's?" If the answers are similar, both teachers feel reassured they are doing a good job. If the answers vary greatly, both may feel guilty. "What's wrong with me?" each wonders, forgetting that youngsters differ from year to year and from class to class, and assuming that it is they who have failed to measure up. Life insurance men working in the same offices, stockbrokers, realtors, and salesmen of all kinds, also compare and make themselves feel guilty in much the same way. Another salesman might be selling more right now. Instead of looking at the circumstances surrounding his sales, or the lack of our own, we immediately feel guilty and inadequate. We compare methods instead of causes, assume there is a right way and a wrong way, and that we must be doing it wrong.

Self-preservation and intense competition may be commonplace in the business world, but few men or women feel good about themselves when they resort to street-fighting methods to get ahead. Guilt is easier to live with than fear, however, and it is fear and insecurity that induce us to pull ourselves up by pushing our peers down. If the good of the corporation is opposed to my good, self-interest usually wins. Thus people don't always promote or back the best ideas, plans, or policies for the company when those concepts come from others. Status-scrambling junior executives often hold back their ideas until they have checked out the competition. Or they refrain from giving others the best help or advice on projects, fearing that they will look good if the project is successful. Department heads do not always groom their best subordinates, hire the best people, or extract the best from existing employees.

Future competition is feared. "What if he gets too good? He might go after my job." Idea-stealing occurs, credit is not given where it is properly due, and road-blocks are intentionally thrown up in front of others, lest they get ahead faster. There is continual nit-picking at co-workers so they will look their worst to the boss. Self-preservation may demand these actions, but those who indulge in office one-upmanship rarely avoid internal twinges of guilt even when they win.

Most of us indulge in another form of nit-picking: belittling the good ideas of others because they will mean more work for us. I've done it to Dick several times while working on this book. He might suggest an addition to a chapter, or a new chapter, and I'll tear his idea apart because at that moment, I can't bear the thought of doing one more addition or writing one extra page. But even while I'm undermining his idea, I know he's right. The addition or change should be made, and eventually it will be made, but not before I make him feel guilty for the imposition.

Lynn Sherman, one of the world's nicer people, tells the story of how she offered to help her younger sister when Sandy had a high school report to type. Lynn, who wanted to show off a little and impress Sandy with her skills, volunteered to do the typing, without realizing the size of the project. She expected an hour's work, not an entire Saturday. As the day wore on and Lynn became more and more resentful at the lost hours, she began to nit-pick unmercifully. "Your handwriting is terrible; I can't read it. And what is *this* supposed to mean? Why does the outline have to be done in such a ridiculous way?" Finally, Sandy broke down in tears, apologizing for the incon-venience. Lynn claims she still feels guilty for the way she behaved that day years ago. Her behavior is typical of the kind of nit-picking we do to each other on the job. "I can't understand this report . . . you realize I have to do all this extra work now because of your carelessness . . . if you'd take the time to organize your material once in a while, Jones, other people might be able to decipher it." Pick, pick, pick. We resent the extra work, and work off our resentment by making the other person feel stupid and guilty. We may win a hollow victory, but invariably feel guilty and small ourselves.

Working men and women feel guilty not only when they look bad in their own eyes, but when they look bad to others. The salesman who loses the sale because the competition actually was better has to explain that loss not only to his employer and co-workers, but also to his wife and family. His self-esteem takes a somersault. Then there is the commonly felt guilt of appearing to let the client or customer down: the real estate agent who can't move the house in a slow market for the couple who have been transferred; the stockbroker who loses money for his customers during a recession or a bear market; the doctor, the lawyer, or mechanic whose best judgment, advice, or counsel fails because of unexpected and unavoidable complications. Even when circumstances are beyond our control, we inwardly blame ourselves for the failure and wonder what others think of us. Whether losing an account, a sale, a client, a patient, or money, each of us takes some of the blame personally, and wonders if others are pointing the finger of guilt at us.

We feel a natural sense of guilt when mistakes are our own fault; when we are late with our work and inconvenience others; when we make a mistake in typing or pricing that embarrasses the company or proves costly. It is more than a fear for our jobs: most of us do have a sense of loyalty to our companies, and can rarely slough off our errors easily. But we also feel guilty when we look bad to others through no fault of our own. "The customer is always right" guilt is experienced by retailers everywhere when they unwittingly sell poorly made products, or offer services, repairs, or replacements the factory later refuses to honor. The retail salespeople are the customer's only contact. They take the customer's wrath, as do unlucky airline stewards and reservation clerks who find abuse heaped on their heads each time a plane is delayed because of bad weather or mechanical failure.

Years ago, when I was an airline stewardess for Braniff, we were routed to Oklahoma City one night instead of our scheduled destination, Dallas. Every airport in Texas was closed down due to fog, and Oklahoma was as close as we could get. Even though it was hardly my fault we had to spend the night there, I felt so guilty about the inconvenience, I offered to buy drinks for an entire planeload of people who couldn't get home that night. Jon Sherman, a friend who was a charter pilot for years, claims he felt the same guilt whenever a charter flight had to be canceled because of poor flying conditions. Because he was getting paid anyway, because he was the company's representative—the only one the customer saw—he accepted the blame personally. A similar but peculiar guilt by association has cropped up since the late sixties: the guilt of being a part of "Big Business." "Who do you work for?" people are asked. When the answer is Dow Chemical (IBM or Gulf Oil), the sneer that is often read into the "Oh" that follows can make almost anyone feel guilty. One cannot walk around saying "I didn't drop the napalm."

When employees cheat their companies, they deserve to feel remorse and guilt. Unfortunately, those who *should* feel guilty seldom do. Those who slough off on company time, pad their expense account, take company supplies, use company phones for personal calls, and take sick days when they are not sick usually rationalize their guilt away by claiming, "It's a big company, they can afford it." It is not unusual for hospitals to have up to 40 percent of their dishes and linens regularly stolen by employees. The airlines have unwittingly stocked many a steward's or stewardess's apartment with miniature silverware, dishes, and liquor. And other businesses fare no better. If it isn't nailed down or locked up, someone is likely to walk away with it. Several years ago, Dick surprised one employee as she was leaving one night with both arms loaded with office supplies. When he asked why, she replied, "I thought everyone could just take whatever they needed. It's only a corporation. It's not like stealing from another person." A similar attitude was displayed when, about five years ago, we had dinner one night in a restaurant not far from the American

Motors plant. At the next table were two assembly line workers and their wives. We couldn't help but overhear as they swapped stories about the tools and supplies each had stolen during the past year. It was staggering—not only the amount, but their apparent lack of any feelings of wrongdoing.

Contrast that to the paranoia the average conscientious worker feels when it even *appears* he or she is goofing off. An executive leaves his secretary or staff a mountain of work as he goes off to a long business lunch or a golf game with a client. He knows he's still working, but it looks very much like play to those he has left behind—and he knows that, too. What are they thinking about him, he wonders. An employee who leaves late for lunch because he was finishing up a job feels guilty walking back into the office a half-hour late. The same is true for coming in late in the morning. Others don't know that we worked late the night before. We feel equally guilty and under suspicion when we return from an errand in the middle of the afternoon. We know the boss sent us to pick up his airline tickets, but no one else knows that. Do they think we've been at lunch for three hours?

Most of us can't even gaze off into space comfortably when we are actually thinking about the job. We feel we have to look productive when someone walks by the desk. Even reading a trade magazine makes us feel guilty when others pass by the office door. Will they think we are reading *Playboy? Better Homes and Gardens?* And invariably, we are making the one quick personal phone call of the week when a co-worker drops by the office. "Do they think I do it every day?" Probably not, but most of us have the feeling others are constantly watching us at work. I feel guilty asking someone to send manila envelopes, typing paper, or paper clips to the house when I'm working at home. It's our company, my own supplies, but still I wonder if others think I'm using them to write letters to my mother.

Those who would never take advantage of their companies or their fellow employees often feel the sharpest guilts when they are slightly off-stride, whether because of personal or emotional problems, or actual illness. One business associate of ours, Lynn Sherman, who usually accomplishes more in an average day than three ordinary people, felt guilty for months because a persistent allergy had slowed her down. She was working at the pace of two normal people instead of three, and felt she was letting everyone around her down. By her own incredibly high standards, she was failing to measure up.

Expending extra energy to measure up to self-imposed standards carries its own guilty plague. Instead of taking advantage of the situation, relatives or friends of the boss often work doubly hard to prove themselves. We have several friends who have been in this position at one time or another, and they continually felt everyone was watching them—and waiting for signs of favoritism or special treatment. Since their self-expectations are higher, so is their paranoia. As one friend, Curt Gorrell, remarked about the occasional projects he has worked on with his father, "There's always guilt—the guilt that builds up from the real or imagined thoughts of your peers on the job that you are someone 'different' than they, that you might get 'special treatment.' You're driven by the desire to prove them wrong, and you can't do that by just being good. You have to be excellent. Besides feeling guilty for the paranoia, I sometimes feel guilty about the extra time and energy I waste trying to prove myself."

While employers suffer less from the "everybody's watching me" guilt, they, too, have their burden to bear. Yes, the boss feels guilty, too. Big Daddy has to hire and fire; but he's human and doesn't always do it well. And at times, he doesn't train his subordinates adequately or can't afford to let go of the reins long enough to let them grow up to responsibilities. Because he is accountable for the bottom line, he can't always afford the mistakes others may make in the growing process; nor can he allow them too much freedom, even though he would like to. He feels equally guilty when he does give subordinates a chance to use their own creativity or initiative, and they blow it. It is *his* error in insight, as it is when he hires people who don't work out, tries new ideas that fail, and makes errors of judgment himself. Dick is probably more supportive than any man I know of women in general and the particular problems of the emerging woman. He continually tries to give those women attempting to get back into the job market after years of homemaking a chance. Frequently, it doesn't work out. Despite the patience, coaching, prodding, and sympathetic understanding, some women are not ready for the business world. Still, when it doesn't work out, Dick feels guilty. He employed them, it was his misjudgment, his failure, not theirs.

No on-the-job guilt is as sharp as the one that precedes and follows firing another person. The manager of the shoe department at Sears may be told by his own superiors to let two of his seven salesmen go because business is slow. But whom does he fire? Joe is the worst salesman, but he has a mentally retarded child. Perhaps the department could get along easily without Pete, but Pete has marriage problems right now and all those kids to support. But then, the better salesmen don't deserve to be let go just because they have fewer problems. How does the manager decide? Agonizingly, in most cases. And often the abrupt, cold dismissal session is only a cover-up for his own feelings and guilt. Torn between his personal morality and his obligations to his company, he can't win.

Managers, employers, and supervisors are human; they make mistakes, too, but their mistakes often cost subordinates time and energy. For the good of the company, it is sometimes necessary to change direction after a project is under way. The supervisor who initiated the project now feels guilty wondering what his subordinates will think of him for changing his mind. He also has the tough job of saying "no" to the reasonable requests of others. He has the total company picture or his division's budget in mind, and while the ideas are good, they may not fit into the plan. Still, he feels the natural guilt of refusal, and wonders just as much as his employees do what others think of him. He knows people never love the order-giver, and he worries about being disliked. Still, he has to ask people to work late, push through crash programs to meet deadlines, and expend extra effort getting the job done on time because of someone's poor planning. When his own poor planning is at fault, he knows it better than anyone else and feels every pang of guilt.

Authority figures, being human, do play favorites, though seldom guiltlessly. The foreman may give the overtime to someone he likes or to someone he knows needs it. The boss may not overload a favorite secretary, but dump the extra work or the boring job on someone else instead. Those in charge do look the other way at times and make allowances for favorite employees or friends when they make mistakes. Honest teachers admit to favoritism. Given two borderline grades, they will often give a favorite student the extra edge. She gets a C while the class clown may get a D for the same grade average. And as one teacher recently confessed, "If I liked Suzie Smith, and she was a good student, her brother automatically starts off with an advantage when I have him in my class two years later."

All of us have our guilts pertaining to work and those who work around us. Some guilts are deserved, some are self-inflicted, others are silly, but they are all real to those who feel them. Since we rarely have as much control over our work environment or as much flexibility as we do in other parts of our life, some of the guilts simply have to be endured. Others may not. We can reassess and ask ourselves if the price of the guilt is less than the price we would pay to change our situation.

Not long ago, I was complaining to Dick about feeling guilty because our lifestyle, due to work, had become temporarily hectic. (I was suffering severe pangs of Good Mommy guilt due to the work load, and bombarding Dick with similar Good Daddy guilts.) He listened, and basically summed up the choice most of us have when dealing with our self-inflicted working guilts. "We can both quit what we're doing any time we want," he said. "We can both get jobs clerking at the local supermarket, live on less, and be home every night at five. No pressure, no hassles, more time with the family, no guilt." He's right; we can. But with that as the alternative, I'll learn to live with the guilts I already have, thank you. And don't most of us have that same basic option? When we begin to feel overwhelmed by guilt at work, we can change—but only if we're willing to pay the price.

17.

Everybody's Paranoid

We have met the enemy and they is us.

POGO

DICK AND I used to think we were the only ones.

I alone worried when the meter man descended into our messy basement. I was convinced that he rushed back to his truck to compare, via CB radio, my basement with those visited by meter readers on other blocks. Single-handedly, I was lowering the standards of an entire neighborhood.

Dick would flinch whenever a neighbor or repairman asked to borrow a tool. Not only did he not know where they were kept, he had no idea which was which. To this day, he has never found either the fuse box or the meter box.

Pediatricians gathered at parties and discussed the amount of dirt lodged between the toes of the youngest McDonald at his last checkup. And, of course, the story of Mike's recent TB shot was told and retold. The nurse swabbed a portion of his arm with alcohol and a white spot magically appeared. "It's not a tan," the doctor whispered in awe.

At the annual Garbage Convention, our garbage men amused the group with endless stories of our trash. They revealed our secrets. Seeking sympathy, they described our garbage when we had a new puppy.

Friends gossiped about the dog hair on my car seats; and the Popsicle sticks and candy wrappers in the car ashtray that made it impossible to put out a cigarette without starting a fire.

Teachers compared our children's unmatched mittens and broken jacket zippers with those of the rest of the class. I'd cringe when one of the children came home and announced it had been weigh-in day at school. "But your underwear is frayed. Now the whole class knows!" Dick would cringe when the children mentioned that the rest of the class had returned their athletic insurance forms weeks earlier. "Where are ours, Daddy?" Was he the only parent holding up the teacher; the only father too cheap to buy insurance; the only person who didn't care if his kids got hurt?

At Christmas time, I'd march briskly, busily past the Salvation Army bell ringer knowing full well she was singling me out as cheapskate of the day, even though I had given all my change at the last corner. Poppy sellers sneered at me on Veterans Day. Should I stop and explain to each one that I had no buttonhole, but the poppy was in my purse? And how does a man explain that he would rather not buy four tickets to the circus benefit for underprivileged children from a colleague at the office because he just spent his lunch money for the week buying raffle tickets—from the boss!—to aid an underprivileged country club?

George Custer's sins hung heavily on our heads. In fact, the demise of the Indian nations was our personal guilt trip, as was gaining our family income from "Big Business," single-handedly causing the population explosion by having four children, and finding ourselves with an Arab brother-in-law during the energy crisis. I was even beginning to feel guilty smoking in the same room with people who wore contact lenses. When our son put a cigarette in the mouth of his Halloween pumpkin and called the pumpkin Mommy, that clinched it. I walked around for weeks explaining to perfect strangers that I had started smoking before the Surgeon General's report.

Then one day my life changed. I was leaving an airport rest room stall and heading for the door when another woman entered. I realized I'd have to go back and wash my hands, lest she think I was uncouth. I was still scrubbing diligently when her stall door opened and she made straight for the door. She stopped abruptly and returned to the sinks, realizing that she, too, would now have to wash her hands because I was there. Red-faced, we quickly finished and slunk away to our separate planes. But the incident cured me. For once, I didn't have nightmares about running into her someday at a party. I knew she'd never tell.

Isn't it reassuring to know that if you're paranoid, so is everyone else? Americans seem to be afflicted with an advanced case of "everybody's watching me," and suburbanites may be in the terminal stage of the disease. You're not afflicted, you say? You don't care what people think of you? Then you've probably never straightened the house "just a little" before the cleaning lady arrived; or heard an automatic apology pop out of your mouth when a friend dropped in and the place was a mess; or carefully counted your drinks when the boss took you out to dinner; or leaped for the closest closet when watching TV in your underwear and the front door slammed. Perhaps some of you have never wondered how you were going to get out of a small, uncrowded store without buying something; or felt guilty walking out on the salesman after trying on twenty pairs of shoes or rifling through forty ties. Congratulations! You may be the last guilt-free people in America who aren't institutionalized. The rest of us are sorely afflicted.

I, personally, am one of those overly conscientious types. I take everything seriously, including my acute sense of garbage guilt. This began as a child when my mother told me it was tacky to allow your property to look like a dead-end lot on Tobacco Road. That attitude has become a fixed part of my suburban pride-of-ownership complex. It even follows me out of suburbia. In the winter, we live a few blocks from

Lake Michigan and are besieged by happy-go-lucky raccoons who prefer our garbage to the neighbors'. Since we've never been able to convince the children that it's smart to keep the garage door closed, our trash is continually strewn far and wide for the world to see. In the summer, the problem is worse. We live in the North Woods of Wisconsin where we are visited regularly by raccoons, dogs, and friendly bears. Since we've never been able to convince our rural mailman that it isn't nice to run over our lids, our country garbage flows colorfully across the fields and meadows. Trash bags are no match for claws, and the local lumberjacks always know what we had for dinner the night before. But will they write to my mother and explain that I'm trying hard not to be tacky?

Even our mothers are afflicted by paranoia at times. How could they be? They live in condominiums and apartments; they have no garbage, no little children, and no tacky backyards. But they have other guilts related to "everybody's watching me." I know of one senior citizen in perfect health who cleans out her drawers and linen closets regularly each week. Why? Because she might die and what will her relatives think if her closets are messy when they dispose of her things? "But, Ma," her daughter-in-law pleads, "you won't care then. You'll be dead." To no avail. Guilt is stronger than reason.

We have it on good authority that others worry about their images. They also fret about saying "no" to the charity collector at the door—even when they really did give at the office. They, too, slink back into the house with guilt feelings, knowing that certain neighbors will henceforth believe them to be tightwads. Even little children soliciting door to door can make us feel guilty. How many Girl Scout cookies did *you* buy this year? How many pizzas to send the high school Spanish club to Mexico? How many bike-a-thons and walk-a-thons have you sponsored at two cents a mile? And how did you feel when you didn't have enough change to tip the paper boy? See?

Some of us even worry about what service people think of us. A friend confided that she can hardly face her dry cleaner since the advent of permanent-pressed clothes. He still makes regular twice-weekly stops at the house, but she has little to give him these days. When she has nothing, she hides and pretends she isn't home. I feel the same way about the milkman. We normally order gigantic quantities of milk. On the rare occasions that I overstock, I feel guilty writing, "No milk today." After all, the poor man did get up at 3:00 A.M. Dick, and probably every other man, feels guilty when he runs into the milkman as he's leaving for work and remembers the bill hasn't been paid.

"What will they think of me" paranoia even extends to our pets. How they behave is a reflection on us. "Sorry my dog ate your tulips" is awkward, to say the least. It's even more difficult to continue talking nonchalantly to a neighbor while your dog is relieving himself on his prize rose bush. The most embarrassing situation occurs when Fido earnestly trots in the opposite direction while you bellow "Come" in your best obedience school voice; running through the neighborhood in your jockey shorts is undignified, especially if the rest of the neighbors are watching from their front porches, their perfectly trained dogs lying docilely at their feet. You try not to look flustered while muttering under your breath, "I'll kill that stupid hound— if I can catch him!"

The vet says your dog is too thin. Another reflection on you, wicked owner. More often the dog is overweight. It's too embarrassing to explain to the vet that the dog is fat because he's poorly trained. He chews and swallows everything—including the latest bestseller. One friend's dog has literally eaten her backyard, Southwest cactus garden and all. Another friend was put in a doublebind guilt squeeze by her dog. Poochie ate a homemade apple pie that the woman's mother brought her. Rather than admit that, our friend confessed to gobbling the whole thing down herself. Having her husband think she was a glutton wasn't as bad as having her mother find out her lovingly baked pie had been consumed by a dog.

How about "perfectly sterile body" guilt? Yes, we

have no bodies in this country, or so we pretend. We certainly have no body odors. It's become a sin to sweat in America, and from head to toe we're now supposed to smell invisible. Bad breath, medicine breath, soda pop breath, denture breath? Take your choice. One will ruin you socially as fast as the other. All of which makes for elevator guilt. The minute modern man steps into a crowded elevator he begins checking himself out. "Is it I who smells?" Sneak a peek at your shoulders while you're at it. Does the dandruff show? The age of miracles has even brought us the deodorized sanitary napkin—flushable, thank God. Someone might think women menstruate.

As a nation, we pretend we don't eliminate—or make noises when we do. Admit it. When someone is nearby, you run the water in the bathroom just like the rest of us, right? One of the most uncomfortable evenings of our married life was spent in a small apartment with a single bathroom directly off the living room. Our host had eaten a massive amount of sauerkraut earlier that day and spent the entire evening racing for the bathroom. The rest of us participated in spurts of frenzied conversation while pretending not to listen. The poor man almost depleted Lake Michigan running the water.

If we neither smell nor eliminate, it's logical that we don't pass gas either. Every home toilet top now carries its own can of lemon spray to disguise what none of us do. Take away our aerosol security blankets, put us out in the big world unarmed, and we panic. Elevator guilt again. "It wasn't me." Dick has the best solution. Look at someone else, walk fast, and scowl. Leave the guilt behind. Unfortunately, you can't do that when using the men's room at the office. If you're the only person coming out when the next man enters, scowling doesn't help. Besides, the receptionist knows you were the last one in there even if you didn't get caught. When the boss reels out gasping, will she tell it was you?

Then there's "did they see me" guilt. Is there a woman alive who hasn't dropped the roast, looked furtively over her shoulder, and put it on the table anyway? Do you wash the fruit and lettuce when no one else is in the kitchen? Has your wife ever asked you to toss the salad and then caught you tossing it with your hands? How many times have you been tooling merrily down the expressway with a finger up your nose when you looked over to see another car next to you? Yank! Or rolled down the window to spit before you realized another car was passing? Splat!

Or there's doctor guilt . . . better known as "I'm sorry to bother you at home." Why do we apologize to doctors when we're sick? Why do we wait until the weekend is over to call when we're running a temperature of 104? We would literally rather die than inconvenience a doctor during his free time. Only when Dick threatens to get a witch doctor will I call, apologizing profusely for my body's poor timing. And my worst fears are always confirmed. My temperature drops to normal just before he arrives. Better to have died.

Dick and I have equal trouble with throw-away guilt. This has nothing to do with being frugal; it concerns those unsolicited freebies that continually arrive in the mail and demand a contribution. The worst are little medals from religious organizations. As Catholic children, we were taught that a blessed object could not be nonchalantly discarded; it had to be burned or buried. Did you ever try to bury something in Wisconsin in the winter? Or burn a medal? Just as guilt-producing are the miniature license plates and key chains that the veterans' organizations send. If you toss them out without a thought, you feel bad. If you use them without sending money, you feel worse. Dick can't even throw away a Jacques Cousteau solicitation without feeling guilty. Will it be his fault if the oceans die? And what mother doesn't experience guilt while tossing out the art papers, the A's in spelling, and the mosaic made of noodles and lima beans? With four children, you can't save a ten-year supply of school papers without renting a warehouse. Yet we're convinced that other mothers do keep these precious mementos to show their grandchildren someday. Other fathers must have endless office wall space to hang the 133 plaques their children have lovingly carved or crayoned for them.

"Not knowing" guilt is a fearful thing for most of us. Not knowing what to wear; which bestseller is being discussed; or how to pronounce *L'Heure Bleue*. French makes me blatantly paranoid. While Latin looked great on my college transcript and Spanish was acceptable on Dick's, neither does a thing for couth today. French is in. Those of us who don't know a *crêpe* from a pancake are out. We feel like fools trying to order in a French restaurant and pointing to the wine we want instead of trying to pronounce it. How embarrassing to have to spell the name of your own perfume. That must be why Charlie is such a big seller; it's the only one everybody can pronounce. *Glamour* magazine recently ran an article entitled "If You Can't Pronounce the Perfume How Can You Tell Him You Want It?" How indeed? Calêche . . . Je Reviens . . . Showoffs!

Almost as obscure are the names of colors used for women's clothes. Once upon a time, ordering lingerie was the only guessing game in town. Today mauve and taupe are slowly creeping into our linen closets and onto our beds. I hate calling up a department store and asking what candleglow with écru looks like. It makes me feel stupid. And I never have figured out what puce is, though it certainly doesn't sound like something I would like. Even the latest direct-mail catalog was designed to make me feel inferior. "This velvety Shevelva of Dacron polyester for the glamorous robe . . . Luscious satin Ravissant of anti-cling Antron III for the femme fatale. Joyfully presented in Danube, Toffee and Candleglow." I didn't order it. I didn't know what it was. It seems only fair that men should suffer the same insecurities as women, and they are beginning to. Dick was bewildered recently by an ad for shirts and asked me for help with the colors. Ha! The choices were Legionnaire Bleu, Neige, Sable, and Gendarme Copper. The culprit? Pierre Cardin, a Frenchman, of course.

There's more to "not knowing" guilt than colors and words. I can feel just as guilty not knowing how to eat something. How long can I drag out the conversation until someone else starts first? Dick has an overbite that makes it impossible for him to eat artichokes. Such poor planning on his part, since artichokes seem to be popping up at dinner parties everywhere. Not knowing what to do is equally embarrassing and guilt-producing. Have you ever been the only Catholic at a bar mitzvah or the only Jew at a baptism? Stand, kneel, sit . . . when? Watch the others out of the corner of your eye. Pretend you have arthritis and move slowly.

What to wear is another new problem for many men. While women have had years of experience with this particular quandary, men are neophytes at the game. Overnight, they've gone from rep ties to chokers, from being gray-flannel-suiters to Serpico lookalikes. Most are not quite sure what looks right with what, how much jewelry is too much, and when campus casual becomes working plumber. "Can I wear my leisure suit tonight?" now echoes through American homes on Saturday night. Poor plaintive peacocks. It's unfair to be made suddenly unsure at forty.

"Not knowing" has another form. Let's call it Mental Midget guilt. It occurs when you find yourself odd man out. You are the only Republican, housewife, company executive, or smoker in a room. Everyone else at the party is into Yoga, TM, feminism, or the art center. You don't know what est is and can't tell Picasso from a Snoopy cartoon. You haven't the faintest idea why people sharpen razor blades in their pyramids. You've been painting the basement for a month and have lost track of both the bestseller list and Elizabeth Taylor's marriages. Everyone's discussing Vonnegut's latest and you don't know if it's a salad or a movie. Your interests aren't relevant. Everyone else's seem to be. You don't even know who your local school board candidates are—and secretly you don't care—but the discussion is hot and heavy all around you. Sidle backward toward the outer fringes of the group, look intelligent, and hope no one asks you a direct question.

Mental Midgetism occurs when either Dick or I

have to take the car in for repairs. Neither of us knows anything about motors and we are immediately intimidated by the mechanic. "It goes tucha . . . tucha . . . tucha," we explain lamely. This is obviously more difficult for Dick—men are supposed to understand motors. How can he argue a $140 bill when he doesn't know what a carburetor is?

Intellectual lapses are always hard to admit. We all have them. We even enjoy them, but seldom confess. Find me ten women who will admit to watching soap operas. I have a friend who has been secretly watching "As the World Turns" for nineteen years but has never confessed to anyone except her husband and me. She and Dick are the only two people on earth I would trust with the knowledge that I go on occasional binges of trashy mystery novels. For others, trashy romances are as well kept a secret as drinking in the morning. But someone must put those books on the bestseller lists besides me. And where are all the Agatha Christie fans when books are discussed at suburban parties? Hiding in the corner with the daytime TV watchers, I suppose. It's like admitting you are a junk food junkie or that you watch "Happy Days" while a National Geographic special is on.

Junk food is a guilt trip in itself, but it's only the tip of the iceberg for guilty eaters. Fat or thin, most of us overindulge or go on an outrageous food binge occasionally. A house guest and I confessed to each other last summer that we each got up and ate a frozen Snickers bar at six in the morning. Fortunately, we didn't bump into each other at the freezer door. Not long ago Dick felt equally wicked eating a piece of his favorite cake after being on a diet for three weeks. The whole family pounced on him, adding to his guilt, and the poor man isn't even overweight. He just wanted to lose a few pounds around the middle. If it's a sin to be fat in America today, we skinny people suffer on the sidelines. Remember what your mother told you about not eating in front of other people without offering them some? Try gobbling a Twinkie when there's a dieter in the house. Most people can't even eat in front of their dogs without feeling guilty. Many of our friends today are conscientious weight-watchers. I feel guilty being thin around them. Not long ago, I was in Phoenix visiting old friends. We went out to dinner with another couple who own the Weight Watchers' franchise for Arizona. Both couples were dieting in preparation for an upcoming vacation. While they sipped tomato juice and munched celery, I devoured their crab, my crab, their gazpacho, my gazpacho, ate an entire basket of bread, and topped the dinner off with two sinful Irish coffees. I still feel guilty knowing that I lost a pound that night while they suffered through my gluttony.

Perhaps you, too, feel periodic twinges of generic guilt. This occurs when you make yourself responsible for the woes of the world. You helped create this mess, right? Or, at least your generation did just by being alive. Because Dick and I are over thirty, we are responsible for Vietnam. We probably had a hand in Hiroshima, too. We felt acute guilt pangs during the sixties when students paraded radiation-burned survivors around the University of Wisconsin campus where Dick had once been a student. He wanted to wear a sign saying "I was only twelve when they dropped the bomb. Truman didn't consult me."

As a matter of fact, the only way you could have lived through the last three wars without feeling guilt was to be Swiss. Why don't we all finally forgive each other? After all, as Lenny Bruce once said, the statute of limitations has run out. Would the Indians forgive me if they realized my relatives were starving all over Germany, Italy, and Hungary when their treaties were broken? I'd give them back their land, but there are houses and apartment buildings on it now . . . owned by Jews, blacks, and Poles, and we can't reclaim the land from them because we feel guilty about Hitler, slavery, and ethnic jokes. Perhaps if we all buy enough turquoise jewelry, the Indian nations will rise again and assuage our guilt.

So many of us cringe today at our parents' bigotry, and let's face it, everybody's father is an Archie Bunker. Expressions our parents have been using for a lifetime now make us squirm in our chairs. "He

Jewed them down." "I met a nice colored cabbie today." "He's doing all right for a wop." When you correct your own parents and receive that innocent, hurt
look in return, you feel doubly guilty. Consider, too,
your own innate bigotry and the mixed emotions it
causes. If you're a liberal white today, you can make
yourself feel guilty wondering why you don't have any
black friends. And why do you still feel a sudden irrational stab of fear when you see a group of blacks
walking toward you? An acquaintance of ours feels uncomfortable and consequently guilty because the black
women she works with dress better and drive newer
cars. She knows she shouldn't stereotype them, but she
can't erase thirty years of conditioning from her mind.
Neither can the rest of us. Flashbacks keep occurring.

If the plight of the minorities doesn't bother you,
try "we've created a rotten world for our children"
guilt. Or "we've created rotten children for our world"
guilt. If you are a parent, the two are interchangeable,
and either way you lose. You bought the products
turned out by all those smelly factories, and you raised
the generation of long-haired hippies that now picket
them. That makes you a polluter of both the environment and the culture by some folks' reckoning. Or
maybe you're an energy hog. Did the little car you
bought during the gasoline shortage give you a back-
ache on the highway? Did you switch back to a big
car this year, rationalizing, as Dick did, that it would
probably be his last chance? Do you throw your gum
wrappers out the car window so they won't start a fire
in the ashtray? Litterbug! Or do you throw the cigarette out instead because the ashtray is full of gum
wrappers? Firebug! Smokey the Bear will get you in
your sleep some night. Did you buy your wife a fur
coat or fur collar for your anniversary? You've contributed to the extinction of some innocent furry creature. If your husband gave you a fur piece, how can
you not wear it without feeling guilty? And how can he
go hunting these days without feeling shame?

We seem to have an unusual talent for taking on the
sins of the world and getting caught in a dilemma.
For two years, I used nonphosphate detergents and

watched our clothes slowly turn gray. Finally, visions of a horrified gym teacher comparing my children's tattletale T-shirts squelched my concern for environmental purity. I switched instead to white toilet paper, Kleenex, and paper towels so as not to pollute our rivers and streams with dye. Now our home no longer meets suburban standards of color coordination. Our decorator boxes never match.

Patriotism has almost done us in several times in the last ten years. All of us have legitimate criticisms of our country, and it had always been an American right to complain about the way things are going to hell until recently. Now if you pass a car with a bumper strip that reads "America—Love It or Leave It," you feel guilty. Watergate makes me prostrate with guilt. I voted for Nixon. Dick campaigned for him. *"You* helped put that man in office?" What can you say after you've said "I didn't know"? Dick used to be active in politics, as were many of our friends. Now we've all withdrawn to lick our wounds and feel guilty about the apathy. How could we have been so stupid, and why aren't we slaving away now to right the wrongs we helped cause? Because we're disillusioned, and in case you haven't noticed, that, too, has recently become a sin—especially in our Bicentennial year.

Did anyone besides us tire of the Bicentennial Minutes halfway through the year? How much red, white, and blue can anyone look at? And was anyone else confused? Didn't we see policemen arresting young people several years ago for wearing flag designs on the seats of their jeans? Hardware stores are now selling Bicentennial toilet seats. What's the difference? Attitude, of course—but whose?

In the early seventies, both Dick and I went back to graduate school. From 1:00 P.M. to 5:00 P.M. on Tuesdays and Thursdays and several evenings each week, we were part of the counterculture. The rest of the time, we were part of the establishment. Try coming directly from the office to campus these days wearing a suit and tie. Try driving a suburban station wagon that gets nine miles to a gallon around campus during the energy crisis. When my car was later traded for a VW bus to save gas, a new guilt occurred almost immediately. Hitchhikers automatically pick up their bundles and prepare to board when a van of any kind approaches because they assume another young person is driving. How can you disappoint them by being a middle-aged mother who doesn't want to get mugged? It helps when they give you the finger.

Car pooling may save our world, but how can you form a group to visit the allergist at two in the afternoon, or make a sales pitch to a client at ten in the morning? Are people staring as you drive your big, empty car alone and whispering "Don't be fuelish"?

Galloping paranoia does take over at times. If we aren't worrying about what others think of us, we're concerned about righting an impossible number of wrongs single-handedly. "It's all my fault" is simply Normal Craziness, and we bring it on ourselves. A friend was recently watching a local newscast and learned that people are healthier today. Good news? No. Our local Children's Hospital is losing money because bed occupancy is running at only 50 to 65 percent. Her first reaction, "Why aren't my children sick? They might save the hospital."

We're all becoming unhinged by unnecessary guilts, but we can't seem to stop ourselves. The Protestants have a group penance service, the Catholics have confession, and the Jews have a day of atonement, but none of these seems to be enough. Perhaps, as a friend suggested, what we need is a National Guilt Day, a nationwide day of atonement for all sins past, present, and to come—real and imagined. The President could absolve us all on network television. We could forgive each other, dance in the streets, and start anew. But will anyone dance with a lady who has bald house plants? Who watches "Mary Hartman, Mary Hartman"? Who pretended she wasn't home when the Jehovah's Witnesses came last month?

18.

Is Everybody Happy?

Let a smile be your umbrella.

Keep your sunny side up.

Every cloud has a silver lining.

There's always a brighter side.

Chin up, kid!

In America, you must live life with a smile, even before your toothbrush has had time to reach your mouth.

VILHELM, PRINCE OF SWEDEN

"How are you?" "I'm fine." The typical American greeting, the typical fib when asked about our present state of mind. "I'm fine." When was the last time you heard someone answer, "I'm miserable . . . I'm angry . . . I'm scared . . . I'm jealous . . . I'm unhappy"? At any given moment, any of those statements might be closer to the truth, but we don't dare tell. Let it all hang out? Don't be absurd! What would people think of us if we did? We've been taught to feel guilty and be ashamed of having negative feelings. Is everybody happy? Of course we are . . . every minute of every day. There isn't a flash of fury, a trace of envy, a speck of spite, a pinch of pettiness in any one of us. We are all great pretenders.

Most of us who are over thirty today were schooled in rigid emotional self-control, but men had more restrictions. At least women have traditionally been allowed to express their positive emotions freely. We can run around squeaking with joy if we choose. We can cry our way through a good love story, our favorite song, a homecoming, or our parents' fiftieth wedding anniversary. Men simply wander around after happy and moving occasions with lumps in their throats, hoping no one will speak to them during the few minutes it takes to pull the façade back into place, hoping the lights in the movie house won't go on too soon after *Fiddler on the Roof* ends. If men cannot be emotionally free when happy, neither can they allow great bursts of empathy, compassion, elation, fear, sadness, or sorrow to show. They can't even get excited without being considered unstable. Staunch at all times is the rule. Emotionless. Cool. How grim for men. And how difficult. Perhaps this is why there are more women in therapy for minor emotional problems, and more male patients who are seriously emotionally impaired. It's acceptable for women to complain of feeling anxious and emotional, and it's permissible for them to seek early help for those feelings. The same admission that all is not well, the same quest for help, is considered a sign of weakness in a man. So, are men really staunch, or have they simply learned to bury the symptoms and hope they won't fall apart completely one day?

In dealing with negative emotions, neither men nor women can comfortably let them all hang out. Anger is a prime example. Everybody gets angry; most of us either hold it in or are quickly ashamed of it when we let it show. Your wife makes a remark in the car that prompts an argument, and you screech away from the next stop sign or take a corner on two wheels. It's a satisfying expression of your feelings, but the moment the anger cools, guilt is waiting to take over. How immature to let your emotions show like that, to let your anger run away with you. Dick and I might have a good quarrel, after which I stomp out of the room, slamming three doors on the way to the bedroom. Before I even get there, the three satisfying bangs have worn off; the angry words seem overstated; the guilt takes over. "I shouldn't have done that. Now poor Dick will be worried and upset. I should have better control." I should, he should, we all should . . . but we're human. Why is it so difficult for us to accept that? A teacher was recently telling us of a temper tantrum in her fourth-grade class—her temper tantrum. "I screamed, I yelled, I threatened to dump one little boy in the wastebasket. It was terrible. I was terrible." "Did they deserve it?" we asked. "Of course they did. They were impossible that day. But I shouldn't let it get to me." How many parents scourge themselves with remorse with that same line after dealing with only one child? But the Scotch tape is gone again; the last ballpoint pen has disappeared from next to the phone; and dammit! Somebody used my razor on their legs again. *Boom!* And after the boom, we are instantly ashamed. "I should be above that," we say.

Above anger? Who is? Still, we were taught it was wrong. "Peace at any price" was the motto preached, if not always lived, in our childhood. Nice people didn't shout and yell; they didn't throw things; they weren't hostile; they didn't become angry. Nice people never let it show. Any expression of strong emotion was quickly squelched, in class, at home, in society. One did not raise one's voice in public, at a party, in a meeting. It made other people nervous, we quickly learned. It made us look irrational. It marked us as difficult. Even strong opinions made others uncomfortable because they smacked of emotionalism. One night while having a discussion of guilt feelings with a group of friends, one of them made some vehement statements concerning family pressures. After talking honestly for ten minutes, he suddenly stopped, looked around, and apologized. "Now I've probably spoiled the discussion for everyone," he said. But he hadn't. We are all simply too accustomed to bland conversation to state a strong opinion without worrying about it. "Be nice," we tell ourselves over and over. "And for God's sake, don't act mad." Smile.

When we're not telling ourselves to be nice, we're telling each other, and it often makes for what psychologist Yetta Bernhard calls a crazy-making situation. For years, the children and I have been urging Dick, who is normally very even-tempered (too even-tempered), to let his feelings out. We keep telling him it's good for him. But do we mean anger? And do we mean at us? One night, not long ago, the family was having a discussion in the living room. It had been a particularly difficult day for Dick, and after a few picks too many at his point of view, he exploded. He did just what we had been encouraging him to do for years; he threw his book on the floor, he yelled, he swore, he got red in the face, and stomped around. Dick McDonald? Old Calm-and-Cool? What did the rest of us do? Instead of applauding, two of the children sat frozen and wide-eyed on the couch, one scurried out of the room in case another eruption was coming, and I immediately began to lecture Dick for unfairly taking his anger out on us, for "making such a scene" over something so minor. I sounded exactly like a scolding mother from our own childhood; in essence, I was telling him he was a "bad boy" and making him feel guilty. The only one in the room who enjoyed Dick's explosion was our sixteen-year-old son Eric. He thought it was superb, healthy, and normal. "Congratulations, Dad. You finally popped your cork." Is that a compliment or not?

Honest expressions of anger are unacceptable and guilt-producing in the American middle-class home. Parents feel responsible for setting the tone and for keeping daily life on an even keel—no hostility, no dissension, no raised voices. We still want peace at any price. Perhaps that's why parents feel so guilty when their children fight—when they act as though they genuinely despise each other. Sibling rivalry does exist, but we try our best to pretend it doesn't. When it surfaces, when doors are slammed, when shoes are thrown across the room, when nasty, malicious things are said, parents are appalled. Why do they hate each other, we wonder. They don't. Our children simply haven't learned to bury all their normal angry feelings deeply and completely. They are learning quickly enough that if they are to get along, many of their true feelings have to be hidden at school, on the street, and among their friends. But for youngsters, there is still one safe place to let it all hang out: at home. And what is more satisfying than that solid smack with the wet towel? That nasty remark they wouldn't dare make anywhere else? "You're fat!" "You're ugly." "Well, you have zits!" They can cut loose at home because they know they are safe; Mom and Dad are continually hovering nearby to referee. Their anger and their emotions can't get completely out of control as they might outside the home, so they can have the satisfaction without the risk.

Most members of our generation have an overdeveloped sense of niceness. It was drummed into us in childhood, and often we find it uncomfortable or impossible to stand up for our rights, to tell off the pest who is bothering us, to deal openly with the gossipy friends, to show justifiable anger when we should. A year ago, I had an unavoidable collision with a large deer that left me scared and shaken, and turned the front of my Volkswagen bus into crinkled aluminum foil. In reporting the accident later, we discovered Dick had inadvertently allowed my auto insurance to lapse; I wasn't covered the day of the accident! It was an honest oversight on Dick's part, but a careless one, and although no one was injured except the unfortunate deer, there were six children in the car at the time. Thinking about the liability for what could have happened, I threw a justifiable temper tantrum. I stormed at Dick, withered the insurance man who had allowed the canceled policy to go across his desk without calling us, and generally made a pest of myself for a month, badgering both of them until I was satisfied there was proper coverage again. And all the while, I felt guilty. I had every right to be angry, but women don't get angry. Especially toward outsiders. Women aren't forthright in their anger—they don't tell their husbands they have goofed, even when they have. Women are perpetually nice. Assertiveness is particularly difficult for us, and each time we stand up for our rights, we feel guilty for cracking the image.

We could all use a healthy dose of assertiveness to

balance the ground-in niceness. Sometimes it helps to have a friend to cheer you on. Dick's assistant, Lynn Sherman, and I practice with each other, and then send each other out to do battle with the world. "Go ahead. March back into the supermarket and make the butcher take the bad piece of meat back. Get your money back, not a credit. I'll hold your coat." It helps to have someone encourage you and dust you off after you've been knocked down. Unfortunately, even a supportive friend can't always eliminate the residual guilt of seeming less than nice. By being firm, I finally had a faulty system in my car properly fixed after two separate sessions at the Volkswagen service center for the same repair job. I did it by standing in the middle of the service department, holding up traffic, and refusing to budge until my car was fixed. But on the way home, instead of gloating because I had finally gotten what I had paid for, I felt guilty. "The poor service manager," I thought, "he's really such a nice man . . . and it wasn't his fault. He didn't build the car." Why, when we have to fight to get what we have coming, do we feel sorry for the other guy instead of ourselves and guilty for winning? The poor butcher, never poor us. Dick feels guilty each time he brings up a problem at home for the same reason. "Poor Paula," he thinks, "look what I'm putting her through. I shouldn't create more hassles for her when she already has so much on her mind." Sigh!

The concept of assertiveness is sound. Of course, we should stand up for our rights, both men and women. But what if you really are softhearted? What if you don't like to fight? Or what if you have a strong streak of jellyfish in you, as I seem to? I don't enjoy browbeating people, and sometimes I am a genuine coward—especially with people I know well and will have to deal with again. Ralph Nader may be able to do it, but how many of us are capable of demanding a lead apron from the family dentist whenever we have a tooth X-rayed? I cringe just thinking about it. Or asking our family doctor what his grades were in medical school? Ralph, you're asking too much. Of course, we have the right to know before he puts a scalpel in us, but dying on the operating table seems simpler than embarrassing the doctor—and ourselves. "What kind of a nut will he think I am?"

Our children, as a generation, seem to be more assertive and more aggressive in pursuing their rights than we are. Many of them have little trouble speaking up to clerks, complaining about shoddy products, and making the necessary fuss to get their money back. Perhaps it is because their lives have always been filled with strangers, whereas our childhoods were filled with plumbers and electricians and merchants the family knew. They gave good service, had pride in their work, and it wasn't necessary to demand that things be fixed properly. It would have been unthinkable to browbeat Mr. Shultz the plumber or sue old Doc McCarthy for malpractice. Maybe that's where our hesitancy comes from—the memory of a personal relationship with the people who rendered services for us in the past. Our children have had no such conditioning. The people they deal with as young consumers are generally anonymous strangers, and for as long as the children can remember, it has not been unusual to have half their toys fall apart on Christmas morning, or find parts missing. With their experience of poor products and poorer service, why shouldn't they be naturally assertive?

Our generation, late in learning, wonders how much of our timidity is really fear of what others will think of us. How many of us back away from the confrontation with the unfair teacher because we are afraid we will be known ever after as troublemakers at the school? Or that our children will suffer later for our assertiveness? A great many parents bite their tongues and look the other way because they judge it to be the wiser course, or because they are not comfortable with conflict. Either way, they feel guilty compromising the principle.

There is a peculiar new guilt experienced by many women who have begun the first steps toward assertiveness but who still have to call on their husbands or other men for help occasionally. After you have asked to stand on your own two feet and claimed to be a big girl now, it's hard to go back and ask for help. But doggone it, we can't always get the job done ourselves, as embarrassing as that is to admit. The world still doesn't take women as seriously as men. A Milwaukee friend recently told the story of her numerous attempts to get the poor framing job corrected on a family picture. The manager of the store ignored her time and again, and all her attempts to remedy the problem failed. She finally swallowed her pride and sent her husband, who is six feet seven inches tall, to straighten out the situation—which he did with no effort at all. As she admitted, "There are some things I still have to have Bob do for me." And there's nothing wrong with that! Couples are teams; we are together to help each other. But to an emerging woman who believes in equal treatment, it seems like a compromise of that principle to have to ask for help.

For many women today, it's very much like saying, "Dammit, I won't cry!"; then crying; then feeling guilty about the tears. We're getting our emotional signals mixed—and our guilts. We don't want to win battles by crying anymore. We realize that isn't fair. But haven't we been encouraging men to let their emotions out? Haven't we been urging them to learn to cry? Are we now saying, "You go ahead and cry—it's good for you—but I can't because it's a sign of weakness for me"? Good God, more false images to live up to! What are we doing to ourselves?

There are some peculiar paradoxes concerning men who cry. With all that has been written and spoken about the unfortunate conditioning of men's emotions, it would seem safer today (at least a little safer) for men to allow themselves to be more open and human. But look what happened to Senator Muskie in New Hampshire. He cried because his wife was insulted. He was openly emotional and it ruined his chances for the presidency. Apparently we're still not ready to tolerate a presidential candidate who is honest about his feelings, who cries. A man must feel totally safe with those around him in order to cry today. We have a friend who burst into tears in a restaurant while having dinner with us one night. They were tears of joy, and he wasn't ashamed—but only because he knew we wouldn't ridicule him, and because he didn't know another soul in the place. He was safe. At another time, in another place, with other people, he might not have felt safe. Do some men now feel guilty for being unable to cry as some women now feel guilty for being unable to assert themselves? And which son feels more guilty—the Christian who keeps obsessively busy arranging every detail of his father's funeral because he needs to cry and can't in public, or the Jewish son who is expected to cry as a sign of love and loss at his parent's funeral and can't? "Maybe I didn't love her enough," said a Jewish friend, after attending his mother's funeral. His brother had stood next to him sobbing; he was unable to cry, and felt guilty for the lack of tears. "Should I have pulled out a couple of nose hairs to bring the tears and look good?" He is still asking himself that question.

Pettiness is another emotion we hide because of guilt. But we're all petty! We're not nice all the time, we're not always fair. We are small and mean . . . and human. We overreact. We overpunish the child who broke the camel's back—our back—or lash out at our husband or wife when we've had a bad day. Little things do get us down: the cookies burn, the car won't start, the toddler makes another mess, the dog leaves a puddle, the TV goes out in the middle of the only program we've been looking forward to seeing. We're crabby and irritable and impatient, and feel guilty because we can't make it through life with a perpetual smile. We keep thinking we should be above all that, we shouldn't let things get to us, but they do. Because our world is supposed to be filled with sunshine, we don't allow ourselves the normal bad day. Teachers have bad days, workers have bad days, mothers have bad days. And all feel guilty when they do. We try to become superhuman, smile through gritted teeth, walk around wincing as we turn down the volume of various things, and work at being extra nice to those around us whenever we feel rotten. Instead of going off alone, as we should, we plunge in deeper. And when we can't maintain the illusion, we pay for our anger, our pettiness, and our guilt later. To soothe our consciences, we take the child we yelled at out for an ice cream cone, we take the person who drove us to pettiness to a movie or bake him a cake. We buy off our guilt, instead of admitting to them and to ourselves we're just people; we have limits.

If we can't allow ourselves to be petty—a minor negative emotion—we certainly can't be resentful, spiteful, jealous, or envious. Those are wicked emotions, vile depths we won't admit to anyone. They don't exist in us, we claim, knowing full well they do. Who hasn't felt a little envious or resentful when someone else got the promotion, the raise, or the praise we felt we deserved? You should be above that, we are told. Why? These are natural disappointments. Who doesn't wish he or she had as much as another, doesn't long for an easier life, less struggle, fewer problems? And which of us doesn't resent it at times because setbacks keep happening to us and not to the Joneses? Love your neighbor? Sometimes neighbors are not lovable. They are not even likable. But we are supposed to love everyone and wish them the best. God said so. Mother said so. Someone said so. A woman at Dick's office felt guilty for years because she absolutely, positively detested a man who worked with her husband. She couldn't stand him (he was not standable), but she had been told it was sinful to hate anyone, and felt like an evil person for years. Why do *we* feel guilty because others have shortcomings or rotten personalities or are not lovable? I know . . . "We should be above that."

"Forgive and forget" is another rule our emotions will not always follow. We forgive those who hurt us, but are not able to forgive ourselves for being unable to forget. We allow ourselves to resent wrongdoing on a major global scale, but not on an individual level. If society screws us, we can become angry, resentful, and fight to right the injustice; we can march, sit down, lie down, be tear-gassed, or jailed. If a friend screws us up, we are expected to turn the other cheek and exude love and understanding. But who has not at some time resented the friend, neighbor, family member, husband, or wife who conned us, hurt us, let us down, or abused our trust? And who hasn't been hustled or used at some time and resented it? Most of us bury those feelings. We can't admit them or share them. They seem more wicked than the wicked deeds done to us because these are *our* personal sins, because we just can't manage the perpetual smile on the inside when we are forced to smile and pretend on the outside. A business associate of Dick's recently lent an old friend a large sum of money because he was in distress. The friend reneged on the debt retirement agreement after moving to another city. He is able to repay the loan now, but hasn't. He is relying on distance and Larry's good nature to get out of it. Larry is left holding the bag, along with his own resentment and guilt. Does one sue an old friend? Or does one swallow the loss, chalk it up to experience, and continue to smile? "Damn," he said, "I resent being put in this position. I don't like having to take legal steps against a friend to get my money back, but I need it now. I don't like the feelings I have about myself when I have to stoop to his level. And I don't like myself for wanting to wring the neck of an old friend." Some friend.

Most of us have found ourselves in that same position at some time or other. We do unto others and they, in turn, do us in. Smile. Swallow the anger. Turn the other cheek. Bury the resentment. Kill the spiteful thought the moment it surfaces. But who hasn't secretly dreamed of telling off the neighbor or friend who has been gossiping about us behind our back? Who hasn't wished to march boldly up to them, at a party, and say, "How dare you stand there and pretend to be my friend after what you said about me yesterday"? Who hasn't secretly wanted to see justice done from on high—just once wanted to see the ones who hurt us fall on *their* faces? My secret wish came true as a child. A schoolmate who disliked me and made my life miserable in seventh grade was a superb skater. She was the only one of our group who took professional skating lessons. She had a little red skating dress; the rest of us skated in jeans, and she never let us forget it. Each winter, as she whirled and twirled around the ice on our little local pond showing off, I would skate around the edges on my ankles wishing she would trip and fall on her face—just once. She finally did. It was early spring. The ice was covered with a few inches of slush, and several small tree branches, frozen into it the previous fall, had begun to poke through. In the middle of a spin, Jane hit one and slid a full ten feet through the slush, right on her nose. There has never been a more satisfying sight or a more guilty memory for a child. I had wished something awful would happen to another, and it had. For years, the vision of Jane's dripping costume and mush-covered face would appear, and I would be torn between glee and overwhelming guilt. It is only now, twenty-five years later, that I can enjoy the chuckle without the guilt. Time and distance have made it safe for me to be a little spiteful, a little human.

We don't allow ourselves to be human very often. The negative feelings of selfishness, of wanting something of our very own—even time—must also be buried. We feel guilty when we say "That's mine," whether "that" is the last piece of cake, the drumstick of the chicken, or the first glance at the magazine, the *TV Guide,* or the book we bought for ourselves. We give in to others, especially our children, submerge our own desires, and feel guilty for the natural feelings of resentment that follow. We fill the needs of everyone else first and are unable to say "I have needs, too." As the world becomes more complicated, as our lives become more hectic, as more and more people make claims on our time and energy, we frantically continue to try to fill all the needs around us. We keep trying to be all things to all people, and feel guilty when we can't manage, or don't want to—when we don't want to visit the sick friend at the hospital; don't want to go to the wedding in another city; don't want to make the duty visit to the elderly relative because our lives are already overflowing with other duties. Taught that selflessness is a virtue, we are often irritable that we can't be perfectly selfless, that we can't completely submerge our own desires.

Dick is a standing donor at our local blood center.

He is on call whenever they need blood in an emergency. A selfless act. But he often feels irritated when the phone rings in the middle of the night, or in the middle of his favorite television program. He expects himself to leap willingly out of the bed or the chair each time, and feels guilty when he groans and rises reluctantly. He should be above that.

Most of us feel guilty saying to anyone, whether it be husband, friend, child, "I'm unable to meet your needs right now. I have needs of my own and they are overwhelming." Instead, we attempt to meet their needs before our own, and resent the drain on our dwindling supply of emotional energy. Because most of us can't admit our resentment, we take our irritation with ourselves out on others. We snap at the nearest child, our spouse, our closest co-worker at the office . . . and feel guilty for that. We wind up fighting, as Dick and I did recently after both of us had a terrible day, over something insignificant. Both of us were unable to say that we were emotionally empty; both of us, knowing the other was empty, tried to be the ministering angel. "I should soothe him," I thought. "I should soothe her," he thought. We had a quarrel about integration instead, and we are both on the same side.

Fear is another negative emotion few can admit to feeling. Fear of physical danger, of trying new things, of not excelling at whatever we try, of looking foolish in front of others, of making a mistake; fear of embarrassment, of being hurt, of exposing ourselves, of asking for help, and—the worst—fear that others will criticize us or think less of us. We are all riddled with fears, but believe others are not, so we irrationally try to hide even legitimate fears. Riding with a slightly tipsy or reckless driver, we feel nervous and uncomfortable, but do not speak up. The guilt of appearing frightened seals our lips. Would we really rather die or be maimed than risk exposing our fear? It's an astounding question.

Unhappiness is the ultimate guilt trip for the average American. "What right do we have to be unhappy," we ask ourselves when we are. We are neither starving, nor oppressed, nor penniless, so how dare we feel unhappy with the middle-class marriage, the middle-class income, the middle-class life? By the world's standards, we have everything, and therefore we have no right to feel despondent at times, to want more, to quietly ask ourselves, "Is this all there is?" Is it sinful for Joe Provider to feel vaguely depressed, for the Happy Housewife to long for an escape from her wonderful life? Feeling down is an American sin. We hide it from our families, our friends, and the world. We feel it is unfair to dump our problems—such trivial problems—on others, to burden them with troubles we cannot even fully articulate. Our fifteen-year-old daughter Kelly felt guilty for painting a somber picture in art class last year. She was feeling melancholy and had been thinking about death, as all youngsters do at times, but the art teacher commented, "Kelly, that's so unlike you," and Kelly quickly slipped the happy façade back into place. We all try to keep the façade in place, and feel guilty when it slips momentarily, or when we admit to ourselves it is a façade. Is everybody happy? Of course. Paint a smiling face, Kelly, because that's what the world expects to see. And when asked how you are, answer, "I'm fine."

In childhood, we were made to feel that our negative emotions were invalid, wrong, wicked. "That's silly," we were told as youngsters when we expressed fear. "Don't be ridiculous. Don't be angry. Don't be spiteful. Don't be petty. Don't be sad. Let a smile be your umbrella. Keep your sunny side up. Chin up, kid. Don't be real." But these feelings are real. The lump in the throat exists. The bitter pill to swallow does stick in our throats. We are human. Our honest feelings are neither right nor wrong; they are simply ours. We have a right to them. If only we could make ourselves believe that.

Who are the most honest communicators in our society? Little children between the ages of two and four. They alone can shout, without guilt, "I hate you! Go away! You stink! Leave me alone! Gimme that; it's mine! I feel bad! I'm afraid." They don't know yet how wicked it is to be honest, but give them another few years with us and we'll teach them to hold it in. We'll teach them to be like us. "Smile," we will say. "It's not nice not to be nice." And we will pass on to them our heritage of guilt—or will we?

19.

Guilty Pleasures

If it feels good, it must be a sin.

LEAN BACK and close your eyes for just a moment. Conjure up a picture of your ornery boss or this year's snooty PTA president. Now imagine your boss facing the company's board of directors. He stands up to make a point and *ping!* The button on his fly pops and his pants drop to his ankles. He's wearing his wife's underwear, and there is a hickey next to his bellybutton. Now envision Madame President at the podium, looking her usual immaculate efficient self. Suddenly, her eyes widen. She starts to clap a hand to her mouth, but too late. She throws up all over the front of her beige double-knit pants suit—in front of three hundred people.

You can't do it, can you? Even when you dislike the people, even when they may have hurt you, badgered you, snubbed you, or driven you to the brink of craziness, you can't take mental revenge by picturing them in embarrassing, shocking, and slightly perverse situations without feeling guilty. Well, relax. Neither can I. We're all far too nice.

Blame it on religion, the Protestant work ethic, the Depression, or immigrant parents, but there is a multitude of innocent pleasures we are unable to take for ourselves. Fantasizing wicked thoughts is only the tiniest tip of the iceberg. Most of us don't know how to relax without feeling guilty. We can't accept compliments or gifts from others gracefully. We can't waste time—or anything else, for that matter—and we can't even crawl into bed when we're sick without feeling guilty. It's difficult and uncomfortable for many of us to stop watching that clock on the wall, to do a sloppy job or leave a job unfinished, or to tell the world about it when we've done a good job. Worst of all, we've been brainwashed into believing that total enjoyment of anything might cause the sky to fall on us. Sex is a perfect example. "I can't believe I ate the whole thing," as in banana cream pie, is another.

Take relaxation. We all understand the concept, but most of us are unable to *do* it comfortably. We have to appear busy, busy, busy every minute or those vague rumblings of guilt begin. Why? Because we have been conditioned all our lives to live up to busy and productive role models—the happy housewife, the dynamic executive, the dedicated doctor, the stalwart blue-collar worker putting in for his overtime. We've also been deeply influenced by those innocent clichés of childhood: "Time is money"; "Never put off until tomorrow what you can do today"; "Nothing ventured, nothing gained." When was the last time anyone urged you just to sit on your tail and take it easy? Even the advertisements for South Sea Island vacations show the happy vacationers surfing, snorkeling, and water skiing. And have you ever seen a person on television doing absolutely nothing—except the man who hasn't had a medical checkup in ten years? (And it is implied he'll soon die if he continues to lie in that hammock.)

Because of our conditioning, most of us are incapable of doing nothing without feelings of anxiety and tension. It's almost impossible to take the day off, lie back, chew a blade of grass, and daydream without guilt. Even though psychologists now tell us daydreaming is healthy, Americans have to call it something else in order to do it comfortably. Some people call it Transcendental Meditation, some people call it television. Dick and I used to call it Mass; now I call it "getting a suntan." Subconsciously, perhaps, I became an artist and a writer in order to daydream in peace. When writers gaze off into space for hours, they can rationalize they are thinking about future articles. When artists spend an entire day beachcombing and collecting driftwood, they can convince themselves they are being creative.

Daydreaming is slothful. Remember that word from childhood? A wicked vice it was said to be, and the very word made little children cringe. "Idle hands are the devil's workshop," and wasting time was, and is, a sinful pleasure. Too sinful for comfort, as a friend of ours, Margie Meldman, discovered several years ago. Margie is a passionate reader, but found it impossible to read during the day without guilt feelings. But, as she is a clever woman, she dug up another old adage to soothe her squeaky conscience: "Money Speaks." She developed a weekly book review column for a local newspaper so she could continue to enjoy herself in peace. Not everyone is so lucky.

While the average man is not necessarily a workaholic, few men are capable of enjoying their leisure time in a nonproductive way. A recent survey of four thousand executives turned up a startling pattern. Forty percent had no outside interests other than work—no hobbies, no recreational outlets—nor did they take vacations. That pattern fits the young bank vice president who recently told Dick he feels tense going to weekend movies, watching television, or playing cards. The only place outside the office he can completely relax is at the symphony. It is an educational and cultural experience, and, therefore, not a waste of time. (His mother probably convinced him as a child it would be an enriching experience.) Factory workers end their work week and putter around their homes all weekend. When they aren't tinkering with the car or the yard, they're putting up a new set of shelves, finishing the rec room, or straightening up the workbench. Very few men are capable of flopping in a chair without holding a newspaper in front of them as an excuse. And is it really boredom that makes Dick take something to read with him into the bathroom? Or is he simply incapable of sitting there "doing nothing"?

The average homemaker is as incapable of relaxation as her husband. "Grass doesn't grow on a busy street" and "A woman's work is never done" are two adages deeply entrenched in the American housewife's mind. Parkinson's Law, which states that "Work expands so as to fill the time available for its completion," might actually be closer to the truth. We've created endless amounts of trivia we call housework to keep ourselves in gear and in motion. The full-time homemaker spends eight hours a day taking care of her house; the employed homemaker accomplishes the same basic chores in five. The moment we find ourselves with a little free time on our hands, we search for new things to polish, drag the stove away from the wall in order to clean behind it, or join another organization. We can't sit still because the busy and productive person is the valued person in our society. And where is the self-esteem for the homemaker who is not constantly making and remaking her home?

One of the saddest casualties of our compulsive busyness is a happy retirement. Men work toward retirement for forty years, and then have no idea how to enjoy it. To be old and useless has become one of America's ugliest stigmas. Psychologists claim the key factor in a happy retirement is the feeling of being needed and valued. Yet how many American men (and, increasingly, American women) can feel valuable without work? It is not enough to be a worthwhile, good, and loving person. We need something to call ourselves, a label such as machinist, druggist, or insurance adjuster. Where is the self-esteem in being a retired salesman? Dick and I have been watching an interesting phenomenon for the past several years. One of our friends was fortunate enough to retire comfortably while in his late forties. Everyone who hears Greg's success story at first expresses envy. It is the American dream come true. But the envy is usually followed quickly by another emotion: bewilderment. "I could never do that," people say. "I'd be bored to death. What on earth would I do with my time?"

Most of us don't even know what to do with vacation time—if we take it. Many men pace nervously up and down the motel room or rented cottage worrying about the office or plant. Many women balk at leaving their children with a baby-sitter. "I really shouldn't go," we say and fret and dream up excuses because it's difficult for us to turn our responsibilities over to others without feeling guilty. Most of us are convinced no one else can handle our jobs as well as we can.

Whenever Dick and I plan a vacation without the children, I struggle with my guilt feelings right up to the moment of departure. And when I finally do arrive at the beach, the lake, or the mountains, can I lower my body onto a soft chaise longue and lie comfortably for a few days without twitching a muscle? Of course not. The tour guide button clicks on in my head immediately and I feel a compulsion to do everything, go everywhere, see everything, and get my money's worth. Relaxing is not getting my money's worth. The same thing happens to Dick at our cottage each summer. He arrives for the weekend and has mentally programmed himself to "enjoy" every minute: now play golf; now fish; now swim; ski, sail. Each day is an unspoken failure unless every available activity has been chalked off. Only the pouring rain and an occasional tornado warning keep him from wearing himself out. And only after six consecutive summers did he stop listening for the phone to ring. He still finds it difficult to lie in the sun and do nothing. Perhaps that's why he and I, and so many others, carry the compulsory magazine or book to the lawn chair, beach, or pier. We might as well get something worthwhile accomplished while we're getting that tan.

If it is difficult for us to do nothing when alone, it is virtually impossible when others are working nearby. How many husbands can comfortably watch television while their wives finish the household chores at night, do a little ironing, or bathe the children? An engineer in Pittsburgh was telling us that he feels guilty every Sunday night watching "Kojak," his favorite program, because his wife chooses that hour to read a story to their children. How many women can chat comfortably in the backyard with a friend on Saturday afternoon while their husbands clean the garage or basement? Only fictional housewives lie around eating bonbons while the cleaning lady cleans. Those of my friends who have cleaning help dream up excuses to go out on cleaning day, or manage to look exceedingly busy around the house themselves. They can't bear to watch while someone else does *their* work, or to have the cleaning help think they are not working equally hard. One friend, who recently stayed home from work with a cold, found herself scrubbing while the cleaning lady watched. Even Ernest Dichter, the nationally known market researcher, felt so guilty watching his gardener work he eventually replaced the gardener with a goat.

A year ago, I was working in my home studio one afternoon while our oldest son and his best friend put on the storm windows outside. When they reached my first-floor windows, I happened to be listening to a taped lecture that had some humorous sections to it. I sat inside, warm and smiling, while they struggled outside with extension ladders and buckets of water in the cold November wind. Did they suppose I was goofing off? I wasn't sure, but after ten minutes, I was so uncomfortable, I stopped working and made them some hot chocolate to soothe my guilt feelings.

Recently, Dick and I were working together on a major project that was overdue. We had reached a point where it was necessary for me to complete the next portion alone, and I decided to stay up all night and finish it. Dick's work was temporarily done, there was absolutely nothing he could do to help me, and yet he stayed up half that night because he could not go to bed comfortably while I continued to work alone. If I was going to feel rotten and bleary-eyed the next day, the least he could do was feel equally miserable.

"Time and tide wait for no man" (or woman) we were once told, and we continue to tell ourselves to hurry. My own clock-watching phobia grew so intense several years ago I found myself accomplishing less because I worried so much about time. "Oh dear! I only have two hours left to finish this. Oh dear! Now, there's just an hour left." I finally solved that problem by giving away my wristwatch and taking down most of the clocks in our house. I replaced the one in my studio with an egg timer that adequately gets me to appointments on time. I can work undisturbed until I hear it "ding." And my life is far more relaxed.

"The early bird catches the worm." "Early to bed, early to rise. . . ." Those innocent words now make it impossible for us to sleep late without feeling a little sinful, a little slothful, a little guilty. Do others deny their wickedness, as Dick and I do at times? Even though we often work late at night and sleep late in the morning, we find ourselves pretending to the person who phones at 8:00 A.M. that we've been up for hours. Or explaining in an obviously sleepy voice that we went to bed at 3:00 A.M. But at least we have basically the same sleep pattern. Pity the poor lazybones who is married to an early bird. A doctor's wife we know has been exhausted for years. She rises with her husband at 6:00 A.M. and stays up with him until midnight. He can get by with six hours of sleep; she can't. Why doesn't she nap? "How can I take a nap," she said, "when he's out there working all day?" Even a well-earned nap can be guilt-producing. What if someone catches you? What will the census taker or meter reader think if you answer the door at two in the afternoon with swollen eyes and tousled hair? He might just think you were sleeping. Or making love. (Maybe he feels guilty for disturbing you.)

One of the advantages of living in the cold and frozen North is an occasional Wisconsin blizzard. It gives all of us an excuse to break the routine and do nothing for a day. "Hurray! We're snowed in!" we mentally shout. Fate has taken things out of our hands; the responsibilities belong to God for that day. We can relax; we can even enjoy it.

Shoddiness is another word from the past that still

makes us cringe. "Well done or not at all." "Anything worth doing is worth doing well." Can anyone (besides our three teenagers) leave a job half-finished without feeling guilty? Or do a sloppy job without experiencing a twitch of guilt? Quitting anything, dropping out of any commitment, is an uncomfortable experience for most of us—no matter how much we hate the job or commitment, no matter how insignificant or unnecessary it may be. Once you begin to clean out the recipe file, you have to finish the job or it will gnaw at a corner of your mind until you do. The same holds true for your tackle box, your hunting gear, or the refinishing of your skis. No matter that you won't be using them again until next season. What would a world of quitters be like?

And what do we think of ourselves when we don't do our best? Not much. We've been committed to excellence for so long that each insignificant act must be perfect. We can't even give the car a quick wash without doing the whitewalls, too. "Sometimes I just want to screw up, goof off," a successful businessman told Dick recently. He can't without feeling guilty, and neither can most adults. We might take a word of advice from psychologist Abraham Maslow, who paraphrased, "Anything not worth doing is not worth doing well." What? Screw up deliberately? Why not? Practice your wickedness with a few small acts of defiance. Go ahead, burn the broccoli just once to see what it feels like.

Delayed gratification is another problem for many Americans. "Never put off until tomorrow what you can do today." Translated, this means we can't take a comfortable break until the entire job is completed. I drive the family wild each Memorial Day weekend with my compulsion to get our summer cottage completely organized, cleaned, and settled for the season. If it's ninety degrees, can I knock off work for a few hours in the middle of the day and come back to the spider webs later? Nope. No rest for the weary until the last cabinet is scrubbed, the last hammock hung, the last fishing rod untangled. Does God chuckle at my stupidity each summer and turn to a nearby angel and say, "Watch this"? He must. Every year, as soon as the last dusty dish is wiped clean, I walk down to our pier thinking smugly, "Now, let summer begin." From that moment on, it rains for two solid weeks.

But I'm not the only one. Few women can complacently leave their homes in the morning before the last bed is made or the last blob of toothpaste is wiped from the sink, even if they will be the first ones to return. And there are not many men who can walk out of their offices at the end of the day without that black leather extension of themselves, the briefcase, comfortingly attached to the end of one arm. A university instructor we know holds afternoon and evening classes several times each week, with a four-hour break in between. She finds it impossible to relax during those four hours, either at home or in her office. Only when the last class is over for the day can she allow herself to turn to other things. I sometimes dangle a carrot in front of my own nose. If the latest bestseller arrives while I'm in the middle of a project, I won't let myself begin it until the project is completed—but I tease myself by reading the front and back cover over and over. Whose voice is that whispering inside my head, making me treat myself like a little child? My mother's, of course. All of our mothers' voices, and those of our former teachers and camp counselors—the combined voices of a society thirty years ago. "You can't go out and play, Paula, until you've finished cleaning your room."

Letting people "do for us" is another innocent pleasure we deny ourselves. It makes us nervous, but what makes us think we don't deserve it when other people want to be nice? Someone pays us a compliment and we immediately belittle ourselves or the item complimented. "You look nice today." "Well, I wasn't sure how this shirt looked with this tie. Besides, my wife said the suit should go to the cleaners." "That's a pretty outfit." "Oh, this old thing. I've had it for years." Why can't we simply say "Thank you"? We can't accept gifts or favors any more easily. "Oh, you shouldn't have done it," we protest. "Oh, I don't want to inconvenience you." Why not? We're great givers, but we have never learned to receive. Which is not surprising when you consider that some of us were brought up on hymns like "Jesus died for a worm like me." How can a worm feel comfortable receiving, being "done for"?

"Love thy neighbor" is another maxim frequently quoted. Unfortunately, somewhere along the way, we forgot the tag line, "as thyself." Supposedly, we are as deserving as the next person, but we cannot make ourselves believe that. A recently divorced friend was telling us how uncomfortable he felt dating a new woman friend. "She spoils me," he said. "Nobody's ever spoiled me before. I don't feel as though I deserve it." Poor Dick suffered through childhood believing he was competing with Christ. His birthday falls on the 23rd of December, and for many young years, he felt guilty allowing people to make a fuss over his birthday because it diverted attention from Christmas.

Even when we're sick, we find it difficult to lie back serenely and allow others to take care of us. I have hobbled around with stitches, pneumonia, bronchitis, and pleurisy, doing "my jobs" after the family thought they had me safely tucked away in bed. I knew Dick and the children would be upset when they discovered the kitchen had been cleaned up, but that doesn't matter when you hear the sound of crashing dishes from your deathbed. Away you go like an old firehorse. Show me the sick female who won't crawl across the floor when she thinks there are dirty glasses in the sink, and I'll show you a dead mother. And men are no better. The only time Dick has ever remained flat on his back for more than a day was ten years ago when the doctors discovered a spot on his lung they suspected might be cancer. The minute he found out it was *only* pneumonia, he got up, dressed, and went back to work. A friend in Pittsburgh broke his leg in an auto accident and was forced to wear a cast for six months. He was miserable, not with the pain and inconvenience, but with his inability to pull his fair share around the house. To make matters worse, his wife had to drive him to and from work each day. How could an undeserving worm comfortably accept so much extra love and attention?

If we are undeserving, then it must be wicked to speak well of ourselves. We were taught not to brag. When I was eleven, a fifth-grade teacher embarrassed me in front of the entire class by calling me a braggart when I honestly answered her question concerning how many books I had read that year. She successfully closed my mouth for the next twenty-five years. To this day, I still feel I'm showing off whenever I share a piece of good fortune with a friend. Though I know the impulse is natural, Miss Salerno is still watching over my shoulder.

Taking for yourself was an equally wicked childhood sin. One did not say, "Gimme that! It's mine!" without reprimand. One did not shout, "Me first" or smile after winning the spelling bee. The smile would have been interpreted as a smirk. Why do you think Miss America always cries when she is crowned? She probably went to the same schools I attended, and joyous laughter in victory is unthinkable. "Me second" was so thoroughly ingrained in us as children that it almost caused the most embarrassing moment of my teen years. As a freshman in high school, I was nominated as class president, and believing it would be a close election, I wickedly voted for myself. (One always voted for one's opponent in those days out of humility. It was the code.) As the ballots were being recorded one by one on the blackboard, I had the sudden, ominous feeling it might be a unanimous vote for me. I would be humiliated beyond belief when the class learned what I had done. Thank God, one unknown enemy voted against me (probably the other candidate). When the election was over, it was assumed the dissenting vote had been my own, and I never told anyone otherwise. It's been my guilty secret for years.

The conditioning in selflessness and "Me second" virtually guaranteed that many of us would be unable to ask comfortably for privacy, items for ourselves, or demand our own way in later life. Whenever there is a simple conflict over which television program to watch in our house, the loser misses a show; and the winner feels guilty. I feel guilty when I insist on the new Barbra Streisand movie when Dick wants to see the Bogart re-release. And if Barbra's latest turns out to be a dud, my guilt is doubled. A friend who has been working to recapture portions of her own life sent this letter a few months ago concerning privacy:

> *At present, I'm assured by the family of two hours per day plus one half-day on weekends. I'll actually have time to get out my paints and brushes and* do *something without having to run out for bandages, butter, or buttons.* They promised! *Program canceled, however, in case of semicoma, severe bleeding, or convulsions. Wish me luck!*

Good luck, my friend. It's difficult to ask for privacy from one's family, and even more difficult to enjoy it without guilt.

Most of us are no more comfortable with success than we are with receiving. Repeat this statement out loud three times: "Everything has been going just great in my life lately!" Now, why were you reaching for the nearest piece of wood to knock on when you said it? Because, like the rest of us, you were warned to distrust the feeling of well-being. Complacency frightens most of us still. When things are going too well, we begin to worry. This life is *supposed* to be an endless vale of tears, so when good things happen consistently, we get a little scared. We stand around waiting for the other shoe to drop. As a Catholic friend told Dick recently, "We were never supposed to be truly happy on this earth. I am happy, and it scares the hell out of me." "Lay up for yourselves treasures in heaven," the Bible said. But what if you're laying them up here, too? Business was booming in a certain Phoenix insurance office last year, and all the salesmen sat around worrying and waiting for it to turn sour. They felt guilty and concerned by the unexpected pile of treasures.

Not long ago, a business associate of Dick's turned

down a promotion two weeks after accepting it because she couldn't cope with her own success—after working toward it for years. When it came, it worried her, upset her, and disrupted her peace of mind at home. She found it easier to reject the promotion than deal with the fact that she had become outstanding.

Another guilty pleasure we deny ourselves is wastefulness. "Waste not, want not" does make sense, but haven't we carried it to a personal extreme? Go ahead, throw it away, I dare you! You can't. No matter what it is, if you have it, you have to find a way to use it—or at least delay the wastefulness as long as possible. If you toss the green and orange tie that Aunt Minnie sent on your last birthday directly into the wastebasket, you're going to feel guilty. It must hang in your closet unused for at least two years before you can comfortably give it to Goodwill. And what about the fruitcake Cousin Mildred sends the family each holiday season? Nobody likes fruitcake, but Mildred made it, and for eleven years, you've guiltily peeked at the package as it sits in the back of the refrigerator until June. Your neighbors now walk through the door and automatically say, "No thanks. You asked me about the fruitcake last year. We don't like them either."

What do you do with hand-me-downs when there is no one left at the bottom of the totem pole? Years ago, to alleviate her own throw-away guilt feelings, I suppose, my mother used to box all her old clothes and send them to me. They never fit, but I couldn't throw them away either. Being the youngest daughter in the family, I assumed they had already made the circuit through my sister's home, so I would guiltily sneak off to the resale shop with them. (Mother, you never knew!) One day, as I was carefully spreading out my mother's designer suits, one by one, for the inspection of the nasty lady who would have looked down her nose at Jackie Onassis's clothes, I pulled out a suit with an enormous moth, long dead, attached to the breast pocket. "We do not want *your* things," Long Nose said in a voice of ice, "ever again!" I crept away with my mother's suits and the biggest single guilt burden of my life. Not only was I now going to have to *throw* them away, but that horrible woman thought I was shoddy. Only shoddy people who do half-baked jobs on their closets in the spring get moths. And it wasn't even my closet!

What else can't you throw away? How about leftovers? Can you dump them cheerfully into the garbage can, or do you have my compulsion to make one more creative casserole out of the single piece of cold French toast, the four squares of ravioli, and the lonely lamb chop? There is one marvelous mother-in-law in this world who alleviated leftover guilt forever for her new daughter shortly after marriage. "Pretend you ate it," she advised, "or get a dog." Can you toss out the house plant you've grown to loathe because it hasn't sprouted a new leaf in three years? Not if you are like most of us. One friend passes hated house plants (and the accompanying guilt trips) on to her neighbors. They have to keep the scroungy things forever because the plants have taken on the added status of gifts. Besides, who knows when Lynn might drop by to see how they are doing?

Another friend suffers each September from a severe case of tomato guilt. She and her husband cultivated a large vegetable garden for recreational purposes two years ago. The primary purpose of the project was to give this couple an opportunity to get some fresh air, exercise, and time together. Unfortunately, as soon as the first tomato poked forth its little pink head, the husband's frugal nature took over. He had been thoroughly indoctrinated with the "waste not, want not" concept by his immigrant parents, but nobody can eat that many tomatoes! After serving them three times a day for weeks, the wife began to sneak them out of the house to friends. Soon all her friends were also serving them three times a day, and still the tomatoes multiplied. Bushels waited on the porch and in the kitchen to be canned. "Help!" she wailed over the phone to me one fall day. "Pretend you ate them," I advised. "I can't. He'll know." No one has seen Chris since. She may still be canning.

Why don't people plant just one tomato plant instead of passing on the guilt to friends? What is this compulsion to be bountiful? Each fall, our generous gardening friends share their overstock with us and with other friends. Soon my own windowsills and refrigerator are bulging, and I am forced to take to the streets peddling the excess. Up and down the block I wander looking for takers. "Does anyone need tomatoes?" I plead. "No," they answer. "We've already gotten some from Hilda, Margaret, Eunice, and Gail." On the 7th of October each year, Lake Michigan turns pink for a full ten minutes as we all flush them down our garbage disposals simultaneously. And the sky clouds over with guilt.

Some people literally can't throw anything away and become pack rats because of their compulsion to make something useful and creative out of every leftover scrap and piece of junk. Creativity is all well and good, but watch yourself. When you begin to make entire Nativity scenes out of the tongue flaps from old shoes, your throw-away guilt has probably gotten the better of you. I confine myself to saving only practical items like the worn-out bottoms of my children's jeans after they have been cut off to make shorts. I now have two rooms full, and keep assuring Dick that one day I will make a quilt of them—or perhaps wallpaper the house.

Spontaneous spending is another difficult pleasure to allow oneself. For those of us raised by parents who lived through the Depression, impulse buying will forever be an uncomfortable problem. Most of our parents worked hard, didn't spend money frivolously, and diligently "saved for a rainy day." When I was growing up, I rarely saw my mother buy anything that wasn't on sale or without "shopping around" first. After seventeen years of marriage and a comfortable income, I still suffer a momentary flashback of guilt when I buy something that just happens to catch my eye; something I don't need, or that isn't marked down.

I can afford the item, but not the guilt that comes from splurging.

Dick suffers another typical guilt related to spending. He can be extravagant with others, particularly with me, but is unable to spend money on himself without feeling guilty. Whenever he buys himself new clothes, no matter how necessary, he usually picks up a little something for me to soothe his conscience. Most of us are uncomfortable with self-indulgence; it's difficult for us to receive, even when we are the ones giving.

Wouldn't you enjoy shedding all those unnecessary guilt feelings and starting over? Wouldn't it be fun, just once, to clean out the closets and not feel obligated to package every old skirt for Goodwill or organize a rummage sale? You could, you know. But first, you'll need to cultivate a healthy dose of wickedness. Start small. Develop your sense of the perverse slowly, and as one friendly psychiatrist has suggested, "Enjoy it." Throw an unanswered survey into the wastebasket; give a leftover pork chop to the dog. Use the children's unused Valentines to write excuses to the school for illness. Save your junk mail for a year and send it to an enemy. Package your hand-me-downs, ill-fitting gifts, and Cousin Mildred's fruitcake in gift wrap and leave them in your unlocked car to be stolen. Fantasize in the bathtub about the most miserable person you know. Visualize yourself at the next party calmly walking up to him or her and saying, "You are the most miserable person I know." Practice it until you no longer slide below the water each time, until the fantasy becomes fun. Wickedness can be fun, and for most good people, it is harmless. What constitutes wickedness for each of us is probably no more evil than stepping totally out of character occasionally. Out of character with our own conditioning and position in life—mother, dad, executive, Sunday school teacher, political committee chairman, Boy Scout leader, church usher, thrifty homemaker. Out of character with the expectations others have of us, and those we have of ourselves. Most of the pleasures we're afraid to enjoy are not wicked, and the guilt they engender is not justified. As a friend recently said, "What's wicked for me may be totally normal for someone else," and she's right. It depends on the conditioning.

Practice makes perfect and someday you may grow as wicked as I. When permanent-pressed clothes became widely available ten or eleven years ago, I allowed the ironing basket to fill with little frilly dresses and little starchy shirts for one full year. After a year, I felt reasonably assured that everything had been outgrown. I called Goodwill and gave them the clothes, the basket, and my iron, lovingly placed like a cherry on top. Never have I experienced a more wicked or more exhilarating moment in my life. And who knows, if I keep practicing, next Fall I may just be able to say, "No, thank you. I hate tomatoes."

20.

Friends

All that glitters is not gold.

THE RAPTUROUS ENCOUNTER with a long-lost friend must be a figment of some fairy-tale writer's imagination. Few experiences are more poignant or sad than visiting an old friend whom you haven't seen for years and finding after fifteen minutes that the two of you have nothing of consequence to talk about. This isn't easy to accept. Friendships change or wither, we outgrow people and people outgrow us. But when a friendship tapers off, ends, or changes, we can't help but wonder if it is our fault. What have we done wrong? Where did we fail?

Often, we've simply moved on—or they've moved on. It's like visiting a class reunion or a reunion of military buddies. What we once had in common, the experiences we shared and enjoyed, no longer exist. Those people no longer exist, and neither do we. Perhaps the needs which brought us together are no longer the same.

For several years after marriage, I made a point of looking up old high school friends on each of my trips home to Pittsburgh. It was impossible to pick up the threads after being away for years. College had intervened, a job in another city, a marriage, and a different life two thousand miles away. All of our lives had changed too much. The girls I once slumber-partied and giggled over boys with were married women whose lives had gone in many different directions. We couldn't recapture the slumber-party atmosphere (and Lord knows some of us tried). But I feel guilty when I now visit my hometown and no longer call.

Dick's hometown experience was a bit different. We married in Dallas, and shortly afterward, moved back to Milwaukee where he had lived most of his life. There was a built-in cluster of friends waiting —from grade school, high school, and college. But what began sixteen years ago as a legion has dwindled to a handful of people who remain close. Why? We've all changed—or more accurately, some of us changed while others didn't. We outgrew a few friends each time we altered any part of our lifestyle or our interests. The gang we once shared tailgate picnics with each Sunday afternoon during football season fell away when our interest in the Green Bay Packers diminished. They may still be there at the stadium each fall, but we're not. As some friends began to drink more through the years, our drinking decreased and parties that centered around heavy consumption of alcohol or barhopping became less fun to attend. We've heard similar stories through the years from several reformed alcoholics who found it impossible to maintain their old friendships once they joined AA. Former buddies continued to swap stories from their bar stools; our friends had to find new recreational interests elsewhere. People who make a conscientious commitment to an organization like Weight Watchers, or who simply want to remain slim, no longer care to be tempted by the gourmet dinner club crowd, or by those friends whose primary weekend activity revolves around dining out. When you no longer participate, or don't want to, in the interests that once held you together, casual friendships drift apart.

Often the course of a friend's marriage breaks up a friendship. Recently, an Atlanta couple confided to us their loneliness over the past few years. They have built a strong and solid marriage based on mutual respect, and it has become increasingly difficult for them to enjoy gatherings where sarcasm, drunken slurs, and put-downs are the norm between other husbands and wives. "And yet," they asked, "where else is there for us to go? Nobody seems happily married these days. We're made to feel out of place when we don't join in." So are many happily married men who travel, play cards, or drink with buddies. When they refuse to join the others in cutting down the "old lady," bragging about other conquests, or finding some action, they cease to be one of the boys. Happily married women find it equally difficult to listen to other women continually criticize their husbands as providers, fathers, and lovers over the bridge table or over the desk at the office. When values change, casual friendships become difficult to maintain.

Our interests change with time. Fifteen years ago, I was a homemaker with small children; so were my friends. We spent endless hours together, amusing small children. Eight years ago, I was deeply involved in the arts and crafts scene; my friends shared those interests. Today, I work. I write full time, Dick and I do a daily television show together, and I have little time left for coffee klatching, browsing in antique shops, or visiting art shows. Many past activities, although enjoyed, have had to be filed away. And many friends who once filled needs and blocks of time have carried on alone now that those hours no longer exist for me.

And it's no different for Dick. Fishing buddies from years ago fell away when his fishing time became sporadic. He seldom has time for the poker games he once enjoyed because new interests have filled those hours. The all-night bull sessions of past years have virtually ceased. As he has grown older, he realizes he can't solve the world's woes in one night—nor get up in the morning after trying to. Hunters, snowmobilers, golfers, and rock polishers all find that as their interests change, so do their friends. It's difficult to find ways to get together with the same couples with whom you have casually played bridge for years when you stop playing bridge.

But there's more to friendship than that, you say. Of course there is. That's why the few close friends remain close through the years. There was always more glue than a bridge game, a golf bag, or a case of beer to seal our friendships. But with casual friends, there wasn't, and we find that difficult to admit as we drift apart. "Was that all there was?" we ask. "Surely there was more. It seemed like more." We felt that way several months ago when we attended a gala dinner dance. Numerous couples we hadn't seen for years were there, and it was startling to realize how many people we had drifted away from in the past ten years. I walked around all evening feeling a little wistful and more than a little guilty. Had we really abandoned all those people? Had we let them slip out of our lives so casually? I felt better after discovering most of them hadn't seen each other for the past few years either. Still, I've often wondered how many other couples felt guilty that night.

Some of our early friendships were based on family ties. Dick's parents had lived in Milwaukee for most of their lives. Many of their old friends befriended us when we moved here as a newly married couple. But when the senior McDonalds retired and moved to Arizona, those friendships slowly began to dissipate. For years, Dick wondered if it was his fault. Was he too busy? Was he not putting forth enough effort? Should he do more for the sake of his mother and father? But it was only that another blob of glue had dissolved. It's been interesting to watch the evolution as Dick's parents now come back to visit and each time see fewer and fewer of their own old crowd. Like me with my slumber-party friends, they've been gone too long to search for the threads with everyone. Still, all of us feel that twinge at times for what once was. "We never see them anymore," we think wistfully, not realizing that they never see us anymore either.

Some friendships cannot survive change because the friends are not changeable. But their expectations and needs demand to be filled, and what you once were to them, they would have you remain forever. "Don't change," they say and resent it when you do. Friends can be as possessive as families, and their voices are second only to Mom's and Dad's in producing guilt. "I think it's wonderful that you're going back to school . . . starting a career . . . getting a promotion . . . opening your own company. But don't change too much. I like you (I need you) just the way you are." Few friendships can survive either success or alteration. The friend who tried to prevent change and failed may be threatened by the new you. And the attacks that follow always stun us. "Why?" we wonder. "I wouldn't have done that to her." Even when we know the answer to our own question, it still hurts.

Curt Gorrell, a young business associate of Dick's who attended college during the last days of campus unrest in the early seventies, was made to feel guilty by his friends for later joining the "establishment." "An old friend from the days of pure ideals heard I'd gone into advertising," he said. "He wanted to know how far I'd made it with 'Packaging the Revolution.'" Not far, but was it fair to make Curt feel guilty for altering a few dreams, for growing up to new ideals? Suzanne, a New York publicist in her late twenties, recently encountered the same hostility and scorn from a hippie friend, an ex-college roommate. Money is important to Suzanne today. An attractive apartment, a varied lifestyle, and a stimulating job now satisfy her, but she no longer satisfies her old friends. Once a California radical, a campus militant, the expectation is you will remain one forever. Why have you sold out?

For some of us, the admonitions and disapproval of friends are softer spoken. "We missed you at church/the Kiwanis meeting/bridge club/the bowling league/the political meeting." The implication is you are letting the group down by moving on to new interests. Change is seen as abandonment. A friend who is a doll collector recently began to sell off her collection to finance a return to college after seventeen years of homemaking. "How could you?" the other doll collectors demanded to know. What could she answer? "Because doll collecting is no longer enough to sustain me as a person"?

Some friends hardly bother to disguise their manipulation. They make friendship an obligation to be fulfilled in installments. They insist that we share their interests, activities, and problems, and make it next to impossible to refuse. Margie Meldman, a close friend of ours in Phoenix, was recently asked by a group of friends to be president of the Sisterhood at her temple. "But I don't go to temple," she said. "Don't worry," countered the group. "We'll get the vice president to go for you." How does one come up with another excuse after that? A friend of Dick's, who is a university professor with many free hours a day, pressured Dick constantly to take time off and to join him on urban affairs projects—his interest. He needed a playmate and still can't understand why Dick, with a company to run, is unable to be one. Last year, a woman friend who holds down a stimulating and rewarding job dated a man who hates his work and gets by with as little time and effort as possible. He constantly badgered her: "C'mon. Take a break. Get out of that office and have some fun. Have a long lunch with me. Take the afternoon off." He couldn't understand her commitment; what made her happy and fulfilled conflicted with his need for a playmate. She finally broke off the relationship because the demands were too difficult to handle, and she refused to compromise an important part of her life.

A Seattle teacher who takes her job seriously was recently confronted by another teacher who accused her of overachieving. She claimed that by reorganizing the curriculum, by volunteering to work on outside committees, by doing the best job possible, Louise, the conscientious teacher, was making her feel inadequate. Louise felt guilty until she realized that if the other teacher wanted to be mediocre, that was her choice, not Louise's. "If you want to be angry with me, that's fine," she said, "but you can't pull me down to make up for your feelings of inadequacy. That's what the unions sometimes accomplish when they threaten to beat up the new assembly line worker who works too fast. But this is a school, not a factory. If you look bad, it isn't my fault."

There are a few friends in each person's life who impose, who ask more than is fair, who recognize the soft heart and abuse it. "But you *have* to drive me over to pick up the kids this afternoon. My car is in the shop and Bob is out of town." Or, "As long as I have to serve on this committee, you might as well, too. If I have to wash clothes on rocks for the Bicentennial program at school, the least you can do is help me. C'mon, you know it will be fun." Even when you state honestly that it sounds like the least fun you've ever imagined, the pressure continues until you give in. And we all do give in at times. Selfishness is wrong, we learned long ago. And saying "no" to a friend who claims she needs you smacks of selfishness, no matter how unreasonable the demands. We forgot that it was selfish of her to ask.

The quietest voices of well-meaning friends can often be as guilt-producing as the quiet voices of well-meaning parents. We feel as much obligated to write back quickly, visit, remember birthdays, as we do with our family. Often we're as close or closer to our friends than we are to our family, and when we disappoint them or feel we've let them down, we feel equally guilty. Even as small a gesture as being lent a book or a record demands time and attention. A friend is giving it because of an interest you have shown, or because he or she is trying to share something precious and meaningful. If you're too busy to read the book, too busy to listen to the record, or if your interests have changed, you feel guilty. How can you say, "Please don't lend me any more child psychology books. That was a phase I went through last year and I'm out of it now"?

One of the most difficult facets of friendship is meeting our own expectations of what a true friend should be. "I will drop anything for you at any time, no matter what" is the burden we place on ourselves. The reality is that the only person who could possibly do that is the person with no family, no job, no interests, and only one friend. Nevertheless, we try, fail to measure up to our own standard of friendship, and flog ourselves with guilt feelings. A close friend of mine was bordering on a nervous breakdown last year. She reached out for help at a time when I was in the midst of meeting a book deadline, a TV contract, running a home with four children, loving a husband, and starting a new business. I almost had a nervous breakdown trying to be what I thought a true friend had to be—available, concerned, and part of her life at a time when I had no damn business trying to be part of anyone else's life.

But I'm not alone. Dick gets caught up with the problems of friends frequently, and he has no more available time than I do. And, he says, if one is looking for a guilt trip, try being forced to fire a friend who works for you, or one who is having medical, marriage, or family problems. Such is the plight of the company president who cannot remake himself out of granite.

Even our children at times feel pressured and manipulated by their friends. Last year, one of our daughters began to drift away from a friend of several years, as adolescents naturally do when their interests change. She was made to feel very guilty because the other girl had an unhappy home life. "Don't leave me. I'm so lonely. My mother yells at me all the time, and if you were my friend, I wouldn't be home as much. I could come to your house." How does a thirteen-year-old cope with that? Or a sixteen-year-old boy who falls in love for the first time and finds that his buddies don't want him dating steadily because that leaves them with nothing to do? Few of us, adults, or children, have the ability to say, "I want to be your friend but I don't want to be owned." Or, "I can't handle your problems right now. My own are overwhelming."

We expect to be all things to our friends, and that's impossible. We expect our friends to last a lifetime, and only the rare and beautiful few can survive growth and change, and be genuinely glad for us each step of the way. We should feel an overwhelming gratitude for those few instead of guilt for the many who have slipped away. But we burden ourselves with two sad illusions concerning friendship. One is that when we and a friend drift apart, it's our fault, that there was something we could have done to prevent it, something more we could have been. It's true, there *is* something we might have done to prevent it: we could have stopped changing, or we could have tried to stop our friends from changing. But would we want to do either? An old, dear, and most cherished friend of ours remarked that the most difficult aspect of true friendship is knowing when it's time to let go—and then being able to step aside without making the other person feel guilty.

The second illusion is that others have better friends, more friends, closer friends than we. From the thousands of people Dick and I have talked to over the last few years, the same wishful comments have surfaced: "We seem to go through friends rather rapidly; we don't have many friends; there are very few people we can count on or feel close to." The truth is, most of us are incapable of maintaining more than a few truly close friendships. It takes time, effort, and a great deal of love to be a friend. We are forced by a frantic world to scramble for inadequate pieces of time and spurts of energy just to meet the needs of our families, our marriages, our jobs. We have little left over, and the illusion of a dozen deep friendships is just that. How can we possibly be a true friend to multitudes? We are lucky instead to be blessed with a few.

21.

The Way We Were
(Guilt and Tradition)

*Can it be that it was all so simple then
Or has time rewritten every line?
If we had the chance to do it all again,
Would we? Could we?*

MARVIN HAMLISCH

You can't go home again.

THOMAS WOLFE

*Call long distance. It's the next best thing to being
there.*

BELL TELEPHONE COMPANY

IS IT GUILT or is it wistfulness? That sadness for what
once was and is no more? That vague feeling of wrong-
ness when the old ways pass? Is something really
wrong, or are some things only different? Life is filled
with transitions; we notice only our own . . . and they
are hard.

Time changes everyone and everything. Traditions
inexorably pass. Families grow apart and change.
Children grow up. We let go, sometimes with joy, sometimes with regret, wishing that life was as warm and
simple as it once seemed to be. Longing for the big
family get-togethers, we forget the hot steamy kitchens,
the work, the separation of men and women, the cleaning up. Which was the last Christmas dinner that
brought the entire McDonald clan together before everybody moved away? Was it 1968? The horrible holiday season of the Hong-Kong flu. Twenty-four sick

316

relatives, sick house guests. Too many people to fit around the table. Christmas dinner on TV trays. Too many toddlers. Too much spilling. Too much everything. It was awful! But as we now eat our quiet Christmas dinners with six around the table, it seems wonderful in retrospect. We said at the time, "Never again!" not realizing that "never again" would actually happen.

Most traditions have centered around the home, the family, and friends. Some fade naturally with each generation, and there are always wistful losses as children grow up. But traditions seem to be disappearing more rapidly now because of the accelerated pace of our lives, mobile families, and working wives. Suddenly there is a great deal to let go of in a very short time. Time itself is in short supply. There is no longer time for gracious living, as we once knew it, for the small kind gestures: fresh flowers for the hostess; homemade pumpkin pies for the family; the coffee pot always perking for those who might drop by. No one is home today, and if they are, a cup of instant coffee will have to do. Everyone is rushing. The kitchen doesn't smell like Gramma's apple strudel or something chocolate baking—at least not every day. And teenagers no longer want to hunt for Easter eggs. We give these things up, bit by bit, at times because we have to or because we want to—but all of it hurts a little and the smallest of passings seems to hurt the most. Perhaps a sprig of plastic mistletoe says it all.

For us holiday traditions have been the hardest to give up gracefully. Is it so with others? The end of Santa Claus was inevitable, of course; we created Santa and had the right to abolish him. We knew he couldn't last forever, but we miss the mystery, the suspense, the trips to sit on his knee; and wish now we had never grumbled. Our youngest is eleven and now helps trim the tree—in broad daylight. It no longer magically appears in the living room one morning, lovingly trimmed by Santa and two sleepy parents in the wee hours of the night. And although we are grateful, it doesn't seem quite right to sleep a little later on Christmas morning. Tiny tots woke us at 5:00 A.M. for so many years because they couldn't wait, couldn't sleep another moment. Teenagers now stumble groggily down the steps at nine, already knowing what most of their wrapped packages contain because they helped to pick their presents out. Little children no longer sit around the tree all of Christmas day playing with their new toys. It's hard to play with clothes, with jewelry, a new watch band, and the teenager soon asks, "Can I go over to Linda's to see what she got? Can she come over here?" The grandparents frequently send money now instead of gifts, and, of course, it's sensible—the sizes are too difficult to keep up with long distance. Surprises in clothing are often a disastrous mistake for teens who have their own definite tastes, and it is silly (and a waste of postage) to buy the record album in Arizona or Pennsylvania when it can be purchased here. But still. . . . And fewer people send Christmas cards these days. Some donate the money formerly used for cards and postage to a charity. Others have simply grown tired of the time and effort necessary to continue the ritual. We have. But every card that comes in is a reminder that we have let another tradition slip away.

And so it is with people all around us. A local grandmother, whose house was always a Christmas fantasy where one held tiny hands and watched small eyes grow big, now spends her holidays in Florida. Does she still decorate now that she is in an apartment surrounded by sand and sunshine instead of snow? The Christmas cookies, once baked to be passed among friends, were bakery-bought this year for the first time. No time to do it—only wistful desire. The outdoor decorating that died during the energy crisis has not been reborn in many neighborhoods. Is everyone saving energy still? Or is it one less thing to do for the busy people who gave it up gratefully? Dick and I felt guilty when we stopped hosting the annual Christmas Eve dinner for homesick friends who had no local relatives; when I stopped making the dozens of little homemade presents for friends and neighbors three years ago; when we started sending cans of popcorn instead. No time—except for the remembrances.

Dick's parents now have an artificial tree—a small

one that fits nicely into the living room of their condominium. I miss their massive fresh trees from the
past. How long will it be before the ritual of picking
and lugging home the tree becomes too much for us?
How much longer before pine needles in the carpeting
become too bothersome? Not long, I suppose. Our
oldest son was away for Christmas for the first time
this past year. We were happy for him . . . but it
seemed so strange with only five around the tree. A
phone call on Christmas morning doesn't replace a
warm body. Long distance is not the next best thing
to being there—there is no next best thing. The holidays are beginning to seem a little empty, a little out
of kilter. Whose fault is it? Some of the customs are
passing naturally; some we are deliberately letting slip
away. We don't miss the baking; we only miss the
cookies.

When did the end begin? Ten years ago when we
took the Cub Scout troop caroling, and only one family
out of five blocks came out to thank the little boys and
wish them a Merry Christmas? Eight years ago, when
vandals began to smash the Halloween pumpkins so
you could no longer leave them safely on the front
steps to guide tiny trick-or-treaters? Six years ago when
the suburban and city councils began to regulate
trick-or-treating hours for the safety of the children?
When a few maniacs began to put razor blades and
poison in the popcorn balls? When the kids grew up
themselves and no longer wanted the front door decor-
ated for Halloween, Easter, Thanksgiving, Valentine's
Day? ("Oh, Mother! It's embarrassing! You make such
a fuss.") Was it only two years ago that we first let the
neighborhood children eat the box of Valentine candy
because none of us wanted to get fat? Was it just last
year that a close friend tried so hard to round up her
children for a family visit to San Diego on Thanksgiving and couldn't? One went skiing; one went to El
Paso; one went out with her boyfriend. Did the children end it by growing up? Or did I end it finally and
forever this year when I burned the hard-boiled eggs
that were to be dyed for Easter? I was rushed, I didn't

watch, I had no time. And no one had wanted to dye them anyway. Except me.

Breakfast in bed makes me gag. My stomach doesn't open for the day until three in the afternoon at the earliest. But I miss the cold toast, the cold coffee, the cold runny eggs the children used to serve on Mother's Day. The food was ghastly, but the gesture was beautiful. Father's Day is diminishing in importance and excitement. A new shirt, a new wallet, or two new fishing lures from the hardware store don't have the same flavor as the handmade posters and plaques that read, "I love you, Daddy." Even our children's own birthdays change dates now for convenience. "Let's celebrate next week instead of this week because. . . ." And there are few surprises left. We ask, "What do you want?" and the gifts are picked out together—in advance. This year, at noon on Mother's Day, our oldest son asked—sweetly, "How long do you want us to hang around and cherish you today?" There was a Frisbee contest going on at the park. Grampa came for a visit not long ago and wanted to take the whole family out for brunch one Sunday morning, as we had often done years ago before they moved away. We had trouble finding a restaurant that served brunch— and where the kids could wear jeans.

We mourn the passing of traditions while hurrying the process along by our lifestyle. Table manners for children haven't been stressed heavily for years. We only notice the gaps when company is present, or when they are occasionally taken out to a fancy restaurant. "Uh oh! We never told them they have to keep one hand in their lap." The rigid rules of etiquette from our own childhoods do not have to be observed when dining at Taco Bell.

There is no more Easter parade, is there? No ritual of patent leather shoes, frilly dresses, and straw bonnets. People hardly dress up anymore, even for church. Perhaps the parade has moved to Florida, where everyone seems to be during Easter vacation these days. The preparations for the first day of school seem strange without the stiff creased new pants, the obviously new little jumpers laid out the night before. Instead, there is the new ritual of jean shrinking and jean fading so that new clothes can look instantly old. Will our children pass that tradition on to their children?

Strange is not wrong, we keep telling ourselves, but the telling is not always enough. Gracious living is dying, and the blame for that rests squarely on our shoulders. Our generation created the new lifestyles. Should we mourn the old, or feel guilty for what once was, when we cannot, or will not, preserve it? There are new ways of entertaining today. "Come to the club" is heard as frequently as "Come to the house." Taking guests out for dinner is easier on the working woman. But if Dick and I are typical, she misses some of it, and so does her husband—not the baking, just the cookies. There is a lack of warmth, real or imagined, to entertaining outside the home. We no longer enjoy large parties or have the time to plan and execute them. Small, casual groups of friends are much more comfortable for us today—and possible. But Dick still gets that wistful look around the holiday season and wonders, barely out loud, if we should have a big holiday party. And feels instantly guilty for putting pressure on me. I feel guilty because I no longer have time to be the gracious hostess.

Little touches once symbolized gracious living: the Good Life. Specifically, for the homemaker, they were the extra goodies for people you loved: the cheese-and-cracker tray before dinner; the planned time for a husband to sit down, nibble, and relax (without having to rush a child to soccer practice); the leisurely, well-planned meals with a touch of sherry in this or that; fussing, dressing up; candles that were all the same size, all the same color; silver cream and sugar bowls polished and filled at all times so that when someone dropped by for coffee, you didn't have to offer the plastic sugar bowl which at any given moment might contain four Rice Krispies and a hard chunk of sugar left when a spoon was dipped back in after being in the cereal bowl. Gracious living is symbolized, one friend said not long ago, "by all the little serving dishes we never use anymore, by all the wedding presents I've let turn black."

Most of the time, we don't think about the little touches and don't miss them. We've evolved happily into a life of coffee mugs and paper napkins. But occasionally, there is a small but jarring flashback. House guests! For the first time in months, I may suddenly realize that the windows we have been unconsciously squinting through are not going to look clean in the bright morning sunshine. And the linen closet is a jumbled tangle of colors, heating pads, and shampoo bottles. Can I get it all done before they come? Is it still necessary? But more than neatness and perpetual tidiness, I miss the thoughtful small gestures I was once able to make: the bouquet of fresh flowers on the dresser next to the guest's bed; the fresh box of Kleenex in the room; the fresh bar of soap waiting in the shower; the little dish of lemon drops on the night stand for someone who might get hunger pangs late at night; the table set the night before for breakfast; the leisurely five cups of coffee in the morning after the children had gone off to school; catching up on news; remembering what people liked to read and having those books waiting for them next to the bed; making paella whenever Burt Meldman came to visit, even though it took all day, because I knew he loved it. The time to do these little things for people we loved is gone, but not the desire. We don't love the people less, but how will they know that?

Society is pushing us onward to a new set of traditions. The other McDonald's has replaced our house when it comes to hamburgers and fries. Years ago, we could return on Labor Day from the summer in northern Wisconsin to find a cake on the kitchen counter, baked by a neighbor or a friend. A casserole was an automatic gesture on moving day, or for the family down the block when their mother was sick. Today it isn't done often, if at all. Colonel Sanders will provide —for moving day, for sick days, on the way home from vacation, and when the kitchen is being remodeled. Visits to the hospital have been replaced by flowers by wire and candygrams. Do we all mourn the losses? We couldn't, or we wouldn't have allowed it to happen.

A friend of mine was sick for a month last winter and I never knew until later. She works. I work. We are both out of the mainstream of local gossip. We keep in touch sporadically by phone and get together every few months. I missed the month she was sick. "Why didn't you call me?" I asked later. "I could have done something to help." "I knew you were busy," she said. Not that busy. Some neighbors got a divorce last year and Dick and I didn't even know until months later when the house went on the market. We have lost track of the small daily occurrences in the lives of all but a handful of friends.

But others are losing track too. There is the acquaintance who recently bought his wife a corsage—a sweet thoughtful gesture—to celebrate a gala evening, never realizing it would look ridiculous on the jump suit she was planning to wear that evening. Never realizing he would feel foolish for making such a silly gallant mistake, and that she would feel guilty not wearing it. There is the woman who lives on a nearby lake, who, like us, entertained family after family from the city every weekend, all summer long for years. "I'm sick of it all," she said last summer. "I'm cultivating friends around the lake. It's easier." It is easier, more relaxing—and yet, it seems selfish, after years of graciously opening your home to the world, to close it to all but a few. To stop cooking and fussing and changing sandy sheets constantly and enjoy the summer with the family.

What traditions will we pass on to our children? The question makes us nervous at times. When we no longer make spaetzles, or pirogi, or gefilte fish, or sauerbraten, a lot of our grandmothers' traditions will die forever. How will our children know how to cook ethnic food in the future if we don't cook it today? When Sunday night dinner now means carry-out pizza because it's Mom's day off? How will people in the future learn how to polish silver and set tables and arrange flowers and write thank-you notes—should *they* ever want to? They don't want to today. The children think the fussing is absurd. They love the more casual lifestyle. And yet . . . ? When I find myself scrambling around for dinner—"Oh no! It's five o'clock. I forgot to defrost something (start the pot roast, get to the store)"—the kids cheer. "Let's have an 'anything you want night,' " they say, and we often do. But I feel guilty and worry that "anything you want nights" are going to become our new family tradition.

It's easy to see why the question of traditions is confusing, if our family is typical, and we think it is. I was raised by a grandmother who believed chubby was healthy, who spent her life trying to fatten us all up, who spent her days cooking for others, and who, at eighty-five, complains about my mother, who is in her sixties. My mother runs a successful real estate firm, and to hear my grandmother tell it, Mother is a gadfly. "She *never* cooks! They run out to eat all the time. And when she *is* home, she *broils everything!*" No one wants all that food anymore, Gramma. No one wants all that cholesterol, and everything fried in a pound of butter. No one wants your strudel, Gramma, not even you. For Gramma has discovered—at eighty-five— Morton's frozen cream pies! My grandmother? The same one who told me when I was sixteen that pizza would eat the lining of my stomach away—It can't be. It's too confusing. It isn't fair to be caught in a time warp.

Those melancholy moments of nostalgia may be no more than a desire to have our cake and eat it too. We want to hang on to the old while we enjoy the new, and that isn't possible. We can't go back. We have to go forward. But neither can we obliterate the past. All right. But what is it that we want to remember? The tree lights twinkling in the dark, or the pine needles in the carpet? The laughter or the pain? The laughter, of course. And remembering the laughter is fine so long as we don't feel guilty about what is gone and can be no more. The farm family doesn't live here anymore. The back forty has been subdivided. Instead of rows of corn, there is an apartment building, a discount drugstore, and a Burger King. Do we mourn the loss? Not when we need a quick hamburger or a bottle of aspirin at 10 P.M. So be it with the family and with our traditions. We will continue to hold on to those that still suit us, and we will be brave and guiltless about letting go of the rest.

I love my life. Dick loves his. We would neither change things nor go back. But last fall, while whizzing down a suburban street, I passed a woman sitting on her front steps, wearing a tennis dress and leisurely arranging mums in a number of vases—for house guests, I presumed. For a minute, I wanted to screech on the brakes, to stop and go back, to be her. For an instant, I longed to be, once again, that gracious liver. But I went on. And for all I know, she looked up at the same moment, and longed to be me, whizzing past.

22.

Yes, I Can
(Coping with Guilt, Craziness, and Change)

We fear our best as well as our worst.

ABRAHAM MASLOW

My definition of a free society is a society where it is safe to be unpopular.

ADLAI STEVENSON

Who indeed can harm you if you are committed deeply to doing what is right?

ST. PETER

Beyond a wholesome discipline, be gentle with yourself. You are a child of the universe, no less than the trees and the stars: you have a right to be here.

DESIDERATA

HALF THE BATTLE with guilt is already won if you recognized yourself anywhere in this book. Knowing you are not alone, knowing there are others like you, is reassuring and freeing. Yes! There are others who are guilty parents, guilty adult children, guilty divorcés, disillusioned suburbanites. Yes! There are other decent, loving women who have had momentary flashes of doubt about the glories of motherhood, and other decent, well-intentioned men who, for a fleeting moment, have wanted to run away from their responsibilities. There are others who experience the same money and status concerns; who have the same

326

difficulty saying "no" or speaking up; who worry about their changing religious beliefs, worry that others seem to have more friends, worry that they are not meeting all the impossible conflicting expectations of this crazy world. And yes! I have even discovered one other person who has burned the hard-boiled eggs for Easter. What a relief!

Half the battle is won when we recognize our guilt feelings as such and begin to understand them: where they came from, when they developed, and why. "What you are is where you were, when," said Morris Massey, associate dean at the University of Colorado. And his statement so accurately describes Normal Craziness. Each of us walks through life with a composite of voices from the past and the present, which simultaneously speak in our heads. Separating the voices and understanding them provides insight, and insight is the first decisive victory in the war on guilt. Still, there is half a battle to go.

Prepare yourself for disappointment if you expect the other half to be won easily. Short of amnesia, there is no magic formula for eliminating guilt. Each pang of guilt has to be warred upon individually, and with each victory, the next battle becomes less bloody. But it will never be easy or painless; we will never become guilt-free human beings.

There are ways of coping, however, of feeling better, of outgrowing some guilts and learning to live peacefully with those we cannot outgrow. That's what this chapter is all about: sharing what we have learned through our own experiences and those of the countless others who poured out their guilt feelings to us. We have already examined the most common kinds of guilt and learned how they became a part of us. Now let's weigh those same guilts and determine whether they are worthy of the pain they cause us. Are our actions—the ones that cause us guilt—really so wicked and wrong? When we have answered that question, we can begin first to change our own concept of ourselves, and then our own behavior, eliminating those guilt feelings that hold us back. We can begin to feel better about ourselves.

Let's start with a rough formula. If we each walk around with 100 percent capacity for guilt, 30 percent can be eliminated just by understanding why we feel guilty and realizing we are not alone. Thirty percent of the guilt connected with temporary impotence, for example, is relieved as soon as we learn it is neither abnormal nor unusual, that millions of other men are experiencing the same problem, and that it is most commonly caused by tension, stress, overwork, anxiety, or fatigue. On that basis, the problem can be dealt with, and another 30 percent of our guilt feelings can be worked through and reduced, though not instantly. It will take time and courage to begin talking openly with a spouse about temporary impotence, and to reach a point where both husband and wife can comfortably face the reality that if impotence exists, it is a shared problem, but not a shameful one.

That leaves 40 percent. With temporary impotence, that 40 percent would consist of those nagging suspicions that you *are* letting her down no matter how understanding she is, no matter how often she assures you everything is all right; that doubting part of you that remains naturally skeptical ("Does everybody else *really* have this problem?"); that secret part of you that will always measure yourself against an ideal standard, because you have been conditioned to do so. So, 40 percent of the guilt remains—or the guilt remains 40 percent of the time. Is that so terrible? It's astonishing! A 60 percent reduction in guilt, a 60 percent increase in comfort. That's incredible progress! As Jess Lair said, "I ain't well yet, but I sure am better." Better means less pain, less fear, more comfort, more freedom. Better means an increased ability to cope with the next guilt feeling. Better is hope, and if the remaining 40 percent is not solvable, we can learn to live around it. We are not perfect people, remember? It is not a perfect world. There will always be conflicts and some residual guilt. But progress is freeing.

What's the difference between Normal Craziness and a guilty conscience? What kind of guilt have we been talking about in this book? We have not been talking about legitimate guilt for actual wrongdoing. People should feel remorse for illegal, immoral, or unethical behavior. There are five varieties of guilt, and only that one category is legitimate; the other four are unnecessary. If you are a hit-and-run driver, you have legitimate cause for guilt. If you crinkle fenders in parking lots and drive away without leaving a note, you should feel guilty. If you mug little old ladies, you have good reason to feel guilty. But these are not the guilt feelings that cause ordinary people so much pain. The Normal Craziness occurs when society changes the rules on us while we are still in the middle of the game; when what we were once taught no longer seems to be valid, but we can't get the old rules out of our heads; when we haven't done anything wrong, but it feels as though we have.

Normal Craziness can be identified in four ways. It is caused by:

1. *Inadequacy*—measuring ourselves, or believing it is necessary to measure up to others in every facet of life. Typically, we could use money, status, or sex as examples. The goals are too high or too confusing; nobody can win. But as long as the competition keeps striving, the rest of us feel we must continue the game too.

2. *Past expectations*—typically from religion, the family, and tradition. These are the conflict guilts that occur when the "Eternal Truths" of our childhood seem to be true no more. "The family that prays together, stays together." "Boys do not like girls who are too smart." "Masturbation will make you go blind." These concepts were handed down years ago by Mom, Dad, the church, and society, and reinforced by a thousand clichés. But the world has changed, and new knowledge has broadened our understanding. While we no longer believe many of the concepts, they are marrow deep and difficult to abandon without guilt.

3. *New expectations*—typically from television, increased affluence, the suburban society, and the

Sexual Revolution. We have been led only recently to believe that other families find instant and easy solutions to all their problems, that other Americans don't sweat, that other couples enjoy simultaneous, multiple orgasms twice a day, that everyone else has more, and is therefore happier, and that every other kitchen has a new garbage disposal. Frequently, the new expectations are in direct conflict with the old expectations, creating a no-win guilt situation. "Sex is dirty" obviously conflicts with the ability to achieve simultaneous, multiple orgasms twice a day.

4. *Manipulation*—guilt most commonly caused by family members, friends, neighbors, and acquaintances when they make us feel we are not measuring up to *their* norms because we don't want to do what they want us to do: join their organization, support their cause, come to Sunday dinner at Mother's, baby-sit for their children, chaperone their field trip. We are made to feel like bad people for not meeting *their* needs or being involved in *their* activities—or their lives—to the same extent they are. Beware! Manipulators are often individuals or organizations posing as institutions. When anyone or anything reaches the point where it can no longer tolerate criticism or dissent, it has elevated itself to the status of Institution. When it demands complete allegiance, it is playing Institution. PTA and the militant faction of the Feminist Movement might be two good examples. When you can no longer decline gracefully or move on to a new interest without being accused of abandonment, selling out, or lack of involvement, you are dealing with a self-proclaimed institution—and a rigid set of expectations. Mom can institutionalize herself and stick it to you, the Girl Scout troop leader can stick it to you, the union steward can stick it to you. They can make you feel guilty for simply wanting to go your own way, or for not being in-

volved in their interests. It is the guilt of the raised eyebrow.

Let's put our guilts in perspective for once. Are they worthy of the anguish they so often cause us? Hardly. When we feel guilty, it is because we believe we have done something wrong. But have we really done *wrong?* Is it illegal, immoral, or unethical to buy Christmas cookies instead of baking them? Of course not. Are you a bad, wicked, or evil person for failing to wear your hair short enough to please your father? Of course not. Charles Manson may be a bad, wicked, evil person. Adolf Hitler was an evil madman. You are hardly evil because you forgot to call your mother last night. It was not even wrong. Killing six million Jews—or one Jew—is wrong. Hijacking planes is wrong. Embezzling company funds is wrong. Leaving the house without wiping the toothpaste blobs out of the sink is hardly wrong. Watching the football game instead of cutting the lawn is hardly wrong. They are absurdly innocent acts by comparison. Making love with the lights on may make you feel guilty and uncomfortable, but it's not wrong. Gang rape is wrong. Child abuse is wrong. Slavery is wrong. Terrorism is wrong. Torture is wrong. But it is not a sin to feed your children pizza two nights in a row because you were too busy to get to the store. And it is not a sin to buy yourself a new car this year even though there are starving families in India. You are not starving them, and there is little you can do about their plight. We are such gentle little munchkins when it comes to actual wrongdoing. Our guilts are so trivial, so inconsequential, so insignificant when we measure them against real wrongdoing that their smallness stuns us. Why, then, do they hurt so much, and why are they so hard to shake? The answer is that most of us are basically nice people; we have no frame of reference for true evil, real wrongdoing. We have only our own expectations, and others' expectations of us, to live up to, and we are never quite good enough. But we are what we believe, and we've got to stop believing we are bad people.

Most of us are very much like little innocents who stick our tongues out occasionally behind Mother's back and worry ever after that we will be struck by lightning. We harm no one, and our guilts are seldom worthy of us. We keep trying to measure up to those imaginary women who are kinder, more loving than we, or those imaginary men who never have headaches after work. But we will never measure up because they are not real.

Perhaps the best way to evaluate any act that induces guilt is to transfer that act to someone else. Pretend someone else did it and see if it still seems guiltworthy. If our neighbor, Mr. Jones, confided that he felt guilty because the company's annual sales meeting was being held on the same evening as his son's first football game, what would we do? We would immediately sympathize with him, try to make him feel better, and remind him it isn't a situation he can control. We would sensibly try to alleviate his guilt. Why can't we be as humane and understanding with ourselves? Another way to put the deed that causes guilt into perspective is to ask if it will still be important twenty years from now, five years from now, next year, or even next week? Will it do permanent damage? Will it permanently affect a relationship, another person, or ourselves? The answer is usually no.

Some of our guilt comes from believing that others are watching and measuring us. But are they really? Is what we are worried about important enough for anyone else to care? Perhaps you have been feeling guilty for ignoring your messy garage for so long. It's cluttered, and you meant to clean it out weeks ago. What are the neighbors thinking? Chances are the neighbors are far too busy to notice your garage. They have their own lives to worry about—and their own garages. Reverse the situation. How often do you notice the condition of someone else's basement, garage, or back yard? Their dusty woodwork and their dirty ovens? How often do you notice who is missing from the open house at school? How often do you notice that a neighbor's child has a chocolate stain on his shirt? And do you care if you do? No. Difficult as it is for us to believe, others are seldom watching us. Nobody has the time.

How do we get rid of guilt? First, by taking stock. We have to recognize our own guilt feelings as such, understand our personal expectations, discover whom we are attempting to measure up to, whom we are attempting to please, and determine whether it is even possible to do so. One of the quickest ways to discover where your expectations came from is to stop the next time you feel uncomfortable or guilty and listen. Which recording is playing in your head? Whose voice is that saying "Bad boy" or "Bad girl"? Mother's? Dad's? The Joneses'? Father O'Malley's? Aunt Minnie's? Whether the guilt feeling pertains to sex, money, housekeeping standards, or relaxation, you can usually identify the speaker if you pause for a moment. Is their message still valid today? Does it conflict with a new or different message also playing? Is it possible to meet both expectations?

A good example of two conflicting messages is the *"Alles für kinder"* (everything for the children) expectation and the marriage expectation. In the fifties, suburbanites were led to believe it was right and proper to sacrifice and dedicate their lives to their children. Today there is a growing awareness of the needs of a marriage. We are just beginning to realize marriages are not necessarily made in heaven, and they do not flourish without continual time, effort, and nourishment. The new knowledge is in direct conflict with the old. If we devote all of our time and energy to the children, as we were taught, the marriage relationship may not survive the strain. In twenty years, when the children are grown, the marriage may no longer even exist. The current divorce rate seems to confirm that fear. We realize it is not possible to be simultaneously a momaholic or a workaholic and the perfect nurturing husband or wife. It is not possible to give our all to both. Something has to be compromised. But even the slightest withdrawal from attending the needs of either side causes intense guilt. Any woman who has ever felt torn between the needs of the children and the needs of her husband can testify to that. So can Joe the

Provider. And that is hardly the end of the conflict. A mother cannot give her all to the children and simultaneously meet the modern woman's new expectation of being fulfilled herself—having a career, or finding activities, interests, and stimulation outside the home. A man can hardly be the perfect provider, the perfect husband, the perfect father, and the perfect community citizen simultaneously. It isn't realistic, it isn't possible, but we expect it of ourselves nonetheless.

What else does the average middle-class American expect of himself or herself? How many different roles have we been led to believe we must play perfectly? Let's list them: good mother or good father, good husband or wife, devoted son or daughter, dutiful son- or daughter-in-law, provider, homemaker, working wife, conscientious employee, good neighbor, good friend, community volunteer, good citizen, active church member, union member, club member, organization member, political party member, homeowner, maintenance man, cook, laundress, chauffeur, animal trainer, handyman, gardener, landscaper, decorator, financial manager, social animal, recreation director, host or hostess. Those are the images most of us expect of ourselves—our goals. And these are the characteristics, virtues, or expectations necessary to maintain those shiny images: clean, neat, organized, successful, capable, devoted, devout, secure, relaxed, concerned, interesting, well-informed, with it, involved, active, sociable, sympathetic, understanding, friendly, sexy, virile, stylish, well-dressed, health-conscious, fit, and exercised.

There is a problem, as you may have already guessed. The time necessary to perfect just those images that apply to one sex would amount to approximately sixty-eight hours—per day! It is simply not possible to be and do and measure up to them all. It *is* possible to go crazy trying. To be well-groomed, you may have to give up the time necessary to be well-informed. In order to maintain friendships, you may have to steal the time from your children or your garden or your mother. If you decide to work for a political candidate, you may no longer have the time to work for the school, or throw the football around with Junior, or visit a sick relative. Whatever we choose to do, we will feel guilty because it prevents us from doing something else. We will continually fail unless we can let some of the expectations go.

How does one let go? Dick and I began by analyzing that impossible list of images and expectations. We asked some honest questions of ourselves and of each other in an attempt to determine what was really important to us, and what was not. You might begin by asking yourself the same questions. First, what are my goals? *My* goals! Not those of my mother, my father, my husband, my wife, my children—but *mine*. Which of those many goals or images do *I* want to live up to? Which are important to *me*? Good parent, good mate, good friend, host? How many can immediately be crossed off as unimportant or secondary? "It would be nice if . . . but I can't." Of the remaining goals or images, can each be realistically achieved in relationship to the other facets of my life? (By current expectations, can I be both a good father and a good provider, or a good mother and a working wife?) Do any of the goals or images I have picked as important conflict? Perhaps the expectations for each goal are too high. Unfair. Impossible. Where did those expectations come from? Who set up the norms? Did I, or did someone else? The previous generation? My parents? My friends? The neighbors? Are they realistic expectations for me, in my life, today? Are *all* the original expectations still necessary to meet each goal, or am I pursuing some out of habit? (In order to meet the goal of Good Mommy, is it still necessary for me to make the children's lunches now that they are teenagers, or do I continue to do it simply because I have always done it?) Are the expectations personally meaningful to me or are they for show? (Do I clean the basement because I like a clean basement, or because I don't want to be embarrassed when the meter man goes down there? If no one ever went into the basement except me, would I still clean it?) Are the goals for myself or for others? (Do I try to be a good provider by the current standards because I enjoy doing so, or because of what I fear my children, my wife, or the neighbors will think of me? Am I convinced piano lessons are important for the children, or was that someone else's idea?) Which of the goals makes me happy? Which ones are good for *me?*

Some of the goals should be eliminated if you answer those questions honestly. Once you have separated what is important to you personally from what is secondary or important only to others, you can narrow the list further. And remember, you are playing *"me* first" for a change. At this moment, you are only concerned with what makes you happy and what is good for you. Now, make a list of the activities in your life, social, work-related, home, church, parenting, community, etc. Which of them do you enjoy? Which do you feel are duty? Which would you rather not do— keep up the yard, attend school-related meetings, invite the Smiths back for dinner, visit your parents on each vacation? Which of your activities are unpleasant? Now ask yourself how you got into them. What pressure, what force, what person, what expectation began that cycle of activity? Is that force still present in your life? Are you continuing out of habit, or on the assumption that others are still watching you? If you were totally free of the expectations of others, what would you stop doing?

You should now have a clear idea which goals are personally meaningful to you, and what you would like to change in your life if you could. Now, list your personally meaningful goals in the order of their importance to you. What are your priorities? Money? Your relationship with your spouse? Your children? Your parents? Your job? Perhaps your children come first, followed by your job, your marriage, and your parents. Remember, your priorities are neither right nor wrong, they are simply yours. If you are married, it would be helpful to ask your partner to list his or her priorities to determine if there is a conflict. If your first priority is your career and your wife's first priority is your relationship, her expectations of you as a husband may be higher than you are willing, or able, to meet. But if her first priority is the children and yours is your career

—if the relationship is second for both of you—there is no conflict. Each can pursue his or her primary goal without unnecessary expectations.

Realizing it is impossible to please everyone, next list the important people in your life—spouse, boss, children, parents, neighbors, friends, etc. Put them in the order of their importance to you. Who are the people you want to please? Who are the people you think you should please? Whose expectations to be pleased would you eliminate from your life if you could? The neighbors'? Co-workers'? Your relatives'? Of those remaining, which people seem to have higher expectations of you than you are willing, or able, to meet? In other words, with whom do you normally feel guilty or inadequate?

At this point, you have a lot of lists. People who are important to you, goals that are important to you, a priority list, and a list of the close people you would like to please in the order of their importance to you. You have also identified a number of negatives in your life: the activities you would like to stop wasting time and energy doing, the people you would like to stop seeing or pleasing, the goals you do not want to meet, the expectations you no longer care about.

Doesn't it seem sensible to pursue your own priorities first? Since none of us can be all things to all people, since none of us has unlimited time or energy—or the sixty-eight hours a day necessary to be perfect—why don't we stop pretending? Why don't we concentrate our time and energy on the people we love, the things we love, and the goals that are meaningful to us? Let's be honest and admit we don't care that much about the rest; that we only do them for the sake of appearances or to keep the guilt monkey off our backs. There will always be some guilt because we can't do it all, but for the first time, we now have a method of choosing the lesser guilt. You know where you stand. If you are caught between the needs of your wife and those of your parents, and your own priority list shows your wife is more important to you, choose her. You will still feel guilty for being unable to meet your parents' needs, but it will be a far lesser guilt than if you had chosen the other way. It's as simple as that. And as you go further down your priority list, the choices become more obvious. Caught between a neighbor's request for your time and your own needs, a child's needs and a friend's, your own needs and those of your parents, look to your priority list. If you choose honestly, your guilt feelings will be minimized. The same method of comparison applies to activities and appearances. When caught between your desire to appear as a concerned citizen in order to impress people, and your desire to spend more time relaxing with your children, your favorite hobby, or the football game, and when there isn't enough time for both, follow your priorities, follow your heart. You'll be happier, more comfortable, more relaxed in the long run, and you can as easily find someone at the party to talk kids, dogs, or football with you as you can the new community sewage system. *We can't do it all. We can't be it all.* Let's be honest, gentle, and humane with ourselves—for a change.

How do we stop feeling guilty about those people we do care for, those goals we would like to meet, and those expectations that are still too high? Again, honesty—but this time with the people we love instead of ourselves. Make another list, but this time, list those people you would like to please and how you feel you are failing to please them. What expectations do you believe they have of you that are difficult for you to meet? What makes you feel guilty and inadequate in your daily relationships with them? Where do you feel you are letting them down? Are you sure you really are? So often our feelings are imaginary, and our expectations do not even exist in the minds of those around us. Why not find out? Take your list of guilts and ask the people actually involved if they have the same expectations you think they have. Dick and I are constantly amazed at how much we assume about each other, and how often we are wrong about our imaginary expectations and their resulting guilt trips. Whenever Dick quits smoking, goes on a diet, begins an exercise program, I sit around feeling guilty for not joining him. "I should," I tell myself. "It's easier to stop smoking or lose weight with someone else. He really thinks I'm selfish and awful because I won't do push-ups with him." But does he? Those are my thoughts, not his, and when I check it out, I invariably find I was wrong. He doesn't expect push-ups of me, any more than he expects me to join him each time he plays golf when I hate golf. I only think he wants me along. Do I expect him to stay up all night and work just because I plan to? He believes I resent his sleeping. I believe he wants homemade chocolate chip cookies more often. We continually overestimate other people's expectations of us and make ourselves feel guilty for nothing. "I never intended to make you feel guilty," he says. "When I moan that I'm tired or overworked, I'm only ventilating—not trying to get *you* to work harder." Surprise!

Check your image out with the people close to you. Ask them to list their expectations of you. Ask for a job description if necessary. Tell them what makes you feel guilty and ask if it's justified. You will probably be very surprised—especially when you realize how minimal your children's expectations are. But whether it be Good Mommy, Good Daddy, Provider, Assertive Woman, or Good Kid to your own parents, invariably others ask and expect less of us than we expect of ourselves.

All right, now you know your children never did expect you to be a Little League coach; your wife was only making conversation when she mentioned the Joneses were off on another trip to Disneyland; and it is a little easier to watch the game on Sunday afternoon now that you know no one has been wondering when you were going to clean out the garage. All of that is progress. The first 30 percent. But—your mother still insists you call once a day, you still have a difficult time saying no, and there are still occasional flashes of guilt when you try something new in sex, when your father asks if the children are attending Sunday school regularly, or when your working wife asks for more help around the house. More than enough guilt remains. The second 30 percent. How do you deal with it?

Before we deal with any specific guilts, we have to

pause to remind ourselves again (and again and again), perhaps each day for the rest of our lives, that *we are not bad people*. We are not wicked, we are not evil, we've been caught in the midst of stupefying changes, and most of what makes us feel guilty is merely change, not wrongdoing.

So you didn't call Mom last night. Some friends dropped by and you forgot. Mom will be upset. You will be made to feel guilty. But was it an immoral, illegal, or unethical act? Of course not. Was it an inadequacy? No. Was it a case of conflicting expectations? Perhaps. Your mother's insistence that you fill every void in her life conflicts with your own needs and the desire to be with friends. Ah. Or perhaps the daily phone calls are a manipulative move on Mom's part. Is Mom a manipulator? Now at least you know what kind of guilt you are dealing with, and that is a beginning. It enables you to determine whether the guilt is legitimate, whether you should feel guilty, whether you are a bad person—*no matter how bad you feel*.

You might even consider yourself lucky for feeling guilty. The only people who don't experience guilt are psychopaths, sociopaths, and fanatics. Those who can put the blame or the responsibility for every action on God, the system, or society feel no guilt. The Grand Inquisitors, the Nazis, the SLA, and the IRA feel no guilt. Those who believe themselves to be divinely guided or who follow a true cause can blow up buildings or blow up people without remorse. The Bible quoters can murder with words in the name of God without flinching while the rest of us feel guilty for the extra piece of pie. But who would you rather be?

The rest of us can begin to fight our small, painful guilts with a support group, whether those guilts are caused by departing from traditional beliefs, by conflicting expectations, or by manipulators. We need to know someone has been in this boat before—and that it stayed afloat. We need a hand holding our own. Support is not imperative in fighting guilt, but it makes it easier, so if you are going to try to change your life, don't make the walk without a friend. It's too lonely. It's too difficult.

Whether you are standing up to Mom for the first time, or dealing openly with sex for the first time, you need a place to retreat to—somewhere safe where you can laugh or cry, depending on the outcome, someone safe who will brush the dirt off your face and encourage you to start again. You need people who are for you, who are not threatened by change, and who do not have a vested interest in maintaining your guilt feelings. Obviously—and unfortunately—if you are a struggling-to-emerge woman and your husband is the primary source of your guilt feelings, he is not the right person to form the nucleus of a support group. ("I know you were late for class, dear, but you didn't take time to kiss Suzie goodnight. She cried herself to sleep, and now she has a fever.") You need people who are willing to travel the road of change with you, or at least attempt to understand your need to take that road. This is a case of "using" your friends in the finest sense of the word. There have been more than a few willing and wonderful supporters mentioned in this book whom Dick and I have leaned on at times, as we have leaned on each other.

The best place to begin a support group is with your own spouse, and within your own family. If the ability to trust and communicate is present, it is not difficult gradually to reveal our guilts, and to ask for help in conquering them. We usually discover those who love us are as eager to help us as we are to help them. Whether it be the painful emergence for both men and women from years of role conditioning, or their equally painful emergence from beneath a mountain of sexual fears, husband and wife can help each other reduce guilt more comfortably and more rapidly than any outside support group. Through openness, we can whittle down the impossible expectations, support each other when it hurts because the progress seems too slow, and slow each other down when the changes come too fast for comfort. We can identify with each other, for there are few guilts men and women do not have in common. We can say, "Don't you ever just want to get away by yourself for a while—without me, without the kids, without any responsibilities?" And when we recognize the affirmative answer as our own honest thought, we can give permission for the other to take some private time, knowing it will be given back to us when needed. If a man and woman can allow each other to be human, frail, and honest, there is no guilt they cannot fight together. And there are few guilts that can stand against a united front. "I'll help you if you will help me." It's an offer few of us can refuse. And two against the world is as invincible as a legion.

If a husband or wife is the likeliest person to begin the formation of a support group, the family is the next best group to begin with, even though they—Mom, Dad, the relatives, the children—often cause many of our guilt feelings. Most of them are not deliberate manipulators. They often have no idea they are making us feel guilty. Since Dick and I first began work on this book, there have been hundreds of discussions in our home about guilt feelings: the guilt feelings children have with regard to their parents; the reverse from parents to children; the guilt of being less than the ideal friend; and the impossible expectations present in all of our lives. There have been many moments of laughter as we identified with each other and realized how silly some of our guilts are, and many sessions of sadness as we first became aware of how we were unintentionally making each other feel guilty. What has evolved in two years is a standing family joke, now heard several times each day: "If you're trying to make me feel guilty, don't bother; it won't work." As we have each become more sensitive to the needs and hurts of the others, manipulation has dwindled because we now work at making each other feel less guilty, not more so. And no one says, "If you loved me, you would . . ." Very few guilt games are played; they aren't necessary anymore. And we all feel we have a place to come home to, and friends right here in the house who are willing to hold us up when we need it.

There are willing supporters waiting outside the home. They will literally rush out of the woodwork if you are courageous enough to speak up first. Declare yourself; talk to people about guilt; open up one tiny area or incident at a time, as we did in gathering material for this book. Everybody feels guilty, and if you are willing to go first, others will open up readily. "Do you ever," we would begin, and make ourselves vulnerable first. "Do you ever worry about what kind of a parent you are because you sometimes feel you can't cope with it all?" "Do you ever feel confused between your image of a good parent ten years ago and your image today?" "Do you ever get scared that maybe everybody else really is right and you're wrong?" "After struggling so hard to get out of the house, after all the help and understanding everyone gave, do you ever get scared and want to go back because it was easier, less threatening?" "Do you ever wish you could start all over and do some things differently?" "Does your mother/father/neighbor/three-year-old ever drive you right up the wall with demands?" Those are the kinds of questions that have started the talk flowing, started the sharing, started the support groups growing for us. Most people, we have found, are anxious to share if only we'll give them a chance, an opening.

Almost three years ago, my best friend sent us her copy of *Fear of Flying,* which had just been published. The book was already dog-eared and passages were underlined from front to back. "Read this as soon as you can and let me know what you think," she said in a note. "This book expresses feelings I never knew anyone else had." I read it, loved it, and sent it back with a long letter expressing my own thoughts and feelings. We seemed to be the only two people in the world who shared those feelings, and I remember the last few lines of my own letter when returning the book: "I love you for sending it and for sharing it, but do you know what's very sad? I can hardly think of anyone else who would feel the way we do about it." *Fear of Flying,* of course, quickly became the number-one bestseller, and the most talked about book of that year. In the homes of Whitefish Bay, the homes of America, men and women were quietly reading, identifying, and trying to put the same pieces of the puzzle together. How little we know about each other. How little we will ever know about what others feel unless we are willing to take the first step ourselves. We can go to the grave with our assumptions, or we can take one small risk.

Where does one begin a support group outside the family? Wherever there are likely to be people with the same problems and the same guilts. The emerging woman, struggling with the many guilts of going back to school or work, has only to look around her to find others like herself. Joe the Provider is surrounded by other providers each day of his life. Joe the Parent is surrounded by other parents, male and female. A sister, a brother, a neighbor, or a friend can be the beginning of a support group. The members of the Human Sexuality Class at the University of Wisconsin in Milwaukee are a support group for each other. Consciousness-raising groups, church groups, weekend marriage encounter groups, growth centers, Planned Parenthood meetings, workshops, seminars, or assertiveness training sessions can all be the right place to begin looking for others. What is it you need support for? Are you a married woman with children who wonders if she should work? Approximately half the married women in the nation are in the work force today. In Milwaukee, 43 percent of the married women work outside their homes. That means there are 195,650 married working women in our hometown. For openers, that's quite a mental support group. It should not be too difficult to find one or two who share the same guilts or doubts. Perhaps you have religious doubts. There are forty-eight million Catholics in the United States. In 1974, only 50 percent of them were attending weekly mass, so twenty-four million people in that religion alone obviously also have some doubts. Surely some of them live in Whitefish Bay—or in your town. Do you believe a husband should share the responsibilities of cooking and cleaning up? There are approximately sixty-four million American men who agree! And fifty-two million American women! There must be a few in your office or your neighborhood. Are you pro–sex education for schoolchildren, but wonder if you are in a minority? Seventy-nine percent of the population or approximately 169 million people agree with your viewpoint. Surely some must live in your school district. Supporters can be discovered at the water cooler at work, over a lunch table, or over a cup of coffee in your neighbor's kitchen, over coffee in the student lounge between classes, in a car pool on the way to work, or on a fishing weekend with your old buddies. Look around, and take the first risk. "Have you ever felt . . . ?"

What do you do with a support group? You use it to learn how others are coping with the same problems and guilts that plague you. A supporter is one who sympathizes, understands, or shares the same problem. Someone who consoles you when you feel you have been taken advantage of or manipulated. Someone who encourages you when you find yourself unable to say "no" effectively. Someone who tells you it's all right, you haven't failed, there is always a next time. Someone who laughs with you when all goes well, and who makes you laugh when the growing pains are hard. A supporter is someone to grow with, who isn't afraid of your growth. A supporter is a friend like psychologist Yetta Bernhard who shared with Dick the world's only foolproof method of saying "no," because we are all jellyfish at times: "I'm sorry, I am unable to do it at this time." *No explanations!* Repeat it if necessary, but no explanations. It never fails (except with your mother). A supporter can give you permission to begin changing your own behavior.

There is safety in numbers, and supporters can often be used to stack the deck in your favor. Years ago, I belonged to a bridge club that had grown out of hand. Not only was the food becoming a production worthy of The Four Seasons, but conversation had deteriorated to husband picking (as in pick-pick-pick), furniture refinishing, and child glorification. I wanted to withdraw, but did not know what excuse I could use and could not muster quite enough courage to tell the truth. A close friend confided that she also wanted to bow out. We decided that when our turns next came up, neither of us would set a date or call a meeting. We would just wait, which we did. We waited for months. There were a few half-hearted questions occasionally when either of us would run into one of the other women. "Say, shouldn't we be having bridge club soon? Whose turn is it anyway?" No one ever pursued it further than that. The club painlessly dissolved and obviously no one cared.

A supporter is someone who gives you permission to let some of the expectations go while assuring you that you are not a bad person. Ideally, husband and wife can best fill this role for each other. Several years ago, Dick and I were scheduled to attend a three-day meeting in Phoenix. We had an extra day after the meeting ended before we had to return to Milwaukee. Tentatively, we told Dick's parents we might drive to Tucson and visit them that day. Both of us were tired going into Phoenix, and at the end of the three-day meeting, we felt overworked and utterly exhausted. The thought of rising early the next morning, renting a car, driving the 125 miles to Tucson, trying to visit all the relatives in one day, and catching a plane later that night suddenly seemed overwhelming. Dick called his father and explained that we desperately needed a day to rest and would not be coming the next morning. "But why?" his father insisted. "You're so close. You can lie around and sleep here. We haven't seen you in months. You can't go home without coming to Tucson. Everyone will be so disappointed."

By the time Dick hung up, he felt so guilty that he had again promised we would come. But there was little pleasure left in the prospect. It was strictly a duty visit to please his father, and under the circumstances, was beginning to sound like torture. I stewed around for an hour, growing more and more upset about the necessity of always pleasing others first. Finally, I asked Dick to call his father back, tell him we were not coming, and blame it on me. "I'll be the villain if necessary," I said, "but I don't think it's wrong to ask for one day to ourselves, even if it does disappoint Grampa. He's thinking of himself and what fun it will be to see you. He's not thinking about you and the effort it will take to make him happy. It isn't fair."

That was all the support Dick needed. He did call back and firmly explained that we were not coming without blaming me. Five minutes of pressure followed before his mother took the phone. "Stay right where you are," she said. "I think you're being very sensible. And we would rather see you another time, when you are relaxed and can enjoy the visit too." We did stay in Phoenix, and felt a little guilty each time we thought about Dick's father. We needn't have. His mother told us later it was forgotten within a few hours, and after getting over his own natural disappointment, Grampa agreed we had done the right thing.

Perhaps you have an intimidating parent who still treats you like a thirty-five-year-old child and often pressures you into doing things you don't really want to do. You have difficulty adhering to your own opinions when he or she is around, or standing up for your own rights. Try stacking the deck in your favor. Mental support is a good beginning. Occasional physical support helps immensely too. If Mother is coming over, invite an encouraging friend to drop by, or ask your husband to stick around. Even an arched eyebrow, a roll of the eyes, or a conspirator's wink between husband and wife, friend and friend, can be enough support in the beginning when trying to break a lifelong habit of submission.

We often need different support groups for different problems and different guilts. Several of our friends are members of Weight Watchers. It is an organized support group that gives them permission to stop baking, buying, and eating the kind or amount of food Mother or Grandmother taught them to eat years ago. It is a support group for breaking habit patterns, as are Alcoholics Anonymous, Smoke-Enders, and other such organizations. But often, one kindred soul can be more than adequate for support. One other dieter, emerging man or woman, working mother, perplexed provider, or honest parent who no longer wants to play one-upmanship; one other divorcé, one other person a little more sexually secure than we are. So often, they are all we need to begin reevaluating our guilt feelings and changing our own behavior.

How do we determine what we would like to change in our lives? How do we know what is important and worth the price of change? Remember all those lists you made at the beginning of this chapter? There were some uncomfortable and unrealistic images to be lived up to; some impossible expectations; some unpleasant or unnecessary activities. Take a look at those again. Ask: Which ones make me feel guilty? Which are holding me back? Who makes me uncomfortable? What would I like to change?

There are two short exercises Dick and I often use to determine what is important to us and what we would like to change. Both exercises are simple, and at times help to click our confused feelings into sudden sharper focus. The first entails taking a few, quiet moments alone and asking yourself: What would I do with my time if I learned this was to be my last hour on earth? Now measure the importance of the various aspects of your life—people, activities, expectations—against that question and try to answer it honestly. Would you use part of that hour to attend a meeting in order to be seen? Would you race through the house with a can of Pledge so the furniture would sparkle after your funeral? Would it matter in the least that the children's underwear was slightly frayed? Well, what would you do with that hour? Whom would you want to be with? And would you still be afraid to cry with them? That little exercise can tell you a great deal about what is important in your life and what isn't, who is important to you and who isn't.

The second exercise is a bit different. Imagine picking up the morning paper tomorrow to find this headline: ARTIFICIAL ORGANS PERFECTED. LIFE EXPECTANCY JUMPS TO 120! Another eighty or ninety years for most of us to live! What would you have to change in your relationship with a husband or wife to survive another eighty years together? If he makes you feel guilty by constant criticisms or put-downs, can you live with that another eighty years? If she makes you feel inadequate as a father or husband, can you live with those guilt feelings for another eighty years? What aspects of all your relationships would have to be changed? With your mate? With your parents? With your children? With your friends? And with eighty more years to make yourself over, what would you like to change about yourself? You should now know what is important to you and what you would like to change. Gather your support group and begin.

But don't try to change your entire life at once. One step at a time; don't overload your circuits. Don't set yourself up for failure by taking on the whole world, or cause yourself and your loved ones vast discomfort, pain, and new guilt by burning all your bridges at once. Make a plan for changing one aspect of your life only. Put one small victory under your belt and then lie back and allow yourself to become comfortable with it before deciding on the next step. Do you need privacy? Don't begin by demanding a month alone in Tokyo. Your family won't be able to handle that much change, and neither will you. It's an unreasonable beginning. Settle for an afternoon alone each weekend. Or take an overnight fishing or camping trip. As a couple, try a weekend visit to a friend's home or a local motel— without the children. If you want to go back to school, don't plunge in with a full semester load. Give your husband and children a chance to become more self-sufficient on a gradual basis. Give yourself a chance to cope with the new guilt feelings of withdrawal (and you will have some) on a gradual basis. Start with a few credits and add more each semester as you become more confident, as the family becomes more confident. If you decide to uncomplicate your life or revamp your lifestyle to gain more free time, don't resign from everything at once. Resign from your least favorite activity first and see how it feels before taking the next step. If you want to put the relationship between you and your mother on a more adult basis, don't go to war with her. It is too guilt-producing, and it is seldom necessary. Gradually disengage instead. If you are too easily manipulated or too dependent on her approval, take a baby step to build your confidence. Plan one small change. "The next three visists to Mother's I will stay exactly fifteen minutes and then have a good and undebatable reason to leave." See how you feel afterward. Wait until you are secure and comfortable with that step before taking the next.

Commit yourself to a small change, commit yourself

to the first step, and then act. No excuses. Don't wallow in self-pity waiting for someone else to swoop down and change your life. It's not going to happen! If you have a long-standing sexual problem, for example, make that first phone call to find professional help. It doesn't matter to whom—your minister, your doctor, your local hospital—make it! Stop saying "Isn't it awful" and take hold of your own life.

Reward yourself for each small victory. They are really enormous victories. Enjoy them. If you want to wallow in something, wallow in achievement: the first time you walked out of the house without making every bed; the first time you said, "I have a right to some time. I would like to watch this football game. *It's mine!*" Don't expect perfection from yourself, and don't rush on to the next victory too soon. Enjoy what you have accomplished, that feeling of getting some part of your life back under control. Tomorrow is soon enough for the next step, for the rest. Slow, steady progress is sweet. Brag a little. Let your support group applaud. Take a bow. You deserve it.

To make the process of change a bit easier, there are a few tips we have learned from our own experiences and from the experiences of those who have been willing to share them with us. First, consider finding an authority figure to back you up. Most of us were raised on black-and-white values and unequivocal opinions. Some authority figure, whether in religion, the family, or society, handed the rules to us. In order to change those rules comfortably, we may need a new authority figure to give us permission to abandon our guilt. A woman from San Diego called Dick not long ago. She had read our first book, *Loving Free,* and was seeking advice on where to turn with a sex problem. She was happily married, but a recent operation had made it impossible for her to have intercourse. Obviously, she was concerned about her husband's needs and the future of their marriage. Her childhood Methodist upbringing had been filled with strict sexual taboos—no oral sex, no masturbation, no sex for pleasure. Dick asked if she had spoken to any Methodist minister about sex since the operation. The answer was no. "Then I suggest you find one," he said. "And if the first minister you talk to is not a permission-giver, call a second or a third until you find someone who will tell you it is not sinful to keep your marriage intact." Shop around for an authority figure? If you have to. If you believe the action is neither immoral, unethical, nor illegal, but you still can't get rid of the guilt because of past conditioning, find a permission-giver.

Second, consider varying your peer group. If you have been immersed in middle-class suburbia for a number of years, consider expanding (not abandoning) your circle of friends. When everyone does things one way, it soon becomes the "right way," and the longer one remains in that kind of environment, the more difficult it is to maintain perspective and to dare to be different. Give yourself an opportunity to discover there are others who have not had the same conditioning, who can guiltlessly do the things you hesitate to do. A move, a job change, even a fresh start in a different suburb can provide the opportunity to begin again with a clean slate—and no preconceived expectations. Even joining a few new organizations or pursuing a few totally different activities can widen your perspective.

It is difficult to change within the old environment because so many people in it have a vested interest in the old you. A woman we know who had been a lifelong Milwaukee resident moved to the West Coast several years ago. She blossomed out there and was happier and more involved than she had ever been. There were no old friends or family members to remind her of the old Ginny, or to criticize her new interests and activities, all of which were wholesome and exciting. Two years later, a job change brought her back to Milwaukee, and within six months, she had shriveled into the same narrow person she had been all her life. Why? "I was happy with the changes," she said, "but when I came home, people wouldn't accept a new me. I had to become the old me to please them and get along."

Develop a new antenna for your own protection. Learn to listen for certain words and phrases like *ought, should,* and *must,* in conversations at the office, at parties, and within your own home. They signal manipulation, witting or unwitting. Ask yourself, "Is what these people are suggesting I *should* do good for me, or good for them?" It usually turns out to be good for them, or the cause they represent. Another way to reduce manipulation is to learn to ask for *opinions* from others, not *advice*. If you ask for advice, you are put in the position of having to accept or reject it. If you ask for an opinion instead, you retain freedom of choice.

If possible, eliminate or diminish the influence in your life of people who make you feel guilty, or who have unacceptable expectations of you, or who make demands on you that you no longer care to meet. Remove yourself from uncomfortable situations and disengage from people who make you feel unwarranted guilt. If the others in the car pool insist on stopping off for a few drinks each night after work, and you would rather go directly home, change car pools or drive yourself. If there are constant digs at the poker club because your wife has gone back to work, get out of that poker club. If there are repeated comments at bridge club about your ability to manage your home properly now that you have gone back to school, drop out of the bridge club. People who continually make you feel defensive are manipulative. They obviously do not have your best interests at heart, or they wouldn't deliberately attempt to make you feel different, inadequate, or guilty. You don't deserve that—you haven't done anything *wrong,* remember? And stop trying to be the *perfect* ——— while letting others fill in the blank. It is far easier to change yourself than to change the bridge club, or the poker club. It is less painful to find a new bridge club than to do battle with the old.

As you change, be prepared to say goodbye. It is a sad truth, but not everyone will wish you well as you change and begin to reduce your own guilts. As old companions see you changing and freeing yourself, bit by bit, from inhibitors, it will remind them of how shackled they still are. A few will love you for the example; many will hate you for the comparison; some will resent you for doing what they cannot do themselves.

Yetta Bernhard, who is a close personal friend of ours and one of the all-time great guilt-reducers and permission-givers, has coined a profound statement for guilt management: "Endure the guilt and enjoy the action." What is she saying? Some new actions are worth the guilt they initially cause—and that guilt will usually diminish with time and the repetition of the action. Only the transition period is painful, and practice makes perfect. In the meantime, suffer the guilt while you enjoy. Enjoy sleeping late, and so what if you feel a little guilty when you wake up. Endure the guilt of saying, "No, I don't want to baby-sit for your children," and enjoy the five free hours. Tell your mother you can't make Sunday dinner this week and enjoy taking a bike ride with your children instead. Accept the small guilt which accompanies it as the price of change.

It is a startling concept: that we can measure the guilt of saying "no" against the pleasure derived from saying "no" or the energy saved by saying "no." A moment of guilt to save hours of doing something we don't want to do. When we first bought our summer home nine years ago, the property had been manicured by the former owner, a retired Chicago landscaper. Three acres of petunias and geraniums in the north woods of Wisconsin. With four babies to watch, I begrudgingly spent the next two summers keeping the property in *perfect* condition, in case the former owner dropped in to check up. He occasionally did. In the middle of the third summer, I looked around one day and thought, "This is our property—not his. I don't even like petunias. And this is the Nicolet National forest! It should look like a forest." I proceeded to let the acres of gardens go back to their natural piney and blueberry state, but I still worried about what the landscaper would think when he next stopped in. When he did, he stayed for only ten minutes and said nothing. His disapproval was apparent. But it didn't matter because I had already learned the value of measuring the guilt against the action—ten minutes of guilt compared to hundreds of hours of weeding petunias in the middle of a forest!

So many of us have difficulty saying "no," it is worth taking the time to digest the idea of measuring guilt. When the telephone solicitor calls asking you to collect, how long does the moment of guilt last after you say "no"? A moment. Just that. Compared with many hours of doing what someone else wants you to do, not what *you* want to do? "Is it better than what it replaces?" another friend, demographer Ben Wattenberg, asks. Of course it is. A woman we know who had been manipulated into running the fund raising campaign for her Temple's sisterhood found it to be an overwhelming job after she accepted. She worried about it for weeks, finally found a moment of courage, and called the president of the sisterhood to resign. This is the note she wrote to us afterward.

> *It was something I just did not want to do—now or ever again. So I called and quit, blaming the pressures of day-to-day life. She was really very nice about the whole thing, and told me not to feel guilty. Then I really started to shake. I called up some friends (who congratulated me for doing it!) because I needed to touch base with people who didn't think I was a shit. I was not very good company for myself. Anyway, that was a week ago and the guilt has practically disappeared. The monkey seems to be off my back. It was just a burden I couldn't cope with at this time. I still think I'm a big shit, but I'm a much happier one!*

Measure the moment of guilt—endure it and enjoy the action or the freedom; find a support group and only the transition period will be painful. There is the whole concept summed up in one woman's act of courage. Is it better than what it replaces? Of course.

In measuring the guilt of saying "no," here are a few other ideas that may be helpful. One does not always have to say "no" in person. Sometimes, as in the case of resigning from a club, an organization, or a group, it is easier to get out by letter. That may seem cowardly, but remember, the bold face-to-face confrontation is someone else's expectation, not ours. There is nothing wrong with accomplishing a difficult task in the simplest, most comfortable manner. Endure the guilt of doing it the easy way, and enjoy the ease.

On a face-to-face basis, stating, "I can't possibly do that!" or "I am unable to do that," while offering no explanation will successfully thwart the usual garden club chairman, the telephone solicitor, the fellow worker at the office, or the man who would like you to join the usher's society at church. Emphatic statements tend to discourage persistence and leave most people wondering just what your problem is. Though they may be curious, they are usually afraid to ask. Sometimes, it is easier to say "no" if we have a legitimate excuse. It does not have to be as important as we make it sound. It only has to be good enough to make others pause.

One friend, when asked why *she* didn't *do* something about the lack of organization in their local swim club, remarked to the friend who was attempting to manipulate her, "I am overwhelmed that you would ask! I am making a 1930s scrapbook on sex role stereotyping, doing my toenails, and flunking psychology! Isn't that enough?" How much pressure can anyone apply after you have made an emphatic statement of your problems, no matter how absurd they may sound? People are left confused, slightly stunned, and sorry they asked. You can say you've gone back to school, back to work; you are working nights in a filling station to put your alcoholic father through dental school; you have signed up as press secretary for Harold Stassen. You can tell people you are studying a rare form of horseshoe fungus on birch bark. It seldom matters what the excuse. With the right note of importance and shock at the request in your voice, the askers will feel guilty for asking; and for once, you won't for refusing.

But that still won't work with Mom or Dad, will it? Often, when dealing with parents or family members, offering a creative alternative to their idea or demand eliminates the guilt, while reversing the situation. Let's say that for years your family pattern has been to gather at Mother's home for Sunday dinner. Now that your children are getting older, there are other Sunday activities your family would like to pursue. But Mother is insistent—and hurt. Offer a firm alternative: Suggest that the family dine out for a change, or have a picnic in the park. Be enthusiastic and insistent yourself; it puts the burden on Mother to say "no" for once. If she does, you can have your picnic anyway, claiming that everyone's heart is now set on it. If she agrees, you are having a picnic in the park instead of dinner at her house. Either way, it is the first break in the pattern. Others can follow.

Change is a slow and painful process for everyone involved. It took years, decades for the expectations we and others have of us to develop. They are not going to disappear after one bold move. The transition period will be the most painful, but the worst is over when you have made a commitment and a first step.

A word must be said about new images. It is tempting to become so caught up in our own new images—liberated man, liberated woman, liberated parent, free spirit—that we stubbornly refuse to compromise those new images for an instant. But that is falling into the same kind of trap we just freed ourselves from. After spending half a lifetime trying to shed one set of expectations, why burden yourself with a new set for the second half? Consistency is stifling. Don't try to live up to your new image all the time. The liberated woman can still enjoy baking bread. The liberated man can enjoy the Superbowl on a Sunday afternoon, and fry pancakes for dinner that night. You can cry and be assertive—at appropriate times for each. You can make soup and sew and still be your own person. You can be tender with a child or a friend, and lift weights and still be your own person. Let's stop comparing once and forever.

If we can learn to understand and manage our guilt feelings, they can work productively for us. Both Dick and I suffer from overconscientiousness. Once we have made a commitment, assumed responsibility for a task, it nags at the back of our minds until it has been completed. Sometimes, the work goes better if we feel a little guilty. This past spring, we had 260 television shows to write, and this book to complete. We both worked until we were dry, but, as the family writer, I dried out at the typewriter first. Production slowed to a trickle—complaints became a torrent. Dick suggested I take a week off and visit old friends in Phoenix. "I can't," I moaned. "I have too much work to do." The next thing I knew, I was in Arizona, lying in the sun and feeling horribly guilty. I came back from that week of vacation thinking I had to justify it, and I did. A good example of "fly now, pay later" productive guilt.

While I was in Arizona, Margie, my long-time, long-distance alter ego, confided she had discovered a way to use her guilt feelings productively to relax. "I can't seem to read in peace," she said, "when there are chores to be done. Even unimportant chores nag at the back of my mind: closets to be cleaned, drawers to be straightened, an anniversary present that doesn't have to be purchased for two more weeks. I find if I make a list, and do one thing (clean the hall closet) and cross it triumphantly off, I can return happily to my book, feeling relieved, productive, and guiltless."

A business associate of Dick's has found a different way to manage her guilt feelings productively. She hates to clean house, so she throws a dinner party once a month for the sole purpose of forcing herself to return all the clutter to its proper place. Let's face it. The guilt is there. If we understand our own natures well enough, we can sometimes make them work for us instead of against us.

A final word must be said about parents. Perhaps it has seemed that we dwelt more than necessary on Mom the Manipulator or Dad of the Impossible Expectations. If we have overemphasized them as guilt-producers, it is because we have heard their names more frequently than any others when guilt has been discussed—in every part of this nation, in every age bracket, from the married and the single, from males and females. People seem to have the greatest difficulty dealing openly with their parents' expectations, and their own resulting guilt feelings. "My mother expects . . . my father insists . . . I have to do it or they'll never forgive me . . . I owe it to them . . . who clsc have they got . . . I can't say 'no.' " We have heard every variation on that theme over and over again, and it brings up the whole question of responsibility. How much responsibility do we have for the lives of others? It is a difficult question to answer honestly. There are too many traditions surrounding family and friendship. We cannot be objective about those so close to us. But others can, and most psychologists would affirm that taking complete responsibility for the happiness of another is the ultimate impossible expectation. For whose happiness are you willing to take total responsibility? How often? And for how long? For a husband when he has a bad day at work? Yes—you will try to make him feel better. For a wife who has a bad day with the children? Yes—you can try. For the children when they have unhappiness, misery, heartaches, as all children do? Of course, you will try. But are you willing to take full responsibility for another's unhappiness? What if you can't alleviate that unhappiness? We all feel guilty about the chronically lonely friend, the lonely parent, the unhappy spouse or child. It does not make us bad people if we cannot eliminate their pain or loneliness. Most of the time we can do little to help them. We can provide understanding and temporarily distract them, but in the end, they can only help themselves. There is devastating guilt when you disengage from the overdemanding parent or child, the husband or wife who wishes to use you as a crutch forever. But you are not responsible for their happiness. You can only be responsible for your own. And what about their growth? They may never grow unless we let go first. They may not see it that way, so we must sometimes endure the guilt in order to let them enjoy the growth.

There is another freedom that comes with the understanding of guilt—the freedom of disengagement. We have often told our children, "Don't make your stand on the edge of a cliff." At times, it is easier to change ourselves than the world around us—and to maintain our silence about the changes. We don't always have to make the choice between compromising our principles and doing battle for them. Everything does not have to be win/lose. We have a young friend who has been at war with her mother for years. Every visit is agony for herself, her husband, and the children. Who will win today? Mommy or Gramma? The hostility is so palpable you can scoop it out of the air. Sandy has been made to feel so guilty, so inadequate, so worthless by her mother (one of the world's true manipulators), that she is fighting for her life—over everything. It is tragic because each visit has become a life-and-death struggle for Sandy's self-esteem. But it needn't be that way. We can withdraw from the manipulators, or we can refuse to play their games. We can disengage. But not until we realize our self-esteem is not at stake over diapers and broccoli.

One friend, whose mother insisted upon a daily call, said, "Fine. I'll get my magazine, call her at the right time, say the appropriate 'Isn't that interesting' every few minutes, and catch up on my reading. There's no reason to hurt her, and it doesn't inconvenience me to make her happy this way." Confrontations are only necessary if you feel you must win a victory. And if we are secure enough, why do we have to win? What do we have to prove? Usually, something to ourselves.

If Aunt Minnie is coming and she enjoys seeing the girls dressed up, take your choice. Dress them up or do battle or disengage. Is it a sin to dress them up today? No more so than to dress them down. There is only a new expectation ("I won't!") we have burdened ourselves with. Opt for the lesser guilt. Dress them up and tell yourself, "So what?" Or dress them down, and when Aunt Minnie fusses, nod and go on to the next topic of conversation. Disengage mentally. It's not important enough to endure the guilt of war. When the neighbor complains that the grass is too long, smile, agree, and go back inside to watch the football game. When someone lays his guilt trip on you, you don't have to fight. All you have to say is, "That sounds interesting." It doesn't mean you agree. No one can lay a guilt trip on us unless we choose to accept it, remember? We don't have to do battle, and we don't have to burn our bridges or blow them up. We can listen, smile, and then do as we damn well please. We have the right not to convert the world.

We may want to cross back over those very bridges on some future day. One of the burdens from our past was the inability to change our minds or think for ourselves. It is another impossible expectation to believe we can know how we will feel in the distant, or even the very near, future. We do not have to be certain that what is right today, what is a norm for us now, will remain so forever. We have personally seen and endured too many changes to be trapped that way again. The guilt of abandonment is too great each time. Take a pit stop occasionally to reassess, without feeling you are abandoning your principles. If you are uncomfortable with your new life and would like to change directions again, give yourself permission. And if the guilt of change has become too painful, give yourself permission to cross back over your unburned bridges. You *can* go back; you have that right.

What will others think of us as we change? Which others? The old or the new in our lives? Dick saw this poem in the Green Bay *Press-Gazette* one Sunday not long ago, and was astonished to learn it had been written by an eighth-grade student, Amy Krawze, of Laona, Wisconsin.

> *They say you're not nice*
> *And they say you're immoral*
> *They say you're no good*
> *And they say they don't like you.*
>
> *They say this because you're*
> *Different from them and*
> *You live a life unlike theirs*
>
> *Don't blame them, they only hurt*
> *Themselves by not knowing the*
> *Reason behind life:*
> *To live to understand each other.*
>
> *I don't listen to them*
> *I listen to me*

And I say that you're
A beautiful inspirational person

And you're unique and lovely
In your own way.
No matter what they say . . .
I still like you.

Out of the mouths of babes comes perspective.

Perspective is what we have to maintain. We can only do that by asking, "What is important . . . to me?" —and by answering honestly. What do *we* want to measure up to? And what will all the rest matter, ten, twenty, or fifty years from now? We can take a lesson in perspective from the very young, to whom all mountains seem conquerable; we can take another lesson from the very old, who have seen enormous changes— far more than we—and have learned that so many mountains are merely a mirage. Few of the win/lose battles matter over the course of time. The neighbors who harass us today about the dog or the children or community norms will move out of our lives in a year or two—or we will move out of theirs, or the norms will change again. The people we try so hard to please today may be gone tomorrow . . . to Santa Fe, Atlanta, or Pakistan. Most of the others whose judgment we worry about exist on the outer fringes of our lives. Only a handful really matter. And what can any of them really do to us? They can no longer spank, punish, or send us to our rooms. We are adults, responsible for our own lives—a heady realization. Others can only disapprove at best. And if we have support, even their disapproval cannot sting much or long.

Everyone feels guilty! Guilt is a natural companion to the distortion and confusion we feel at being caught in a period of vast cultural change. Yet, it is quite an exciting world and most of us would not choose to live in any other time or place in history. We play at nostalgia, but would not go back if given the choice. Our problem is learning how to live fully here and now—not half-buried in the past, not half-expectant that on some unknown future dawn all things will become simple and painless again. It is not our fault that much has changed since our childhoods, or that some people in our lives have changed while others have not. Nor is it our fault that the old voices and the old messages continue to play in our heads while new ones attempt to drown them out. We didn't create the din, and we do pretty damn well surviving in the midst of it . . . and coping as we do. We may never know complete peace, we may never feel totally guiltless, but we can help ourselves. We are *not* bad human beings. We are simply human and we are trying. Give us credit for that.

Anger, resentment, militancy against the past does little to relieve guilt. It creates more. The past will not be changed, nor can those who live there be changed. We do not have that right. Battles to change others are painful and usually futile. We can only change ourselves. We are imperfect—guilty of deeds and omissions that were never meant to be sinful. Who will allow us to be human if we do not allow ourselves to be? And who will forgive us if we cannot forgive ourselves?

We feel fragile and unsure at times. Afraid to reach out and ask others for help; to make ourselves vulnerable first. Like the women on the couch, we each travel daily through unfamiliar territory. We are all strangers here ourselves. But from our experience, for each time we miscalculate and are hurt, ten times a spark, a sharing, a recognition of common needs occurs. Other strangers are out there longing for support. We have met them. They live in your town, in your suburb, on your block . . . as they do on ours. They, too, need someone to laugh with. Someone to say: *Enjoy! It is* NOT *wrong! You are a good person. Keep trying.* They, too, need someone to counterbalance the past. To say, "I give you permission . . . be human . . . be yourself."

Where are they? Waiting inside all those houses that look alike and untroubled from the street. Waiting for someone to take the first step, waiting for a knock on the door. Waiting for you. And crying out against the impossible expectations as we all have cried, "Times change. But why is it so hard?" We need each other more than ever right now. And it doesn't have to be so hard.

Reach out and touch another hand. Knock on a door. Take a baby step. Find someone loving to say, "I give you permission." And be gentle with yourself.

Enjoy!

IN 1942 THE U.S. RATIONED GASOLINE

The basic ration for passenger cars

A

MILEAGE RATION

"A" DRIVERS
MUST DISPLAY
THIS STICKER

That was wartime and the spirit of sacrifice was in the air. No one liked it, but everyone went along. Today we need a wartime spirit to solve our energy problems. A spirit of thrift in our use of all fuels, especially gasoline. We Americans pump over 200 million gallons of gasoline into our automobiles each day. That is nearly one-third the nation's total daily oil consumption and more than half of the oil we import every day ... at a cost of some $40 billion a year. So conserving gasoline is more than a way to save money at the pump and help solve the nation's balance of payments; it also can tackle a major portion of the nation's energy problem. And that is something we all have a stake in doing ... with the wartime spirit, but without the devastation of war or the inconvenience of rationing.

ENERGY CONSERVATION - IT'S YOUR CHANCE TO SAVE, AMERICA
Department of Energy, Washington, D.C.

A PUBLIC MESSAGE FROM BALLANTINE BOOKS

Witness the drama of children in search of themselves.